LIVERPOOL BANK ROBBER TO HOLLYWOOD BUTLER

BOOK 2

MY LIFE WITH MARLON BRANDO, FARRAH FAWCETT AND JOAN RIVERS

TERRY MOOGAN

SPELLING DIFFERENCES: UK V US

This book was written in British English, hence US readers may notice some spelling differences from American English: e.g. color = colour, meter = metre and jewelry = jewellery

DEDICATION

The most wonderful gift I could ever ask for, and one that I still marvel at, is my beautiful daughter, Kelly Moogan.

Non-judgmental and loving, she has brought me great joy during the times of my darkest memories, and her lovely smile never fails to light up my heart.

CONTENTS

AUTHOR'S NOTE

My long life has been an unforgettable journey as an urchin child from the tenements of Liverpool, a street kid born in the city of fire among crumbling factories and idle dockyards, with a smoke-filled skyline and an uncertain future echoing with silence and boarded-up windows in our homes.

The police knew my name before they knew my face. You would either fold or fight. Most parents had empty wallets, and we lived in desperation fueled by a growing rage. Opportunity never knocked. We were arrested and discarded on the slagheap of institutionalized throwaways. Poverty stricken, I walked alone. The separation, the isolation, the loneliness of rejection and the burden of heaviness, were trials that were too hard to bear.

That was England in the 1960s and 70s. At aged 12 most children were learning football, but not me; I was caged. Yet, I was able to use a prison guard strike, of all things, to get the hell out of a never-ending cycle of agonizing violence and robbery, to make my escape to sunny California.

I cherished breaking the chains around me, as I carried on as a child. Desperate, I couldn't bear another courtroom, a suffocating space filled with the weight of the accusations against me. I took the chance to embrace the opportunities that lay before me in the greatest country in the world.

I worked with the ultra-rich and famous in Beverly Hills. I knew the wealthy who were brought up in the biggest of mansions, attending schools and universities, and with servants all of their lives. How ironic that they asked this poor lad from the slums of Liverpool for his advice on how to properly set a table and throw a dinner party in their grand Beverly Hills mansions.

Thank you for reading my memoir. This book is dedicated to

the people who have suffered from any kind of abuse or mental illness and who are still alive today, past and present. As I outlined in my first book, *Liverpool Bank Robber to Hollywood Butler,* we were never young and afraid. No one ever told me who I was. So begins the untold chapters of my life. The resilience, revelations, revolution, and finally, the last man standing.

I was born a scouser in Liverpool in the United Kingdom, one of the country's most infamous and dangerous places at the time. I spent part of my childhood being abused in government Homes and ran away many times.

I lived in a chaotic and brutal world. Liverpool lads like us found ourselves in street gangs to survive the harsh childhood that only we knew. I considered bravery a top priority and never used violence – only when necessary to defend oneself. I couldn't dream when my brain was numb from the abusers. I lived constantly on hyper-vigilance, which formed into anxiety.

All during my childhood, little gang members unfortunately passed away young: Franny Jones to cancer; David Brooks to complications from mental illness; Ronnie Gibbons to murder; Tony Sinnott also murdered; Joe Maran to suicide; Dave Brown to suicide; Tosh Tomo, to an overdose of drugs; Eddie Lingstone to suicide; Jimmy Walker to suicide. And the rest live on; many suffering from depression and anxiety.

I remember the abusers, the tigers coming out at night, their voices only as soft as thunder as they tore my hopes apart and turned my dreams into shame. I struggled with good and evil, even though I lost myself in my own labyrinth.

Liverpool's beleaguered civil servants at the time knew the deceitful homeless imps I hung around with. But they also knew my personality well. The people who knew my name then undoubtedly pictured me ending up in Borstal Prison and other youth correctional institutions. That was England's most abundant fertile breeding ground for sociopaths and psychopaths.

Indeed, in time I would become a Borstal boy, residing for two years at the nation's best-known youth prison among other well-locked accommodations that were provided for me in my youth by Her Royal Majesty. Those same bureaucrats and police could not possibly have pictured the subsequent stretch of years that I would reside in a $120 million-dollar mansion in Beverly Hills, a 1920s masterpiece with 10,000 square feet of elegant Italian Mediterranean charm set on rolling park-like grounds, while populated with some multi-million-dollar paintings and various statues by artists such as Giacometti Cezanne, Kandinsky Hockney, Harding Miro, and Magritte next to Picassos, as well as the infinitely posh digs in Holmby Hills that I later occupied. The two areas were the crème de la crème of Beverly Hills, the sun drenched and fantastically opulent neighborhoods.

And yet, the best side of Beverly Hills is precisely where I set foot one day in the guise of a quintessential English Butler, who would soon become friends and a confidant to billionaires, movie stars, and some of the most powerful people of their time. There I was, rubbing elbows with such as Marlon Brando, Clint Eastwood, Liz Taylor, and Richard Burton, along with Sir Lawrence Oliver, and waving familiarly almost every day to such neighbors as Lucille Ball and Desi Arnaz and others, while working my trade in the former Elvis Presley mansion.

None of the luminaries would ever know of my sordid criminal past, or my close connections to many of Liverpool's most notorious criminals. I found out failure is the best path to success!

Thank you all once again, to those who read this book and to those who are struggling. I wish you all the best. Don't let the demons win. The demons did not win against me as I peered into the void and slid away sitting on the ledge of hope. The hope would come as our case in the battle against the highest court in the land for justice. I became the lead man, Moogan versus the Catholic Church and the Nugent Care society. Our objective was to change the laws so that no beast, teacher or priest in any children's homes could put a hand on a child in care.

I represented a voice echoed free for all those children who had passed away due to abuse in care and those who brought death upon themselves. I felt like a man of courage fighting for the victims and for justice; my broken heart still fueled by hope while battling evil. We fought back in the darkest nights; my voice echoing once again to the lawyers for justice, loud and clear. They thought that I was weak, but I never chose to hide in the name of justice or defender of the free. Let it be a warning to the past, present, and future beasts and abusers. I felt I was the beacon who stood strong for what's right. Justice, justice, justice for all no matter what it costs. If you're walking through hell, walk faster.

POEM

The judge said step down boy.
Dry up your tears you're going
To Borstal for a term of
Two years.
So kiss me, my darling
Say you'll be mine
Two years in that scum Borstal
Is a mighty long time.

He came home one day to find
His true love went away
Then one day just by chance
He met her at a local dance

When he asked her why she left him
The words in her reply
If you would have lived an honest life
I would have been your loving wife
But you chose a life of crime, Borstal Boy
And go and do your time.

Later on the same night
Borstal Boy cried like hell
In the morning they found him dead
In his hand a letter that read.

Dig my grave. Dig it deep.
Place some red roses at my feet.
Above my head
Place a white dove
To show how
I died for love

All you girls
Bear in mind
A Borstal Boy
Is hard to find.
If you find one
Love him true
Because a Borstal Boy
Will die for you.

CHAPTER 1
THE FRIDAY NIGHT GUNMEN
1978

It was a bitter winter day, and the stormy weather was followed by sleet and snow. Sitting in the Hermitage pub on Queens Drive in Walton, Liverpool, I was waiting for the phone to ring. The time was 11.30 a.m. on a Monday in November, 1978. I was staring out of the window wondering what the next move in my life would be. Sipping on my orange juice, I watched a couple of old men whose lives were probably over, with their grey faces, deep sunken eyes, and sitting with their old black overcoats on their backs, trying to keep warm from the miserable day outside. They took another drag on their cigarettes, and smoke filled the air as they sipped on their pints of beer, clenching their cold glasses. They had probably worked all their lives and had nothing to show for it. Just like my mother and father.

As the little red-haired barmaid, Mary, shouted, putting her mop down after cleaning the stale ale from the night before from the stench of decay, her groggy scouse voice echoed all around the pub.

"Another pint, Kenny?"

There wasn't another soul in the pub, just the four of us. Kenny nodded politely, bowing his head like a gentleman. I thought to myself, I want a better life than this. Was a better life somewhere else in the future? It certainly was. Had to be. I stood there waiting anxiously. It was the same pub where the police arrested me in 1972 and pushed me through a plate glass window, almost severing my arm and nearly killing me.

All of a sudden the phone echoed out. Ring! Ring! Immediately,

I grabbed it. Mary's ears perked up as she was trying to listen to my conversation. The man on the other end of the line spoke.

"Hello, mate, how are you?"

It was Bobby Hughes, my old friend, a local gangster from Huyton. He had a twin brother, Billy. They were known for their underworld connections. In Huyton they were absolutely fucking ruthless men who would eventually become millionaires and control the club scene in Liverpool, plus one club in Tuebrook: the Coconut Grove. That was their favorite place. Bobby was putting me in touch for a meeting here at the notorious Blue Bell Pub.

"Your man will see you tonight at 7 p.m., mate."

"OK, lad," I replied.

That was the code to meet one of the most ferocious gangsters to ever come out of Liverpool. He was also from Huyton. His name was Peter Connolly, whom I had met in Walton prison in 1974. He had a reputation like no other. But that didn't matter to me, he was just another scallywag.

One Monday evening in November, I left home at 7 p.m. The year was 1978, and I was approximately 15 minutes away from my destination. The location was the notorious Huyton where they bred some of the craziest bank robbers in Liverpool's history. In the future they would become notorious as The Friday Night Gunmen. The destination was the Blue Bell Pub, known for local baddies that were absolutely fucking crazy and fearless.

I pulled up across the street on Blue Bell Lane. I knew I would be safe. But you never know. I was meeting two old friends from my days in Borstal. *Scum*, the movie, is a British prison film – a powerful uncompromising drama about the struggle for survival in the nightmare world of the brutal custodial institution for young offenders, which we had survived, me and my friends. The movie was banned in 1977 but the BBC and its director, Alan Clarke, finally got the go-ahead from the U.K. government. It was released in 1979 and portrays the life of what really happened in Borstal. However, it doesn't tell the whole truth of many of the youth who died later on in life. Margaret Thatcher eventually closed down the place. It was inhumane, cruel and heartless.

The night was cold as I stepped out of the car on Blue Bell Lane, the flickering streetlights on the lamp posts in the street were dim. You had to be careful where you parked. The car would be stolen in a few minutes. I put a long black parka coat on and grabbed a claw hammer from the back seat, placing it inside my coat just in case there was any funny business.

The rain started pelting down on my face and the wind was howling. I locked the car door and slowly walked over to the pub. Blue bells were displayed outside above the door. It was only for local residents, one of the few that had a ruthless reputation like the Eagle and Child a mile away. Rarely would you find a stranger walking into the bar, they had to be fucking crazy.

After I opened the old wooden bar door I stepped inside where a cloud of smoke stung my eyes. I approached the bar, staring straight ahead, not looking around. All of a sudden, the many voices that had just filled the air in the bar seemed to go silent. The bar was clammy. The locals might have thought I was an undercover cop or maybe a detective, but no way would a gang of locals intimidate me, especially when Alan Spencer was watching. He was disguised as an old man with his cap on and a dark overcoat, sipping on his pint from a distant corner to make sure there was no funny business. He was a man you could trust in Huyton and was well-known throughout the Huyton estate for his ruthless reputation.

I could smell the stench of the old stale ale throughout the pub. I reached the bar full of stinking smoke and ale and dirty glasses all over the counter.

"What are you having?" the barmaid snapped with a smirk on her face. She was middle-aged, about 50, with a thick scouse accent and a suspicious look on her face once again. "What are you having?" She was a short woman, about 5 '2", with dark hair and teeth missing from the sides of her mouth as she kept her eyes on me, probably thinking, Who the fuck is this fella?

Looking around carefully, I noticed four men in a corner that were sipping their pints, their eyes gleaming at me. They relied on the notorious reputation of the Blue Bell. But these men had pitiful lives, and no existence, and didn't know fuck-all and probably had never been outside Huyton. Just a gang of shitheads and drunks.

"A Britvic orange juice, please," I said in a calm voice.

"That'll be 40 pence, please," she responded, her eyes rolling in the air and glaring right through me.

I kept my head straight. Within 30 seconds a man came up from the right side of me. "Cheers, Terry! How are you?" He slapped his heavy hand on my right shoulder.

"Alright mate, how are you, my old friend?" Peter had become a key figure in Liverpool's underworld. My serendipitous encounter now, after not seeing Peter for years, led to an enjoyable chat about our experiences. "Come and sit down in the corner over here, mate."

All of a sudden people realized who I was with. They carried on with their conversations; their voices perked up once again, going back to their comfort zone.

"My friend can't wait to meet you," Peter said, ushering me over to where the other man was seated in a corner of the pub.

"Terry, this is George."

Watching closely was Alan Spencer in another corner, his eyes getting intense. I realized straight away who George was.

"He was in Borstal a year after you left, Terry."

"Yes, I met you in the city centre on a door at the She Club. You and Mickey Bennett worked together. You were the bouncers, right?"

"That's right, Terry," George said, rubbing his flat nose. "Did you see the movie, *Scum*, they made of us Borstal boys? It was a load of shit, Terry. They never told the real truth even if it was harrowing and brutal." George's voice got angry as he added, "Worse than that, the bastards."

"I know, mate. Bad news," I replied. "It was excruciating, mate. By the way, are you related to Johnny Aspinall?"

"Yes, he's my cousin."

We had a few more eyes staring at us once again. The locals would love to have known what was being discussed. I said no more. I sipped my orange juice, staring around the room at the sorrowful souls, but I knew we were safe. So did they.

I was in the presence of the Friday Night Gunmen. Seemed normal to me. They were making a lot of headlines in the news. They seemed to be flawless, always striking on a Friday night, holding up pubs, liquor stores, shops, you name it. The two bastards, Peter and George, were the real fucking thing. Eventually there would be a massive manhunt for them in Liverpool by the entire Serious Crime Squad, including for me at one time.

"We read in the news, Terry, about your innocence and acquittal at the trial at the Crown Court. Fucking brilliant that, Terry," George said.

"Yes, mate. All good."

"Do you have anything, Terry?"

I pondered for a minute. Peter was excited, rubbing his hands. I could see his piercing blue eyes. He loved the thrill of a robbery. He'd heard about my reputation.

"Can you leave your shotguns at home?" I said to Peter.

"No fucking chance."

"Keep your voice down," I said. "Peter, are you fucking barmy?"

I knew he was impulsive due to his tendency to act without considering the consequences.

He spoke with a deep Liverpool accent that would scare the life out of most men just sitting in his presence. However, he could plan and execute a crime while the others might be aroused by his acts of violence, or domination over a victim, but not me. I was not impressed. They could tell I was displeased, and gave me a dirty fucking look.

"The fucking guns, Terry, they'll do the trick. It's way better, mate."

"What about a hammer?"

"Calm down lad, don't make me fucking angry."

They went quiet for a few seconds. These men craved guns.

"We'll carry what we fucking want," Peter said with a weird look.

"No, you fucking won't, lad. Calm down." True power doesn't shout but whispers do. "Listen, Peter lad, you're gonna get us 20 years if we get fucking caught."

Then all of a sudden Peter had another proposal: "What about an imitation gun?"

"There ya go, Peter lad, that's even better." I cleared my throat with a sip of orange juice; I decided that I would not have this conversation again.

Peter was one of the safest men; we found out later on in Liverpool that everybody could trust him in the Blue Bell pub in Huyton and throughout the whole of Liverpool, especially since he kept watch on the elderly people. If there was anybody that ever stepped out of line, Peter would fix it. We thought he was sound.

"Go on then, Terry, what have you got?"

"It's a security van picking up all the money that's paid into all the post offices in Lancashire and deposited in the main Safeway store."

"You've seen it, Terry?" George asked with excitement. You could see the thrill in his eyes and the glee from defying societal norms.

"Yes."

"We're in, Terry."

"OK. I'll take you Monday evening. You'll see the operation there. There are seven pickups of money that's been taken from the post offices and deposited into the security van. You'll have to train to be fit for this one," I said to them.

"Yes," Peter spoke for both of them.

"OK, then. It's done. Just the three of us."

'We will fucking bladder them, Terry."

We all shook hands. We had a sophisticated operation now.

"So, let's have a pint!"

We had now laid the foundation between us; however, one

slip or overheard word would fuck us up. I could see most of the customers' eyes were on us. Once again, they were commoners. I knew they were sound, though. But they knew nothing. We settled down and finished our pints and had a bit of a laugh to ease the stress. I looked over to see Alan sipping on his pint and looking over the rim of his glasses.

"OK. I had best get home to my wife now. I'll see you Monday night in the car park at 5 p.m. OK, lads?"

George was 5'11" with a chiseled face, black hair and deep brown eyes. He would scare the life out of most people without his mask on. His frame was complete with massive shoulders and his hands alone looked like shovels – a complicated man. Peter, on the other hand, was just a regular guy, 5'8" with dark hair and good-looking, with deep blue eyes. He had a five-inch scar down the right side of his face that made him even more scary. However, he was a manipulative person. As I left the Blue Bell, Alan Spencer was still in his corner watching every move.

Peter shouted: "I'll let the twins Bobby and Billy know that I had a pint with you, Terry."

Monday evening at 4:45 p.m. on a windy night, I waited outside the Blue Bell. A high-powered red Jaguar pulled up. Peter and George jumped out.

"Get in the back of my car," I said. "I need to talk to you both."

I sped off up the M57 towards Manchester in my Cortina, my hands tight on the steering wheel, keeping one eye in the mirror,

"Where to?" Peter asked. He was smoking a thick joint and blowing the smoke inside of the car.

"You'll see."

The rain started pelting down once again and turned colder that night. I put the heater on in the car for a little warmth. The car filled up with smoke from Peter's bad habits.

"Put those fucking ciggies or joints out, will you? I can't see out the fucking window."

"OK, Terry," Peter replied.

"No more smoking in the fucking cars. OK? Especially that shit you smoke."

Everybody went silent. Thirty minutes later we were nearly there. We arrived in Wythenshawe, Manchester. In the distance waiting for us was a massive Safeway store. Sitting on a corner close to the highway motorway. It was a perfect getaway for us. I parked the car.

"Peter, George, listen. In ten minutes, two men will be getting in that van. They're going around Manchester to seven post offices. We will follow them. When they get back here, we will take the two of them down to the floor before they deliver the bags and boxes to the Safeway store.

"Sounds great, Terry," George replied. "Can't fucking wait, lad."

I told Peter and George that the two men in the van would be the same men every week. They nodded and gave the go-ahead sign.

"OK. Let's go and have a pint," Peter said.

"You drive home, George."

"OK, Terry, fine, mate, along the M57."

"Have you ever done a Group 4 security van before, Terry?"

I just winked as he looked at me in the rear-view mirror. He was trying to say that he knew I was all business, which was the banter out of the scousers, as usual, crazy.

We had a pint once again in the miserable Blue Bell. This time we went into the lounge where it was a bit more civilized or was it? We would have our rendezvous in approximately three weeks. We sipped on our pints of lager smiling with excitement and Peter inhaled a massive joint to calm his nerves.

"Do you want a puff of that, Terry?"

"No, thanks, mate."

"OK. Let's go to the bar and have a game of pool. Whoever loses has to take the boxes off the guards," Peter said, laughing.

"They will give us the boxes, mate, don't you fucking worry about that."

All of a sudden music came on the jukebox, "I love you, baby, " from the new 1978 movie, *The Deer Hunter*, then Peter jumped on the pool table and started singing, "I love you baby, you're just too good to be true, can't take my fucking eyes off of you." Then all the bars' customers joined in and started singing, "Can't take my eyes off you." This was the Blue Bell in the day. It was fucking crazy.

However, the eyes were all over us because we were well-known hardened criminals. They would think twice about their actions as they were not in our league. We all stumbled out of the bar into the cold air into Blue Bell Lane half drunk, especially Peter. He was stoned out of his head still clutching a joint between his lips, then suddenly he stumbled, bent over, and spewed up all over the Blue Bell wall.

"I'm OK, boys." He seemed embarrassed.

"How much do you think is in the security van, Terry?" George belted out in a drunken tone.

"I don't know lad. Oh, £50,000 to £75,000."

"Wow," Peter said. "Nice few quid that, lad? Happy days, you bastards," his words echoed down Blue Bell Lane. Alan Spencer was overseeing every move now that the gang's ambition was set.

It was the last week of October. Winter was setting in now, which would be perfect to put our parkas and hoods on without any suspicion. Our plan would unfold in three weeks. We would watch the van every Monday after the delivery for three weeks and follow the moves from post office to post office, then drive back to the Blue Bell. In the meantime, Tommy and George got fit as fuck. I'd told them they had better be fit lads, so all three of us went up to North Wales three times a week to run up and down the hills. Four miles we'd run, and a quarter of a mile we'd finish sprinting. Carrying ten-pound weights on our backs, I was surprised at how fit they were, especially Peter. He was nothing but a street fighter.

Of the two men who were collecting the money from the post office, one was young and about 5' 8." The other, more middle aged, was about 5' 11." We would have no problem with taking them down, they were just regular citizens.

We would sit in the Blue Bell bar on Monday and Wednesday evenings, organizing the plan, sipping on our pints of lager, with the locals glancing over now and again. They knew we were up to no good, but they were sound people which made them comfortable with us.

We'd have two cars, one parked in front of the van, and one behind the post office. When the Group 4 security van pulled up, George would emerge behind it. I would be by the door of the post office in a wheelchair, sitting there with a blanket over my legs with a cap on and makeup on to cover my face. George thought that was a great idea.

"Where are you going to get the wheelchair, Terry?" Peter asked.

"The Royal Infirmary Hospital, mate, in the city centre of Liverpool," I replied. "I'm going tomorrow. You both can come with me."

"We can use my van," Peter said.

Peter and George burst into hysterics when I told them I was going to get the wheelchair from the hospital. "That's fucking brilliant, Terry."

We met the next day in the afternoon on London Road in a pub in the city, called the Legs of Man, for a pint near the Royal Infirmary Hospital. I parked the van and walked towards the Emergency Room and to the Reception Desk with Peter and George following behind me.

"Excuse me, nurse, I need a wheelchair for my friend. He is very sick," I said.

The nurse at the desk got up to get one and swiftly pushed a wheelchair towards me without hesitation. I thanked her, and within a minute the wheelchair was ours. We pushed it out to the van, then we drove off, Peter and George laughing their heads off once again.

We organized our plan, so each man knew his responsibilities. I would jump out of the wheelchair as the men put the bags in the back of the security van. George would get one guard on the ground and Peter would take the other guard down to the floor and hold him with the pin-down move pressing his foot on his arm to lock his muscle, a move we always constructed. Putting a foot on his arm when he was on the ground would disable his muscle. Then we could take the boxes.

The day drew closer. We had one week left to train. We were fit as hell from running up and down hills, boxing training, and lifting heavy weights. We were ready, and understood things could go wrong. We were prepared for that. Peter insisted he bring his imitation handgun, but I also told Peter and George we should carry hammers as well.

"But don't use them, only threaten them, and don't let anybody see them. If you bring a handgun, it's got to be imitation. Peter, do you fucking understand me? Otherwise, that's 15 fucking years in jail. If you bring a real gun but we use the hammers, that'd be only five years in jail from the judge. Our intention is no violence, Peter."

Our last meeting would be on Sunday night, in the Blue Bell. Once again, the eyes of the patrons were on us. However, they all felt safe with Peter and our presence. I looked around the pub, at its patrons. It was filled with old chairs and tables, and stinking empty pint glasses on the tables and big thick ashtrays with cigarette stubs in them that were signs of weak men and the suppressed lives they led, never knowing anything else. The people in the pub had been constantly inhaling smoke into their lungs and filling their stomachs full of alcohol with such shitty surroundings for years. I wondered if they had ever worked, and about the pitifulness and their waste of life. What the fuck did they know, anyway? They got a lot of excitement just observing the Friday Night Gunmen, which was their entertainment but only if they knew Alan Spencer was in the corner, scrutinizing the whole scene.

"OK, are you ready?" I said. "Meet here tomorrow at 3:30 and don't be fucking late." My anxiety was rising. "Peter, George?"

"OK."

We all agreed that hammers were only to be pulled out if we got into trouble.

But George was a loose cannon, he didn't care. Peter was at least more conservative and listened to me, but he was a dangerous man and impulsive. He knew I was the real deal. He felt safe with me.

A couple of nights before, on the last Saturday of our training we headed to a well-known upscale local spot, Childwall Five Ways pub, and waited for the locals to come in for their night out. Our target was a high-powered Jaguar with a 3.8 engine, one of the fastest cars in Britain, along with a four-door Sedan, a Ford Granada Saloon. The two cars were fast enough to get us away from the scene of the crime. We knew if we were chased the police would have no chance of catching up with their underpowered cars.

Then suddenly, there she was. A Ford Granada pulled up with a young guy and his girlfriend. We had keys from the local car thieves already.

"Wait till he goes into the pub, give him 20 minutes to settle with his pint, mate."

Within two minutes, Peter was in the Granada, forcing the ignition with a screwdriver. He was on his way to Huyton within seconds, it seemed, laughing as he drove past us, waving his hand with his thumb in the air. We had a safe house to park the cars. We waited another 30 minutes then all of a sudden, a Jaguar pulled in.

"That'll do, George. Take the Jaguar right now."

As George jumped into the car he played with the ignition with a screwdriver and finally started the engine. He slowly pulled away from the car park. We were on our way now. The cars would be parked close to the safe house. The license plates would be changed. We would all meet at 3.30 a.m. the next day.

"Hello, boys." I said.

The wind was blowing a cold breeze, and the streets were empty. It started to rain heavily, fucking perfect for a hold up. Again, we'd convened at the Blue Bell car park. We had parka jackets, gloves, and boiler suits on, all in black, of course, and ski masks on, just like British commandos. The operation was now on. There was no turning back. George and I were in one car and Peter in the other.

"Just keep calm, George. OK?"

"Sure, Terry, lad."

George was relaxed on the drive to Wythenshawe. We made small talk.

"I've got two kids, Terry. I want a better life for them, mate."

I just looked at him and said, "You've got to stop playing around with shotguns, mate."

"I know, Terry."

I gave each man a piece of gum, Juicy Fruit, to chew on to calm our nerves. It was a dark evening, and we knew the convoy was on its way.

We arrived at 4:30 a.m. The van would arrive at 5 a.m. We were ready. At 4.50 a.m. we would take the wheelchair out of the Ford Granada.

"OK, George, you stay in the Jaguar. Peter, stay tight in the Granada. When you see me move towards the van when he opens the door, make your move. Put the men on the ground, OK?"

"Right, Terry."

I sat outside the Safeway store in the wheelchair. Suddenly, the security van arrived. I pushed the blanket over my legs and had my cap on. It would take the security guard a minute to come out.

I removed my cap and took my ski mask out of my boiler suit and slipped it over my head. The man came out and headed to the security van. I came up behind him and as soon as the guard opened the door Peter sprawled himself over him effortlessly, wrestling the guard and crashing him to the ground, suffocating the guard's ability to move by placing a foot on his arm. That's how fast Peter was. The man was screaming on the floor. Peter put his hand over the guard's mouth. Then the handgun into his face. Oh my God, I thought, Oh no, but it was too late. Peter had betrayed us. The dirty bastard's gun was real. My heart hammered against my ribs. I was furious.

George jumped inside the van, grabbed the bags and boxes, and threw them to me. I loaded the bags into the car, and we drove along the M57 to Liverpool in the Ford Granada.

George shouted, "Fucking easy! He was on his own, Terry! Just one of them!"

"OK, keep calm, lad."

I kept the speed limit intact. The windows of the car were steaming up from our anxiety. I rolled the two back windows down to get circulation. I felt the cold air coming through and our anxiety slowly descending. I motioned to both of them. Especially Peter.

"You cunt! You brought a gun!" I felt a deep sense of betrayal. "You're finished!"

Peter blasted out, "Fuck you!"

Keep calm, I said to myself. Gripping the steering wheel, the tension with my leather gloves on was agonizing. My arms were going into spasms, or was it my nerves? Shaking, I again told myself to calm down.

On the M57, we arrived at Huyton, and drove past the Hillside pub, down to the Blue Bell estate, and into the safe house where we unloaded the bags and boxes. We placed them in the bedroom, on the bed. By this time, the morning was getting light.

Peter seemed to be getting excited now. All of a sudden he blurted out with his big mouth, "When's the next one?"

"No chance, you cunt, you're fucking finished, lad."

He just looked at me with his piercing eyes. "I love ya, lad. The gun was only imitation, Terry."

"You lying bastard," I was whispering under my breath.

Our count was £45,000. We split the money evenly three ways, giving the safe house £1,000. We departed.

"See you in the Blue Bell Monday, Terry!" George shouted.

As I walked down Bluebell Bell Lane a high-powered Jaguar pulled up.

"Get in, lad!"

Alan Spencer drove off slowly, the fracture in our relationship widening with each passing argument about Peter.

My friend in the safe house burned all the evidence, the clothes and ski masks, and dumped the car in the scrapyard to be cut up into pieces. I met the Friday Night Gunmen the following Monday at the Blue Bell for a pint. They discussed coming in on the next robbery, but they wanted to use real guns once again on their next big job. I declined, saying I'd let them know. George, one of the Friday Night Gunmen, was a hothead and was captured a year later by a force of armed police officers at his home early in the morning at 6 a.m. and taken into custody to await his trial. He was given a 15-year sentence for an armed robbery with another armed gang from the Huyton firm. As for me and Peter we had successfully slipped under the radar once again. Alan Spencer that night was protecting and guarding me and keeping one eye on the Friday Night Gunmen.

Many years later, Peter was arrested in his home at gunpoint by the armed Serious Crime Squad for armed robbery. The sentence was 14 years in jail. Peter's life crumbled. Years later, there was a contract to assassinate Peter by my friends for betraying us.

I told them, "You will end up serving a life sentence and rot in a cell. Think about that."

I persuaded them to look after their wives and children, and most of all their freedom, instead of spending a lifetime in a prison cell for a scumbag bastard. After some persuasion, they realized I was right, and obliged.

Years later, Peter Connolly would pass away, a long life of crime finally taking its toll on his well-being. Peter thought he was unbreakable but that was the end of the ferocious Friday Night Gunmen. As for Alan Spencer, we are still friends today. My daughter visits his son on the outskirts of Liverpool where they are good friends.

CHAPTER 2
TRAUMA IN THE MIDDLE OF THE NIGHT
1964

The notorious Scotland Road is one of the neglected areas in the city centre of Liverpool. Growing up there, I was the youngest of seven children, with an ear for secrets. We were five brothers and two sisters. Scotland Road had a history for local gangs and tough guys, especially the highly infamous rip gang that used belt buckles to beat the shit out of people in the early 1900s. These gangs also included Peaky Blinders, the most terrifying. They targeted dockers and sailors who came into the busy city port and it was even suggested that some of its most dangerous members had links to Jack the Ripper.

In December, 1964, Liverpool was grimy, wet and miserably cold. This was especially true in the city centre, the toughest section of our neighborhood. The river Mersey was dotted with coal-fired smoke belching from factories. Places in the city centre's streets were well in the running for the meanest in England.

Flashback: a look at my home in Gerard Gardens, Liverpool. It was a tenement block. The homes off Scotland Road were loved by those who lived in them.

While our future enemies were plotting war, Liverpool's city planners were visiting other countries to come up with ideas for homes that would replace cramped and disease-ridden slum housing. A delegation went to Germany and Austria to see the facilities of projects including Vienna's Karl Marx Hoff blocks, which as well as decent-sized flats included kindergarten, public laundry, library, and even an office and business section.

In 1958, a year after I was born, the tenements' reputation took a bashing when the film, *Violent Playground*, starring Stanley Baker and David McCallum, was shot in Gerard Gardens. The movie dealt with street gangs and youth crime. Its makers embellished the real-life location by replacing the clean white washing hanging from the balconies with ragged gray clothing. My father, Patrick, was a seaman, one of the great many Liverpudlians who served in the Merchant Navy, making him a cohort of the local sailors who brought home infectious American rock and roll, and rhythm and blues.

Forty-five R.P.M Records got kids like John, Paul, George, and Ringo to start begging their mums and dads for drums and guitars. My mum, Frances, was left home to care for the flock of seven children with the pittance of wages my father brought home on those rare and widely separated occasions. I was the youngest of the Moogans, a clan with Irish roots, ragged clothes, not enough pairs of shoes to go around, and empty little stomachs more often than not. My ancestors may have come originally from County Clare, or perhaps Monaghan, trying to outrun the potato famine, but it was a sure bet they entered Liverpool Bay with little more than a few pennies between the lot of them. But Gerard Gardens lives on in my mind, and my beautiful childhood memories under the arches and its gossip over its washing lines.

Early in a cold damp morning my brother and sisters were cramped into our two-bedroom house overlooking the courtyard tenements to the playground. I would often peek out of the little frosted window at night to see if there was anything going on. When I couldn't sleep my mother would keep the little lamp on for me at the side of the bed. All night I was petrified of the dark. Most nights were silent but every now and then we would be awakened by a child screaming in the background, echoing around the tenements. If it wasn't the baby's voice, it would be a married couple drunk out of their heads screaming at one another at the top of their voices, caused probably by the mental illness no one recognized fueled by alcohol. In those days, my father was away at sea. My mother tucked me into her side of the bed to keep me warm and keep an eye on me. I had a tendency to get up in the middle of the night and wander the streets. We didn't have much in those days, but we weren't homeless. My mother would call me after playing out in the square.

"Come on now, Terry. It's time for bed!"

It would take quite a bit of calling until she would physically get a hold of my little arms and gently bring me into the house. There was a small single hanging light bulb that gave a little light. Sitting on a bed stand was a cup of hot chocolate my mother gave me before I went to sleep.

"Come on, Terry, get your shorts on and wash your face."

The bar of soap was twice the size of the palm of my hand. My mother would hold it for me as my hands were black and dirty from playing with the stones in the square. "Come on now, you have to learn to wash your hands," she would say, smiling at me.

My other brothers and sisters were always watching TV in the living room. We only had two stations in 1964: the BBC and ITV.

My mother tucked me into bed with my grandfather's old war overcoat. She would put the coat on top of the bed to keep us both warm at night. He had left the coat after he passed away. It was one of the memories from the war. After Hitler bombed the shit out of Liverpool, the war hung over Europe. My mother always said the overcoat was lucky. She would always place it on me. Every night of the cold winters, I had a hot water bottle on top of my feet, and she'd kiss me on the cheek.

"Goodnight night, Terry," she'd say with her soft voice. "Don't forget to say your prayers."

"Hail Mary full of grace, the lord is with me," I would mumble. "Amen."

"Your grandad would be proud of you, Terry. He won the war and left the coat to keep us warm."

The mementos in the bottom of his trunk were in a messy pile: several faded leather-bound journals and a packet of aged postcards tied together with a blue satin ribbon in a cardboard box.

"That's all his belongings there," Terry.

I was sleeping soundly next to my mother in the early hours one morning. My eyes opened. There was a small pain in my stomach. I stared out the window. The morning was still dark. I noticed the snowflakes descending as winter was approaching. All of a sudden, I felt liquid flowing out of the side of my mouth and onto my chest. I began to cough. More liquid flowed. My whole body was now wet. The pain in my stomach began to pound over and over again. Liquid sickness began flushing out – more and more. Eventually, I would fall unconscious and pass out.

I didn't know until later on that my mother had rushed to the nearest phone box down the end of the street to call 999 Emergency Services.

As I was lying in the Royal Infirmary Hospital, I woke up to see my mother's worried expression. Her shaking hand was on my face. She was petrified that I was going to die.

"You're doing fine, Terry," she whispered in my ear, rubbing her face along my cheek, blinking her tears back.

One of the nurses at the hospital would get me out of the bed to bathe me. I asked her, "Am I going to die?"

She replied with her soft Scottish accent, "Oh, no, my love. We got you just in time."

My stomach was painted pink all over, and there was a six-inch scar below my stomach with the stitches intact and white bandages around my body. The sensation of fear was racing through my little heart, but I was too young to know that. My hands turned into fists with anxiety.

My mother would visit every day and night. After work, she would ride on the bus in cold, dark nights in the miserable winter. My dear mother worked in the jam factory, Hartley's packing the jam into the jars on the assembly line. The pittance of the wages they paid her must have been nothing in those days.

After she rushed to the hospital after work, I was isolated in a hospital room for observation by myself. For days, a man came in wearing a white coat and a smile on his face. He never said hello.

His discussion was with the head nurse, talking softly: "Let me take a look at his stomach." After the nurse removed the bandage, the doctor said, "Looks good," and left the room.

"Am I going to die?" I said again to the nurse.

"No. You are fine, Terry."

The kind, warm nurse put me at ease. My appendix had been removed, a finger shaped organ that comes out of the first part of the large intestine. It can leak bacteria and infect your entire belly, which can be life-threatening. I would recover after a week in the hospital. And eventually, I would be sent home.

I wonder today: did this have an effect on my life?

With the trauma in the night, the battle would get tougher.

CHAPTER 3
THE EVIL AT WESTFIELD CHILDREN'S HOME, LIVERPOOL
1965

On a cold winter morning, my mother got me out of bed. As usual, she always made a pot of porridge to fill our hungry little stomachs, the most inexpensive meal at the time. It was quiet around the table with Brian, Alan, Tony, John Frances and Pat, especially early in the morning.

Thinking I would not get found out, I had not been to school for months. Instead, I wandered the streets in the city centre with my small gang. Our little caper was robbing the money from the buses at the depot with my friend, Philip Shields, from Soho Street.

In another area of the tenements the city centre was as rough as it could be. It bred tough young men, from generations of history, from the Liverpool gangs, including our generation now. I waited outside Gerard Gardens for Philip. He was a cute lad, with blond hair and blue eyes, a skinny frame and a pasty face. He came from a notorious family: the Shields.

"Where are we going today?" I asked.

"The Pier Head," Philip said.

We headed down to the city centre. We noticed all the buses parked in their lanes at the depot. They came from all over the city to park there. The bus drivers would probably be in the cafe getting their breakfast and smoking their heads off. Philip's friend had told him all the money was left in bags on the buses. There was an emergency valve to open the bus at the side. All of a sudden, Philip pushed it. Bang! The doors flew open. I dove behind the driver's side of the bus. There it was! A satchel bulging with coins. Along with it, a black wallet full of pound notes. We stuffed it into our plastic bag and made our escape.

We headed to the Leeds and Liverpool Canal on the banks of the River Mersey and counted our haul: £28. We hid the bag under a bush close to the River Mersey. We thought we were safe. We took a few pounds each and headed to the city centre where we stuffed our little bellies with hamburgers and Coca Cola at the Wimpy Bar, and walked around the city like little gangsters, smoking Benson and Hedges cigarettes that were popular at that time. We were nine years old.

The next morning, as usual, my mother made the porridge in the big old silver pot on the ancient gas stove. She said that she was taking me to the doctor's office for a needle in my arm. I was getting scared now as she rubbed my little head.

"OK, son, you'll be fine," she said, putting her gentle hand across my face.

Then suddenly there was a knock at the door. My mother opened it and she instantly knew. After my mother invited them into the home, two big men stepped in.

"Terry, can you sit on that chair?" one said with a stern voice. "You have not been to school, Terry."

My mother interrupted: "Will he be needing anything?"

"No. He is fine. Stand up, Terry."

One got me by the hand with a tight grip. "Come on. Let's go."

My little mind was blank. As I was ushered into a car, my mother said, "Goodbye."

"I'll see you soon, Terry."

The tears began to flow from my eyes and down my cheeks while confusion set in.

One of them said, "You're going to Westfield Home, Terry, for your own good."

We arrived at Westfield Children's Home early in the morning in an old 1960s beat-up car.

"Get yourself out, boy! This is Westfield Children's Home, Terry." That's all I kept hearing: "You have to change your ways."

Westfield Home was in a massive Victorian brick building on lush grounds in the south of Liverpool. The local authorities' children's home housed 26 kids, aged 6 to 16, mostly from disturbed backgrounds.

They marched me into the headmaster's office. I could not hear much in my confusion. All I heard was, "You're going to behave yourself!" The headmaster had an angry tone. He was a huge man with a bald head. He marched me up the stairs to a dormitory. "Here is your bed," he said, once again shouting like a sergeant major, "and your uniform. Go and change your clothes quickly!" A few minutes went by. "You ready?" he snapped. "Call me Sir. Do you understand?" He grabbed me by the ear – that bastard beast of England.

After I was ready, he marched me downstairs to a garden where all the children were playing, some laughing and some sad. I noticed we all had the same uniform on: striped shirts and grey pants with grey socks and black shoes. There were older children and young children. We would all eat our dinner together in a massive dining room. Then, when it was time to play on the grass outside, we were all marched out.

I remember that first night going to bed at 8p.m. after we washed our faces and changed into our pajamas. We read a book till 9 p.m. then the lights went out in the dormitory. A small boy, Eddie, next to me, was crying and grasping his little teddy bear under his arm, beneath the covers of the sheets.

"I want my mother!" he cried out loud.

Nobody could sleep with the moaning and the crying. Then, the night watchman screamed, "Go to sleep!" As he expressed his anger, there was silence.

But then Eddie's sobs worsened and grew louder. He was getting frightened now.

"Go to sleep!" the watchman screamed. "You little bastard!" Another beast of England, his voice even louder now as Eddie's cries became slow and shallow, and faded into the night.

At 8 a.m. a bell rang.

"Up, up, up!" a teacher shouted.

As we slowly got out of our beds the horrible teacher snapped, "Make your beds!"

We made our beds, got washed, cleaned our teeth, and stood in line for breakfast. The headmaster was shouting, "You boy, outside my office." He was waiting for his next prey saying, "You've been talking, boy."

He took me into his office, snatched the cane from the top of the cabinet, and rolled his shirt sleeves up.

"Hold your hands out!" My anxiety kept my hands clenched. "Open your hands, boy!" the bastard shouted.

He caned me three times on each hand. I could see the joy he was getting out of the abuse. The tears started streaming once again down my face. With my hands throbbing, they turned black and blue a few days later.

As I was marched to the garden before school I asked to go to the toilet. I ran to the front door so fast, to make my escape down the street to the nearest bus stop. I gave the bus driver my name and address, and told him my mother would pay the fare.

"OK, son, hop on."

I was once again at Gerard Gardens in the tenements. My mother was shocked. After she saw me I never went back there again. I was classed as a liability and a bad boy. The community was now hardening me.

In 1965, a few months later, the headmaster, a beast of England, was arrested and found guilty of buggery. The offenses of male rape did not exist then, so he was charged with indecent assault against several of the boys and sentenced to four years in prison.

In the courtroom, the judge said with a stern voice that the state of affairs in that home were shocking. There was outrage in the city, and many called for a public inquiry. The files show that the Home Office was unenthusiastic about this, and officials were relieved when the council decided to hold an inquiry in private.

Queen Counsel G.W. Guthrie Jones noted: "It is plain that if a man, particularly unmarried, lives in such a community, the strictest supervision is required. Indeed, it is possible that such a man might himself, in one sense, be the victim of boys who have already been corrupted."

He didn't get to raise that voice in prison. I hope he rotted in his prison cell, the dirty no-good bastard beast of England.

We got to keep our money, the £28, with no investigation from the police. As for Philip, he went under the radar with no arrest. I would fight evil in the future in British care homes, the haunting memory still lingers like a lamp to my feet as I ran and ran.

CHAPTER 4
DANGEROUS YEARS: THE FORGOTTEN CHILD

In the winter of 1970, our gang consisted of me, Philip, and his friends from Soho Street, Austy McCormack and Tommy Gilday. Our main enterprise was the docks and its cargo, when the drivers would stop for breakfast at the cafes on Liverpool's Dock Road. All we needed was one box of vodka or whiskey or whatever we got our hands on from the wagons. The wagon drivers would stop to fill their stomachs up, usually at Molly's Cafe. On Dock Road you could smell the bacon and egg sandwiches a mile away. The place was ancient but the lorry drivers and dockers loved it.

A little old woman called Betty with dark red hair worked at the café. Everybody loved Betty, who was a typical Liverpudlian with her little squeaky voice saying, "Good morning, love," to every lorry driver and docker who entered the door of the café. She was proud of being the cook at Molly's Cafe that served the best bacon and egg sandwich, which she would repeat all morning for the customers and local scousers. The wagon drivers loved her.

Tommy would wait outside by the door, keeping watch. Austy would jump on the back of the wagon with knife cutters, or sometimes Stanley knives to rip open the cargo. Austy would shout at Philip and me: "Get hold of that box." I would put the box on a little go-cart and push it down the dock road towards Soho Street. We were successful most of the time.

One morning, we stole a box of vodka. Here we were, laughing with our haul, down to the Liverpool-Leeds Canal, our hangout. Austy always had a buyer for the vodka. Most people in the Soho Arms pub were deprived and would gladly give a couple of pounds for a bottle of vodka or whiskey. Most were already alcoholics due to the stress in their lives.

Soho Street was in the heart of Everton; it was rough, next to the four tenements squares that bred some real tough guys, Austy just being one of them. He would sell the vodka to the local people in the pub for a couple of pounds, our little pot of gold, netting £25. However, the police were documenting us. Also, the bus heist at the Pier Head was documented by the police in the city centre while we carried on for quite a few months with our escapades. The police were hearing my name more often now.

As we lay fast asleep in our tent after eating hamburgers and drinking Coca-Cola on the banks of Liverpool-Leeds Canal early one morning, hugging our little coats to keep us warm, four policemen descended on the tent with a detective.

"Come out now, you little bastards!" they screamed and shouted.

We froze. We were arrested and taken to a Black Maria police van to the Liverpool City Police Station and charged with the theft of cargo and theft from stealing the money from the bus depot. We were put in the cold dungeons of the underground police station cells awaiting our fate, before going to the magistrates' court where we were given a cold cup of tea and a piece of dry toast for breakfast, from an old miserable policeman.

"That's all you're getting, you robbing little bastards," he would mumble under his breath while locking the door.

We were paraded into the Juvenile Court the next morning, keeping our heads bowed down with shame as our parents looked on. The three magistrates whispered among themselves with their hands over their mouths.

"These children need to be taught a lesson," the magistrate was telling the other magistrate. "Put them in custody, for probation to Menlove Avenue Assessment Centre Children's Home."

Britain's ruthless institutions were set up by the British government, and the Beasts of England couldn't wait to have us. In custody, all of a sudden, Philip started crying with the policeman shouting at him.

"That's enough now, boy."

We were carted off to Menlove Avenue Assessment Centre Children's Home, in the Black Maria police vehicle, where the abuse was introduced into our lives by monsters of men. The following week we were returned to the magistrates and sentenced into care by the court; me and Phillip, for three years; Austy and Tommy received probation. We got the stiffer sentence because of the bus shelter heist of £48.

I wouldn't see Philip for many years, or Tommy or Austy. They would hold me and Philip at Menlove Avenue Children's Home, once again a ruthless, sadistic chamber, an assessment centre, with our destiny unknown, a wicked place that would be famous in the future for the abuse of children on every level by the staff and its teachers: the Beasts of England.

The doors closed in the 1970s after concerns were raised in the House of Commons in London with relation to poor facilities and staff behavior towards children in care. The council was told that offences consisted of rape, beatings, you name it, every level of abuse. Most staff were the Beasts of England who would be arrested but too old to prosecute. What a shame, they should have been brought to justice for their serious crimes of sexual rape. The home was so bad the government ordered the place to be demolished; so many scars on a young generation, and lost lives, and death.

Phillip was allocated to St. Gilbert's Home for Disturbed Children in Wales. As for me, I would be sentenced in my youth to Britain's institutions, approved schools on four occasions, totaling 12 years. I escaped from them all. I would become one of Britain's many forgotten children. Detention in Borstal and prisons were places I would also reside in.

History is full of child abuse. But the scandal that unfolded in British children's homes is inexplicable for a modern western nation, with a tradition of caring for the weak.

Indeed, thousands of children were put in residential care homes where they ended up battered and sexually abused. This phenomenon poses many questions, but there has been little will among policy makers to ask them, let alone answer them. Most of the sexual abuse in children's homes had been by men on boys. And the widespread public perception of the Beasts of England pedophiles preying on young children in their homes is largely wrong. Most of the victims were teenage boys because male teenagers formed a majority of the residents.

These were our feelings: You all pretend to care. You all say, "I know how you feel." But you didn't. A few sympathetic words were your strength. You refused to dig deep and see what the real trouble was. You were all meant to be qualified for the job. But how could you when you have never experienced what we have? I wrote a poem:

The shop was overcrowded, no more room
It's a buyers' market during the baby boom
Defenseless, afraid, alone, and sad
Placed in a home with other kids
Vying with them for the highest bid
Buyers could inspect us and our hair
They don't like black hair, only the fair.
Many were shop-soiled and returned to stock
Damaged and spoiled with emotional blocks
And freezing hearts, they rejoined the sale
Constructed lovers, eyes empty and pale.
Black shaved priests who could only love one another, and to the stocks
Our surrogate fathers
Administering blows and cod liver oil
Between endless prayer and righteous toil
The stock was cleaned, the shop closed for the night
We huddled together when they switched off the light
The priests retire to Jesus for more frustrated love
While piously withholding it from dormitories above
Our emotional time bombs, temporarily defused
While we struggle with adult life, married and confused

Still trying to escape that unwanted long night
Scrambling through aged files in search of some light
The homes are now updated to suit modern taste
But still the containers of unwanted fetal waste.
The cold children's homes WILL continue to stay
While adult Beasts of England still involve children in their
dark play
The abusers still prowl through children's lives
Smiling, caressing, or threatening with knives
The kids still cling together through terrified nights
Manipulated like me, still stripped of all my rights
Until their death they departed.
God bless all of them
Rest in peace.

CHAPTER 5
LET THE GAMES BEGIN: SCOUSE GANGLAND WARFARE
1977

I had served a total of ten years of an 18-year sentence in Britain's institutions and got lost in that system; however, I survived it with many scars in my brain because it was basically a life sentence. I had lost my youth and most importantly, my mother and father and my love for them and my cognitive function due to the biological process. The list goes on; however, I was resilient and adaptable to physical stress. Most of the children and prisoners would have died from the abuse and the harsh life. I would say I was unhinged and looking for bigger and better things. Objective: money. My life had a gloomy outlook due to negative thinking: pessimism, cynicism, defeatism, and worst of all, expecting disasters, plus a fucking chip on my shoulder. I was angry at the world.

I teamed up with Phillip once again. He had done his three years and was a free man now. I noticed he had developed into a handsome young man, with his blond hair and a great physical appearance. But also, he had intelligence. It was in the city centre that I met him at the Wine Lodge pub, where all the men were drinking larger, cheap white wines, getting drunk off their heads in the presence of Gerry Bennett and Mickey, his brother.

Joe Evans, a Liverpool docker, was a good source of information from the docks for many years to come. A certain Liverpool docker would drive a wagon load of whiskey or whatever they could get their hands on out every night and make his fortune off the docks, but it was only a matter of time when Joe and his boys got too confident. Joe was followed one evening after driving out of the Clarence dock with his load of scotch whiskey. The port police were on his tail straight away. Joe was arrested, his trial would start at the Liverpool crown court in 1979, his charge was the Theft Act of 1968, and the evidence was overwhelming.

I decided to get to the jury before their decision and pay them off in exchange for money for a not guilty verdict. When the judge asked the foreman on the jury, "What is your verdict?"

The foreman pronounced, "Not guilty, your honor."

The court was dumbfounded. Joe walked out of the Crown Court when the judge announced: "You're free to go, Mr. Evans."

We all followed and went to the Legs of Man pub across the street from the court and celebrated singing: "He's a jolly good fellow, he's a jolly good fellow and so say all of us, hip, hip hooray," with our voices growing louder.

Phillip suggested we go to the Soho Arms, in the middle of the city.

I said, "Fuck that place."

Phillip got annoyed: "Calm down, Terry."

It was known for its brutal tenements, and tough underprivileged people. The Soho Arms pub was in the middle of the tenements, an old pub building just as bad as the tenements. The place was booming with gangsters from the city and nobody giving a fuck because nobody cared. It was a way of life in the Soho Arms.

One night I was there I noticed a little old woman sitting by herself drinking a glass of Guinness in the corner of the bar. I saw from a slight glance she had seen better days. I ordered a glass of Guinness and took it over to her.

"There you go, love."

She smiled with her toothless mouth. It made her day and mine, with all of the drunks with their big loud voices talking over each other. The Soho Arms reminded me of the movie, *One Flew over the Cuckoo's Nest*, an American film with Jack Nicholson and Danny DeVito. The pub stank of smoke, barrels of stale ale and musty sweat. When you exited the bar to the streets, they were filthy with litter, also.

"Oh, we might even bump into our old friend, Tommy Gilday," Phillip said.

We flagged a taxi down on Dale Street.

"Where are you going, mate?" the driver asked.

"The Soho Arms mate. Soho Street."

"OK. Rough as fuck that place, mate."

We just smirked. What the fuck did he know?

We arrived at the Soho Arms, paid the driver and thanked him. Soon as we walked in we saw the place was packed, people smoking and getting drunk, talking shit, but good people. I ordered two pints of beer from the barmaid, Rita,

"Here you go, Phillip and Terry. It's on the house, love."

All of a sudden, Austy comes from the lounge into the bar. There he was. Short, a little thinning hair, with a flat nose. As soon as he'd seen us, he ran from behind the lounge bar and hugged us.

"Fucking hell, lad. Lovely to see you!"

He and Tommy Gilday had served a couple of years each for an assault on a police officer, and probably fucking deserved what they got. One night a massive fight broke out. Tommy waded into the police beating the shit out of them on Scotland Road and Austy got some kicks in.

As Austy puffed on a cigarette with a long inhale, he shouted, "Three more pints, Rita!"

I quietly said, "Where's Tommy?"

To my amazement Austy said to me and Phillip, "He will be in soon."

I couldn't wait. Sipping on our pints, we laughed as usual with our special sense of humor. Austy told me and Phillip that he had bought the pub, which was impressive for a scallywag from Soho Street. As I looked out of the corner of my eye, the door of the bar swung open. Tommy walked in, all patrons' eyes fixed on him. Within a second he laid his eyes on us.

Austy shouted: "Here they are, lad!"

Tommy had changed. He was stocky, with a bent nose, and short hair. I noticed the development in his body. I patted him on the back, and he was fucking solid muscle. He gave us all a warm hug, saying, "Hello boys." His reputation had gone through the Liverpool underworld. You could not mess with him. No man would. We talked all night, drinking a few Scotch whiskeys, and smoking large joints and laughing our fucking heads off.

At about 10 o'clock another old friend engaged us at the bar. I knew of him. He was better friends with Austy.

"You know Terry and Phillip," Austy said.

I reached out my hand and gave him a friendly shake, so did Phillip. Austy introduced him: "This is Dennis Kelly"

Philip had told me all about Dennis, who was absolutely crazy and would kill anyone. He had short black hair and wore gold-rimmed glasses. Phillip told me he was a hard bastard and would fight any man. As the night was coming to a close that Thursday evening, Austy got excited and wanted to go to a club.

"Let's go to the Babaloo nightclub in Toxteth," Tommy said, which was in the south end of Liverpool.

I knew the Babaloo, my friend and Phillip's brother-in-law, Jake Abraham, owned the place, though we never gave it much thought. That night it was run by the West Africans who had settled in our city on Upper Parliament Street. We thought we would see Jake anyway, as Phillip's sister, Marie, was married to Jake.

We arrived by taxi at the entrance of the Babaloo. I noticed the bouncers at the door were tall, at least 6'2", stocky, and protective of their territory. Relationships at the time in the 1970s were not good with the people of Liverpool, however, we thought everything would be sound. As we entered the club, one of the head bouncers said with a bark in his voice, "That will be £5 each."

Phillip commented that his brother-in-law owned the place. The bouncer's reply was: "I don't give a fuck," raising his voice once again.

Dennis piped up. "Well, we're not fucking paying, mate."

"Well, you can fuck off and leave," the bouncer said.

I motioned to Phillip, "There's going to be big trouble here. Come on. Let's go get something to eat."

We ended up in Chinatown for a meal, which was far calmer compared to the Babaloo and its bad vibes. We entered Mar Bows, a Chinese restaurant, and we talked about the old times and the future, drinking bottles of white wine. I noticed that Dennis had consumed a large bottle of white all by himself.

Then Dennis blurted out, "I'm going back to that fucking club. My mates are there!"

Phillip said, "Don't be stupid. Relax, mate."

"I fucking won't."

Phillip and I decided to leave, while Tommy piped up, "Leave it out, mate," which was unusual for Tommy. We arranged to meet the following night at the Soho Arms to talk about some business. Intoxicated, Dennis and Austy went back to the club. As they tried to enter, the black bouncers said once again, "That's £5 each to enter."

A black bouncer, Billy, said to Dennis, "You will have to leave."

A fight erupted and spilled out into the street, with Dennis and Austy fighting Billy. Some of the other bouncers tried to break up the fight, but to no avail. Then, even more suddenly, a knife was pulled out and forced straight into Billy's chest. He was lying on the floor moaning, "Help me, help me."

He collapsed. Within a few minutes, he was dead. Austy and Dennis ran away. There was a manhunt in Liverpool for the two men: Dennis Kelly and Austy McCormack.

Eventually, Dennis was arrested while Austy stayed low. He was nowhere to be seen. The news hit the headlines. The papers read: Man Charged with Murder is Dennis Kelly.

Dennis' trial came up a few months later. We packed into the Liverpool Crown Court: me, Phillip Shields, Leslie Shields and Tommy G. The news was everywhere. After the jury deliberated, Dennis was found guilty. In his testimony, he claimed it was self-defense. The judge sentenced him to life in prison. Austy was still nowhere to be seen. We believed in his innocence, and formed a campaign headed by Philip's brother, Leslie Shields. We wrote on the walls over the city: FREE DENNIS KELLY.

He said he was innocent on the grounds of no evidence. His appeal was granted, but he was turned down once again. He would continue to serve his life sentence. We marched through the city: "Free Dennis Kelly!" Dennis would serve approximately 18 years of a life sentence. As for Austy, he was never caught as there was no evidence against him. This was the start of gang warfare in the late 1990s.

After Dennis's initial release, he was jailed once again for 27 years. He was found guilty of plotting to flood the U.K. with 166 million lbs. of staggeringly-high-purity cocaine. The judge told him that he was likely to die in prison. Once again I got a call from the Huyton mafia a few weeks later that there was a warm-up fight at the Liverpool stadium. John Conteh, a former world class champion, was on the headline card to fight Len Hutchinson, an American. We all decided to go with John's brother, Jerry. He was a friend of mine as well as Tommy and Phillip. The place was booming. All the boxers came to the fight and local gangsters we knew from all over the city. We were sitting ringside when I noticed a massive 6' 7" man walk past.

"Tommy!" I shouted. "Lad, how are you?"

"Alright mate! Who's that tall fella? I was in jail with him in 1974."

"Paul Sykes." Paul Sykes was a British professional boxer who had spent most of his adulthood life in prison where he became notorious as one of the most difficult prisoners in the country. He would serve 29 years for violent acts. After being released from prison he became a nuisance in Wakefield, Yorkshire.

"Piece of shit!" Tommy replied.

John Conteh entered the ring and put on a great performance. He won the fight. As we were all leaving the stadium it was mayhem. Paul Sykes bumped into Tommy going out the door.

"Watch where you're fucking going!" Tommy snapped.

Sykes was fuming.

I said, "It's OK. Paul."

Having a few drinks down him, Tommy shouted, "Fuck you, you big cunt!"

Sykes was on his way over to Tommy. I jumped in the middle, saying, "It's OK, lad."

It was about to go off big time but thank God it never did. Phillip had a gun on him. He blurted out that Sykes would have got it in the fucking knees, waving the handgun in the air.

That night outside the stadium if there would have been a brawl in the street, Phillip would have stepped in and shot Sykes, but no problem, it never happened. Phillip would have spent a lifetime in jail just like our old friend, Dennis Kelly.

Eventually, Sykes would turn to increased drinking and that would cost him his life due to cirrhosis of the liver. His two sons would be convicted of two separate murders: Paul Leighton Sykes for a frenzied knife attack; Michael Sharp for killing an ex-police officer while attempting to rob his house. They would spend the rest of their lives in prison.

Liverpool would erupt once again that year, the headlines reading in *The Liverpool Echo*: Chicago warfare when a gang of bouncers on The She Club door were confronted by a mob from Kirkdale.

The mob underestimated the bouncers, and all hell broke loose that night. A battle erupted in the street. My friends from Kirkdale were in the middle of it. They were Les Powell, Oliver Golden and Steven Owens. Their homes were attacked early in the morning, with the bouncers carrying machetes and hammers to break into their homes on the hunt for the men and causing a lot of destruction.

Most of the men on the door were arrested and charged with battery, Jobo Jones being one of them, and Big Fred. However, they got to the jury once again. Most got a not guilty verdict. Some went to jail.

In the 1980s, the Liverpool nightclubs had a rapid expansion set against a backdrop of Liverpool's economic challenges and social change. The city's club scene became a focal point for both entertainment and organized crime. This led to Liverpool taking its part in the infamous door wars. Liverpool was tagged by the media as a smack city or skag city after an explosion in gang crime and heroin abuse. This would flow over to the 1990s. The door wars were a series of gang-related shootings and criminal-damage incidents that took place in Liverpool going into the 2000s.

The violence began as a petty rivalry between young men and anti-social youths but escalated into full-blown gang war. This left a few of my friends dead whom I have mentioned. It will continue into the future, just like in 2024. Two men were sentenced to 64 years for the murder of Nyle Corrigan in 2020. Nyle was 19 years old when he died from a single wound to the back after being shot in Boode Croft in Stockbridge village in December, 2020. It was formerly known as Cantril Farm. Thank God my friends took my advice not to kill Joey Wright. They are free men today.

CHAPTER 6
ROBBERY AT DAWN
1978

I was having a drink at the city centre in Rigby's pub in November on a cold afternoon in 1978 in Liverpool when an old friend walked in. "Hello, Terry!" he shouted. "I haven't seen you for a while, mate." Taking his cap off and placing it on the table, he rubbed his hands, adding, "It's fucking freezing out there, lad."

"You too, Freddy. Nice to see you, lad."

Rigby's pub was located in the centre of Liverpool. It was one of the main pubs in that area. All the local Liverpudlians would visit the pub on weekends because of the atmosphere and it being a vibrant attraction for women and a great place on the weekends to socialize.

We sat and talked for a while in the corner of the pub, Freddy knowing my reputation. He had gone away to sea in the Merchant Navy with my brother, Alan. They had become good, solid friends in the time they served together.

"I've got a good job now, Terry, with the Corporation in Liverpool. They sent me to Rochdale to look after the textile mills. I'm on their security."

"Oh, good, Freddy. What do you do on security?"

"Well, I'm at the gate letting people in and out. It's a piece of cake, Terry."

"Lots of people work there, Freddy?"

"Oh, yes, loads of them."

Rochdale is a market town in the north-west of England and nestles in the foothills of the Pennines. It is surrounded by outstanding, beautiful scenery. Originally, when cotton was king, there were around 300 mills spinning and weaving, producing the fabric for which Lancashire was famous.

"That's an interesting job, security, Freddy. Do you want another drink?"

"Yes, Terry. Pint of lager, mate."

I thought I'd ask him a few more questions. "Is the money good, Freddy?"

"Shit, Terry, not enough to keep the family going. My wife works too, mate. Got to keep the kids going you know, Terry."

"Lots of people work there?"

"Oh, yeah, Terry. I do the night shift. It's fucking horrible."

"That's tough, lad."

"Oh, yeah. Tell ya what, Terry, thousands of people work there mate."

"Really? I wouldn't mind taking a look."

Freddy gave me a weird look, the cogs in his mind were going. "What day do you get paid, Freddy?"

"Thursday morning."

I knew, straight away. "Could you do with a new car, Freddy?"

"What do you mean, Terry?"

"Do you ever see the Securicor van come in, Freddy? That delivers the wages?"

"Of course, I let them in at five o'clock Thursday in the morning. I'm on the gate lad."

Fuck me, this is perfect! "What's the name of the mill, Freddy?"

"There's a sign that reads Textile Mill, on a massive hill." He informed me once again that there were hundreds of people working there.

"Want another pint, Freddy? Go on, how about another small scotch? Shot of whiskey. I'm buying."

His lips were getting loose now; he drank the Scotch in one shot.

"What about that new car for your wife?" He gave me a funny look.

"Well, Freddy, you're at the gate right?"

"Yes, Terry."

"Does security bring the wages?"

"Yes. Thursday morning at 5 a.m."

"I can have that Freddy, with my gang."

He burst out laughing.

"Don't fucking hurt anyone, lad will you?"

"No, mate," I replied,

"Is that right, Terry, Thursday morning? Ah, ha ha. I've heard about you, lad."

"I'll take a look at it, Freddy, OK? I'll get that new car, mate, for your wife. See you here next week lad."

"OK, Terry."

"It's on, Freddy. OK?"

He gave me the thumbs up with a wide smile.

I walked down Scotland Road to my old friend's house. This man knew nothing but crime. I'd worked with him before. Few people could get near him. We had done a few snatches, grabbing money from the banks together.

"I need to talk to you. I've got some graft work," one of our words for robbery.

"OK, lad."

I explained it. Brian got excited.

"It's a big one lad. I think over 100,000 quid."

"Really? Fucking beautiful, Terry! You got it. I'm in."

"Let's go and have a bevvy."

We stopped at the Green Man Pub on Dock Road and banged on the window three times. Tommy knew that was the code to let us in. We sat in the corner of the pub; it wasn't special and it was fucking freezing,

"Can you put the fire on, Tommy, lad?"

"Alright, Terry, lad."

The Green Man had seen better days in the early 1960s and 70s. It was rough as fuck, but we loved it and felt safe. An old friend of mine owned the Pub. Tommy OB, an underworld criminal, so we were safe to talk. Tommy poured a couple of pints of Guinness then left us in privacy to talk.

"I will know more next week when I meet my man, lad. OK?"

I needed another tough guy. There were many to choose from.

"Are you thinking the same thing as me, Brian?"

"Yes, I am."

"It's got to be Tommy G, right?"

"Yes."

"OK, you go and ask him, Brian, and I'll see you after I speak to my man, OK, lad?"

I couldn't wait to meet Freddy at Rigby's Pub on Dale Street again on Thursday afternoon.

A German owned Rigby's. I often said hello to him. You could walk in and nobody would know your business; sometimes you would get undercover cops on the lookout for information, however we would outsmart them. The manager of Rigby's was our friend and he would pass the information back to us as to what the police were looking for.

Freddy walked in on the spot.

"Pint, mate?"

"Yes go ahead, Terry, mate."

"Are we all good?"

"Yes."

We sat in the corner on the old red leather stools with a brown scratched-up mahogany table to place our pints on. I knew Freddy loved his Scotch.

"Here you are, lad. I'll get you a Scotch."

He threw it down his neck in one go.

"Are you going to have the guards, Terry?"

"Yes, Freddy. I'm bringing two tough guys in, OK? Why don't you drive out there next week? Take a look at the security van delivering the wages at about five in the morning mate."

"I will, mate."

Tommy, Brian, and I would drive out to Rochdale one early afternoon. Freddy gave me the address: Castleton, Rochdale. I had no problem finding the place, a massive five-story building with a sign that read: ARROW. It wasn't any different than the

Victorian buildings. The most important thing once we'd done our business was the getaway. With hundreds of people there, this would net us a small fortune.

We set a plan: one month to do the operation. I would see Freddy every week for the information at Rigby's pub on Monday afternoon. Brian Tommy and I would arrive at Rochdale the following Thursday morning at 4:45. a.m.

The morning was dark with a light layer of fog that was perfect for a hijacking. We turned the headlights and watched from a distance for the security van to arrive at the mill delivering the wages. At 5 a.m. on the spot, there it was, its engine crawling in the early morning coming down the street towards the mill. It arrived at the gate and stopped.

Tommy raised his voice: "Group 4 security van my arse, lad!" That meant they were nothing in Liverpool language.

The gates opened. It was perfect.

"OK, Brian, drive slowly back to Liverpool. Let's see how long it takes to do a dummy run."

We drove back towards Liverpool on the M62. Under the rising sun there was a lot of excitement in the car.

Tommy said, "I can't fucking wait!" He took a cigarette out and started to smoke. He passed one to Brian. They knew I didn't smoke.

I was dying to say to Tommy, "Put that fucking ciggy out." If I ever did I knew he'd be the type to shout back, "I'll fucking knock you out." That was Tommy. I kept quiet.

We then made our way onto the M56 and all the way to the M57. The drive was approximately an hour and ten minutes as dawn broke, marking the beginning of the cold day.

We went back to the Green Man on Dock Road and knocked on the side window as usual of the pub. Tommy was expecting us. He made us a beautiful bacon sandwich with a nice cup of tea. There we would discuss the next move. They had filmed a series all about Liverpool's tough life, *The Boys from the Black Stuff,* in the Green Man, which followed five unemployed men as they navigated their lives. It became famous in the 1980s, starring Yosser Hughes and Shake Hands and Lavero from Kirby. It was a great success for the city of Liverpool and put the Green Man on the map. The pub was most memorable for being the place where the well-known Shake Hands scene played out, whereby Yosser head-butted a menacing character known simply as Shake Hands, who had been approaching random people and demanding that they shake hands. The show had won the BAFTA award.

We weren't any different, except we were bank robbers planning our heists in the Green Man and no one knew, only my friend, Tommy. Our plan was to put a car in front of the gate at 4:45 a.m. just before the Securicor van arrived, then we'd come up behind the security van in the second car so they would be locked in with no place to move, then we'd jump out with pickaxe handles on both sides of the security van, smashing the windows in on the passenger and driver's side, yanking the security guards out and onto the street and holding them down, using the pin-down maneuver. Then, we'd get the boxes out of the back of the van.

The operation was set for two weeks away, on a Thursday morning. However, we still needed another driver. "No problem," I told the boys. I brought Dave Knox in, a gangster from a Huyton firm. He was a real ruthless man and a brute. He was about 5'6" with black hair and had a permanent weird-looking eye half closed. He loved to smuggle guns all over the country. I met him in Walton prison in 1974 when he was serving his three-year prison sentence for robbery with Tommy Smith, another member from the Huyton firm. Later on in the 1980s, he was connected to the London mob. His mate, Frankie Fraser, an underworld gangster, was the infamous Richardson gang enforcer.

We all had a drink together in the Green Man the night before, Tommy serving us pints of Guinness. Dave Knox would get to know my friends well. Dave got the high-powered stolen Jaguar from an auction in Liverpool, where he falsified his name.

We would meet at the Hillside Pub car park at 3 a.m. the next morning. The operation was all ready to go now. This was the real thing. I went home that evening and tossed and turned all night waiting for the early dawn to arrive. It was a short night.

We all met the next morning at 3 a.m. and piled into the Jaguar. It was absolutely freezing with white frost on the ground. Each of us was dressed in all black like British commandos, once again secretly carrying claw hammers hidden in our black jackets – and you never knew what else they were carrying!

Another car was behind us for backup. My friend, Paul Williams, was driving a ford Granada. I explained this as we were driving the Jaguar. They all agreed the Granada would be the one parked out by the gate to block the Securicor van from coming in.

"Great plan," Brian said. "Good lad, Terry."

We arrived at 4.40 a.m. We parked the Jaguar about a hundred feet away, Paul behind us in the Granada.

"Go park the Ford Granada outside the gate," I ordered Paul. "Wait in the Jaguar. And be prepared. Paul, you drive the Jaguar back, OK? Tommy, you're with me on the right side of the van. Dave, you're with Brian. Whack the windows in. Once they smash the windows, you can open the door. Davey, you jump in the back, get all the boxes, and throw them out to me while they've got the guards on the ground."

The Securicor van arrived. It slowed, making its way to the gate of the mill with its high beams on. The driver must have been confused, as the Granada was blocking the way into the gate. We were slowly behind the rear of the Securicor guard's van in the Jaguar. The Securicor van came to a halt, so they were locked in now.

I ordered, "Let's go!"

We came along to the side of the Securicor van. Whack! Whack! Both windows smashed in with the pickaxe handles, the noise had broken the morning silence.

"Get out, you bastards!" Tommy screamed. "On the ground!"

They followed the orders. They froze. Both of the guards were tossed onto the frosty ground.

"Please don't hurt us," one mumbled.

Davey jumped in the back and threw out four boxes to Brian and me while Tommy had his knee on the guard's back lying face down. We all escaped to the waiting Jaguar that Paul had strategically positioned with the boot open. We tossed all the boxes into the boot.

"OK," I ordered Paul. "Let's go, slowly."

Keeping to the speed limit, we would disappear before the police could blink. The anxiety level inside the car was high. Tommy took a packet of cigarettes out of his jacket and passed them around. Even though I didn't normally smoke, I took one this time to calm my nerves. Paul rolled the window down on the Jaguar to let the smoke out. You could feel the cold morning air floating through, releasing the smoke and high anxiety.

"Tommy, Brian, Davey, keep your heads down. All OK, Paul?"

"Yes, Terry, mate."

There was a bit of tension and talking as the sun was peeking over the horizon.

"Shut up!" I ordered. "Be quiet. You know the fucking score, lads."

Then there was silence. They would always listen to me. It seemed like hours before we reached the Blue Bell pub. When we finally arrived, my mate from the safe house was waiting in his Bedford van. We loaded the boxes into the vehicle. I ordered Paul to take the car to Cantril Farm and burn the fuck out of it that evening. As for the rest of them, Brian, Tommy, and Davey, they came to the safe house with me in Huyton. We were anxious to see what we had netted.

We went into the back of the bedroom in the safe house and broke open the boxes and emptied all the brown envelopes from the four boxes onto the floor, the wage packets for the employees at the Mill Company. It took three or four hours to count all the money. In the end it totaled £115,000.

We all had a change of clothing. My friend at the safe house would burn all the rest of the evidence of our clothes. Tommy,

Brian and Davey left on a bus a few hours later down the street just like regular people getting a bus to work outside the Bluebell Bell pub. Our share was £25,000 each, between Tommy, Davey, Brian and me. I kept £15,000, and gave Paul, the driver, £10,000, and £3,000 to the safe house. A week later, I walked into Rigby's pub.

"Hello, Freddy. You want a scotch?"

"Yes go on, lad. I'll celebrate with you. Fucking easy, Terry?"

"Here you go, Freddy," I said. "The police didn't have a fucking clue who did it."

"The police were informed though, Terry. When they arrived, the witnesses told the police that the robbers had gone in a flash. The guards were taken to the nearest hospital and provided treatment for shock. The police took statements from any witnesses, they asked me, Terry, a couple of days later. I said I was off work, never seen nothing at all, fuck that, Terry. The nearby areas were scanned for forensics for their investigation, lad."

"Here's £2,000 for the car, Freddy."

He just smiled at me. "Let's have a toast, Terry!"

We drank a shot of whiskey down our throats. As for the rest of the gang: Davey Knox would die several years later; Tommy would cause mayhem on the streets of Liverpool; all the gangsters feared him in the city. All the way up until his death during an accident at his farm in Lancashire, he will be forever remembered as one of Liverpool's tough guys. Brian went into business and bought a few pubs in Liverpool.

We are still friends to this day, and I get to chat with them at least once a month. Paul would burn the Jaguar, and if I recall correctly, move to London for a better life. Freddy wouldn't be a suspect, but that week that was his day off work, he never heard a word. He was still my friend all the time until I left for the U.S.A. I'd like to believe he is still alive today. The raid on the mill was successful. The Green Man pub would be demolished in 2017 another icon bites the dust on Portland Street, the dock road. I never heard from Tommy O' Brien anymore, but we had prosperous wealth once again.

CHAPTER 7
HELLS ANGELS CONFRONTATION
1978

I arrived at my girlfriend's house on a beautiful Thursday night in May. The house was situated in the middle of an industrial housing estate in the centre of Huyton, Liverpool. It was notorious for its crazy men, nutters, and gangsters. Just across the road sat the Blue Bell pub.

Annette and I met in a nightclub in the city centre of Liverpool in 1975. We formed a beautiful relationship. She was the love of my life. I knew that in the future she would be my wife.

I had decided to buy a new car, a new Cortina from Ford Motor Company, a special car, a yellow G.T. – exceptionally fast. Annette had not seen the car until I pulled up to her home to surprise her. Her mother and father, Annie and Alfie, rushed out to see the car.

"You like it, Alfie?"

"Yes, Terry, beautiful."

"I'll let you use it any time you want, OK?"

Alfie was in the British Army and had spent three years in solitary confinement in Germany after he'd been captured in World War II by the Germans. His wife, Annie, was a beautiful woman. They didn't have much in life, and if they did, they would gladly share with you even their old Ford Escort that was falling apart.

"Where you going, Terry?"

"Oh, just down to the pub called the Clarence, about half a mile from Anfield stadium. I've got to see my friend."

Annette came down the stairs, she looked beautiful as ever, with her pink polo neck on and grey jeans and red shoes. She just gave me a wonderful smile.

"You ready?"

"Yes," she replied. I opened the passenger door to the Cortina.

"The smell of the leather and the mahogany wood is beautiful, Terry."

"Get in."

"I bet this is fast."

"Oh yes." I put my black racing gloves on.

"Where are we going?"

"The Clarence."

"OK."

I sped through Huyton down Queen's Drive. Annette made another comment about the car's intense speed. I turned on Utting Avenue in between Anfield and Norris Green, two places that are notorious for gangsters and violent men. Most of the kids from those places would love to try to steal this car because at the time it was so popular.

As I stepped out of the car, I walked around and opened the door for Annette. We walked into the Clarence. The bar was long and was a young person's pub. It had lush furniture, beautiful round glass tables that were unusual and had been modernized from old to new and had a bowling green in the back of the grounds. As we walked in an old friend, Les Collins, was sitting there with his friends. We were good friends when we were kids. We did a lot of mischief together.

"Alright, Les? How are you?"

"Good, Terry."

We had a chat, and I approached the bar. "Two glasses of lager, please," I said to the barmaid.

As I was sipping the lager, I noticed two big men with Hells Angels jackets on, one staring right at me. I tried to ignore him, but I kept my eye on him. Just then, an old friend from Scotland Road walked in: Jimmy London. I was in Borstal with Jimmy in 1972. We talked about the movie, *Scum*, that they had made about the Borstal boys, and how brutal it was and how the BBC had banned the movie because of its violence and sexual content.

However, in 1979, it was released and became one of the most violent movies at the time. People were horrified, which led to Margaret Thatcher, Britain's prime minister, to close the institution down for good. We had a good laugh however, because we were the survivors of that horrific movie. A lot of young adults would not survive. Some of them couldn't take the hard regime, and committed suicide, the poor souls.

"Hello, lad! How are you? This is my wife, Annette. Well, she will be soon," I said.

"Hello, love. Nice to meet you, my name is Jimmy."

He had come to discuss some really important work, a job on the outskirts of Liverpool.

"I'm glad you're here, Jimmy."

The two Hells Angels kept glancing over at him.

"Cheeky cunts," Jimmy commented, raising his voice. They were really big guys. One was about 6 '2", with black hair and a thick mustache. The other was smaller, with a large bulky frame and a black beard. They both wore leather jackets with the Hells Angel logo on the back.

Jimmy was from Scotland Road and could handle himself well. He was the "daddy" in Borstal, the meanest of the meanest. No one would fuck with him, so these two Hells Angels were in for a fucking surprise. As the night went on, the pub got busy, and the bar was packed. They called for a last order of drinks as the bell rang, the manger shouted, "Last orders!"

I went up to the bar, and as I did so, found myself only a couple of feet away from the two Hell's Angels. The one that was staring at me came up beside me, he was the bigger one and made a comment: "We don't like robbers."

I ignored him, got the drinks and sat down. I looked over and he was pointing at me.

"There's gonna be trouble in here, Jimmy."

"Is it them, Terry?"

"Yes, those two twats."

My mind started racing. I had some tools in the boot of my car. A hammer and a hatchet handle about two feet long.

"Let's drink this and go," I said to Jimmy and Annette.

We went outside. The bar was going to close in thirty minutes. I told Annette to go home.

"Take the car."

"You sure, Terry?"

She pleaded with me to leave. Before she left, I opened the boot and took out my gloves, a ski mask, and a black overcoat which I always carried in case of an emergency. Annette took the order and left. Jim knew the score, what I was going to do. I knew they were loaded with booze, so I had the advantage. Plus, they were about ten years older than me. Jimmy stood there, ready.

"Here's the axe handle. Jimmy. When they come out fucking wade right into them."

I waited ten feet from the door for them to walk out. As they did so I walked towards the tall one and head-butted him right in the face. He went down like a ton of bricks. His friend tried to run but Jim caught up to him, whacked him with the axe handle in the back and beat the shit out of him. We left the two of them in a pile of blood.

"That will teach you a fucking lesson, you bastards!"

"Terry, your head has burst open, mate, There's blood all over you! You have a deep cut on your forehead. It's bad, mate. Come on, get in the car. I'll take you to the hospital."

All the customers from the Clarence were just staring at this point as they were leaving the bar. Jimmy took me to another area of the city, West Derby Village. I went into the emergency room at Alder Hey Hospital and told them I had fallen over. They did fourteen stitches in my forehead and gave me some medication for my pain.

I found out later on that the Hells Angels' jaw was broken who I had head-butted. They both went quietly. This was a lesson for them, and I never heard a peep from them or the police. I could've been arrested for a stupid thing like that over a fucking stupid comment, but it was all good now. I decided to drink outside the city, in the countryside, where it was safer and more peaceful.

Years later, my old friend Les and his family would become a notorious gang from Liverpool. They were given 82 years in prison for conspiracy to supply class A drugs. They would be known as one of the top crime families in the city.

CHAPTER 8
CANNIBAL FARM DEN OF THIEVES

In 1979, the City Council informed me by letter that they had a flat for me and Annette on an industrial estate. It was located in the heart of Cantril Farm, next to Huyton, and was close to Annette's parents in Huyton. I thought it would be a good idea to be close to them as they were getting older now, especially as Alfred had survived cancer. His wife, Annie, took care of him.

The flat was located in the tenements. The creation of these self-contained communities started in the 1920s, driven by a need to tackle slum housing and provide a better standard of living for working class families. From the mid to late 1930s, tenements really took off in the city with a number known as bull rings also being built. The city of Liverpool includes a diverse variety of historical housing architectures, some dating back several hundred years from small working-class terrace houses to larger mansions mostly from the Victorian era. While there are still many that remain in the present day, large numbers were demolished and redeveloped during the slum clearance of the 1960s and 70s. Of those that survived, many have since been refurbished. The flat that I viewed was refurbished. Annette and I were grateful as I would be offered a two-bedroom maisonette on the first floor, which we accepted. This would be the start of our new life.

The tenements were called Mosscraig, overlooking the whole of the city. We had moved in just before we were married in 1978. We furnished the flat out completely with beautiful furniture. I kept the address to myself and did not disclose it to many people except for family members. This would be our home for the future. The tenements were designed for our generation for a better quality of life and were miles away from the Liverpool skyline.

You had Carlyle Gardens in the Dingle. You had the bull ring in the town centre in Liverpool, Kirby, on the outskirts of the city, and the rest goes on. Within these tenements and the surrounding area amenities were also provided, which consisted of a local grocery store, a local bank on the corner, a bakery, and a sandwich shop with a butcher and community petrol station. Most of all there were new schools to educate the next generation which gave the people a sense of security.

Perhaps most important of all was the post office where people in tenements could cash their unemployment benefits and their pensions and pay their bills. People could also save some money in their bank account which the post office provided. They even built a pub on each corner of the tenements so people could socialize at night and weekends.

There was quite a lot of money flowing in the area of Cantril Farm at the time. There was also a generation of wild young thieves coming up looking for an operation. This was when the government was negligent. One pub was called the Black Angus. We decided to go out one night, me and Annette. It was a Friday evening when Annette finished work. We had our evening meal and watched a bit of TV. Annette had a little orange Volkswagen Beetle at the time. It was about 8.30 p.m. when we drove over in the little Beetle to the pub located at the other end of Cantril Farm. We walked into the lounge. It was a pleasant place with filtered maroon carpet and bar-room tables with ashtrays in the middle of the table where you could smoke freely. I went to the bar, ordered two glasses of lager and we sat down in the lounge. The place was packed with young couples. This was their new life now and a new generation.

Most of the people were local, but you would also get new people moving into Cantril Farm to start a new family from the city centre. In those pubs, you would always get a gang of tough guys. Well, they thought they were tough. Most had loose lips which sank ships. I noticed a couple that sat at the next table. It looked like they were married. I knew from experience that this guy was tough. I noticed him staring at the tattoos on my arm. After a few pints, he blurted out to me: "Been in jail, kid?"

I just smiled and laughed. Another tall man came over to his table. He was drunk.

"Hello, Alan, lad, how are you?" I thought nothing of it. Eventually the man left when Alan said, "I'm with my wife."

They made some small talk for a few minutes. Alan was looking over at me once again, asking, "Well… what jail were you in?"

I turned to him. "Plenty."

He started to laugh. "Do you want a drink, kid?"

"I'm fine, thanks," I said. Both of our wives were smiling at each other.

That was my first encounter with Alan Spencer. Then I told Alan about the sentences I had served. He was shocked to say the least; Alan was a well-known Liverpool tough guy.

At the time, I was working on the cruise ship, Queen Elizabeth II, and Annette was working in the city centre of Liverpool. After my dismissal from the ship, I became unemployed and received my first unemployment cheque from the government. It's called a Giro cheque. I had to find the nearest post office in Cantril Farm, located in the shops area. In the middle of the shops there was a post office named The Withen's Post Office. I decided to cash the cheque one morning after Annette left for work. I walked over to the shops at the Withen's and waited in line for the post office to open.

Upon waiting, two men approached the post office door with brown sacks over their shoulders and entered the post office. I didn't think much about it until I got to the window to cash my check. My eyes looked over. There, on the back of the counter, were two large stacks of money. I cashed my check from the post office employee, and walked home, thinking constantly about the large amount of money. We decided to go to another pub on a Friday evening called the Barley Mow. It sat on the corner, facing the tenements. As we walked in, the whole place was packed with people talking and smoking. I finally got to the bar and got two beers. Then, all of a sudden, I noticed a man in the corner, an old friend of mine, Tommy Cavana. He was waving at me.

"Alright, Tommy, how are you lad?"

"Good, Terry."

"This is my wife, Annette."

"Pleased to meet you," she said as they shook hands.

"What are you doing here, Tommy?"

"I live here, Terry, in Booth Croft."

Tommy was 6 ft. tall with dark hair and acne all over his face. I had known him from my days in Norris Green, a local tough area. He was a sound fella you could trust. He came from a family that was a wild bunch of thieves. I also knew he was game.

Tommy piped up, "Terry, there's loads of people that live here you know, lad. You know them all, Terry."

What I heard next from Tommy got to me: "Have you seen that post office, Terry?"

I couldn't believe what he just said. We had another drink, then I had to get going.

"Annette has work tomorrow, mate. We'd best be off. I'll tell ye what though, Tommy, here's my address. Come over tomorrow morning for a cup of tea after nine o'clock. OK, mate?"

"OK, mate."

When we both left the Barley Mow we were thinking exactly the same thing, me and Tommy: the post office.

At about 9.15 the next morning, there he was. Bang! Bang! On the front door.

"Come on in, Tommy."

"It's cold out there, Terry lad. Get the kettle on."

"OK, Tommy."

We both had a cup of hot tea together, as it was a cold morning. I knew Tommy had served a couple of years in jail, but I didn't know what for. We kept that private. As we sipped on our cups of tea, he began to stutter with nerves. The poor bastard, I thought.

"Do you wanna have a look at the post office, Terry?" he stuttered with anxiety once again.

"Yes, of course, mate. We can walk over there after the tea, mate."

Within fifteen minutes, we were on our way. We looked at all of the directions we could take if we ambushed the post office. I looked at Tommy.

"I'm game, Terry. I've got fuck-all to lose, mate. I need the money; I've got nothin'." There was desperation in his voice.

"Let's meet Monday morning, Tommy, here at the Withen's post office. We'll take a look, 8.45, mate?"

At 8.45 a.m. Tommy was waiting by the post office, eating a doughnut from the bakery next door.

"Wipe your face, lad, come on," I said.

"Let's wait downstairs; see if the post office van arrives."

It arrived at the back of the building at 9 o'clock. Two men got out, one went to the back of the van and reached in and loaded the brown post bag with parcels of money, putting the bag over his shoulder, then locking the door of the van. We slowly followed them towards the post office. We stood outside. Tommy went inside and took a look. He was excited when he came out.

"Terry, there's two big bags of cash, lad!"

We made a plan. We would follow the van the following week from Cantril Farm. The guards delivered nine bags of cash to nine post offices in the region of Cantril Farm and Huyton. Tommy, again, was already planning the robbery.

"Calm down, lad. Let's have a drink tonight in the Barley Mow pub."

"OK, Terry."

We sat in the quiet lounge on a Monday evening. We would plan on hijacking the van in two weeks' time. Tommy would bring a friend in on the job, and I would bring an experienced bank robber.

"That would be four of us to tackle the men and escape into a stolen car where we'd have a second car to pick us up."

"That sounds great, Terry."

I would contact my old friend, Jacko Fitzy. Without hesitation he was in. Tommy would bring the driver in, a man he'd worked with before, Paul Williams. We all met at a cafe in Huyton Village. We munched on our sausage rolls on a brisk April morning. A steady breeze was blowing with light rain coming down and passersby running to get out of the rain.

Jacko Fitzy was all of 5' 2" with a small-framed body and jet-black hair, he was an experienced man, and I also had heard about his fearless reputation. Paul Williams was Tommy's friend. I knew him well. He had long blond hair, a medium build, large blue eyes and an extraordinarily big nose. He also had a brilliant sense of humor.

As we were sipping our tea, Paul blurted out, "What's the gang called?"

I said, "The Mad Four."

Jacko was quiet and then just started laughing while Tommy blurted out, "The Den of Thieves."

"That's brilliant. That's great, Tommy," with Jacko laughing his head off, "and we're all from the tenements, lads."

This time there was no training, not for Jacko, Tommy or Paul. Only for me there was plenty, running five miles a day and lifting heavy weights as usual. The first Monday of April, 1979 was all set for the ambush at the Withens post office in the tenements. We all met the night before at the Barley Mow around a table, drinking whiskey. We all had our instructions. Tommy and Jacko would hold the men up, and I would jump in the back and grab the bags, and throw them to Paul. Paul would then throw them into the boot of the car and drive us all to Knowsley Lane to a pub called the Hillside where an old friend of mine would pick us up and drive three miles to Prescot outside Liverpool to the safe house.

We all met at Cantril Farm at 8.30 a.m. at a pub called the Ploughman, a short walk from the post office. We were all dressed in large overcoats with hats on, balaclavas in our pockets and nylon gloves. The surge of adrenaline started to kick in now. Paul had got the car the night before and was in position at the back of the post office. The breezy morning was overcast with dark clouds and damp, which was perfect.

"Put your gloves on, boys," I said.

This was do or die. We did not give a fuck for anyone. The government had fucked us. Now we were going to fuck them for the money. We had been persecuted since we were born. We're going to fuck you all back. The drive was in our souls for the dirty, despicable things they had done to us.

The car was a dark yellow 3.5 Rover engine four-door sedan, which would leave the police behind in a chase.

Tommy snapped, "It's perfect, lad."

The people from the tenements who worked in the city centre would be at the bus stop going in for the pittance of wages they earned to support their families in their meaningless jobs. Then there were the children going to school. We had to be careful of children crossing the roads. We all stood at the top of the stairs, waiting anxiously. My heart was pounding, and my neck was sweating and the palms of my hands were tingling with nerves. I noticed the van coming in.

"Get ready, boys!"

The two post office drivers got out and opened the back to retrieve the bags from the van. Then there we were, in a flash suddenly leaping up to overpower the guards. Tommy put a sawn-off shotgun to a post-office-worker's face, and Jacko drew a revolver to the other guard's neck. They froze instantly and didn't say a word.

I jumped in the back of the van and threw nine green bags to Paul. He loaded them into the boot of the car trunk while Tommy and Paul held the men at bay. The two guards were slim of build, ordinary-looking men. They must have got the shock of their lives. And, just as quickly as we came, we were off. Faster. In the car.

"Take it easy, Paul, no rush, mate," I said, while Tommy and Jacko sort of relaxed in the back. "Why did you point that gun in his face? There was no need for that, you soft twat."

Tommy was shocked. He had never seen me like this before. Paul and I took our masks off while Tommy kept his tucked into his forehead, Jacko's still fully covering his face.

"Take them fucking masks off, will you?" I said.

"OK, Terry," Tommy said. "Sorry, mate." He sounded just like a little kid; however, this man was tough.

We drove out of Cantril Farm at moderate speed to Knowsley Lane, made a right turn to the Hillside pub about two miles away, and parked at the back of the pub. I had an old friend waiting in a van. We loaded the bags, and all jumped into the back, making our way to Prescot to my old friend's house, Shuggy Boyle. We could relax now.

As the tension and anxiety subsided, we all entered my friend's house and made our way to the back garden shed, where it was all set up with a change of clothing for everyone. We took all our black clothing off and dumped it on the floor in the back of the shed. I knew Shuggy would take care of it. I broke the seals of the bags open and counted the amount that was attached to the seal.

"Add that up," I told Tommy. I leaned over and picked up a bundle of £5 notes to smell it. "Look at that, lads. Brand spanking new. It's beautiful!"

I fucking almost jumped for joy.

Tommy kept going: £50,000, £55,000, £60,000, £65,000… We had hit the jackpot. In the end, we all got a total of £15,000 each.

The men were picked up by their friends. Before Tommy left, I gestured for him to come over to where I sat. I blasted him for bringing a shotgun and the revolver he gave to Jacko.

"That's the last time I will work with you, mate, that's a 20-year sentence," I said.

The news headlines read that night: Ambush £65,000 stolen from the Withen's Post Office in Cantril Farm!

Shuggy drove me to Chester about 30 miles south of Liverpool. I booked into a bed and breakfast called The Cheshire Cat and stayed a week. Only my wife, Annette, knew where I was.

"Don't forget to burn the Rover, mate."

"OK, Terry. I will," Shuggy replied.

Tommy never had so much money in his whole life. He went to the city centre of Liverpool with his girlfriend and bought a load of jewelry for her and himself, and new clothes and big fancy leather coats. The police were now out in full force, looking for the Den of Thieves. They went to every pub in Cantril Farm. A few nights later they watched Tommy in the Barley Mow Pub with all his new clothes on and his girlfriend. They were dripping in jewelry. Jacko was also in their company.

The following morning, the Police Special Squad burst open the doors of their home at 6 a.m. They ransacked his house, looking for the cash, but found nothing. Nothing, until one policeman picked up a box of cornflakes on his way out of the home. In the bottom, lying there, was £5,000 in new pound notes. This was a gift for his girlfriend. Tommy was automatically arrested and put into a police car. His girlfriend was released when Tommy announced, "OK, you got me."

He would be charged that night with armed robbery and appear in court the next morning. He was put into custody with no bail. Jacko was also arrested and charged with armed robbery and put on an identification parade when a man picked him out. He was also put in custody. Paul went home; his house was also ransacked the following day. The front door was kicked off its hinges. He admitted to the robbery for a lesser charge.

As for me, I was nowhere to be found when the police burst my door down. My wife was at her mother's house. There was no one home. I called my old friend, Jimmy Mullen, to get some information, he was the lawyer representing Paul Williams. I always wondered how they got my address.

"Terry, I don't think they have anything on you yet, mate," he said when he left the police station after speaking to Paul Williams. I trusted Jimmy, he was sound as they come, a great scouser.

"Let's front them in the police station for the interview," Jimmy said with confidence. "I think you will walk out, mate."

"OK, Jimmy."

"That is unless Tommy, Jacko or Paul make a statement, which I don't think they'd dare to do."

"I don't think they will, Terry," Jimmy said. "The police would have given him some kind of indication.

"Thanks, Jimmy."

A couple of days later I met Jimmy Mullen at St. Anne Street Police Station at around 3 p.m. As we walked in four detectives were waiting for me. They took me into an interrogation room. The first thing one detective said was, "Tell us about your part in the robbery."

I answered, "I was in bed with my wife."

"Because at 9 a.m. that's where you would be."

Then I told them I would not answer any more questions.

When the detectives keep asking questions, it means they don't have anything.

I used the power of silence.

"Do you know Tommy Cavana?" I declined to answer. "Do you know Jacko Fitzy?" Silence again. These were the instructions from Jimmy, my solicitor. I did not answer.

"Place him in a cell," a detective said. I heard another detective mutter, "Mr. Smith." He would be the one who would follow me for many years later.

Jimmy now had done his job and left the police station. But why was I in the cell?

An hour later, a voice came from a detective: "Mr. Moogan, you will be going to an identification parade. There was a robbery in Sefton, we believe you were involved."

I knew the men who had done the robbery. A few hours later, I was put on the identification parade. I thought, I've got nothing to worry about, I will be going home. As I stood there, an old lady, 68 years of age, Elsie Seanor, picked me out of the line and tapped my shoulder. She was wearing bottle-thick glasses. That was enough to charge me on Section 68 of the Theft Act, the same charges as Tommy, Jacko and Paul.

I was put in a cell, thinking to myself, Oh my God. What happened? Paul Rooney, the solicitor, was informed I would appear in the Magistrates' court the next morning and be put into custody, charged with the robbery of £33,000. I was on my way to Risley Remand Centre once again, where Tommy, Jacko and Paul were on remand awaiting their trial. I would spend six months in Risley until my trial would start in September of 1979.

The judge had a trial within a trial, explaining there was not enough evidence. The evidence had to be calibrated with other evidence. There was none.

"Mr. Moogan on the 30th of April was involved in a daring armed raid which took place at the Withen's post office. The men escaped with a total of £65,000. Mr. Moogan was involved in a robbery in Sefton, Liverpool, stealing £33,000 from the Moss Lane post office."

The judge explained to the jury that the crown court did not have enough evidence in either case, therefore, I would be found not guilty.

"Let him stand up. He is free to go."

I was a lucky man for staying quiet and not giving in to any police questions. Like most men, they were feared. But not by me. One of the Den of Thieves was now back on the streets of Liverpool. As for Tommy Cavana, he would receive a 15-year sentence. Jacko Fitzy was found not guilty. Clever man for keeping his mouth shut. Paul Williams would receive five years for his part in the robbery, for driving the getaway vehicle. However, we found out later that Paul Williams had given the police the robbery information. But, by British law, there was still not enough evidence to go against me.

But now, I was a tagged man. I kept in touch with Jacko until his death in the late 1980s. I would never see Tommy again, nor Paul. The Den of Thieves was the biggest robbery ever in the Liverpool tenements, the place where thieves were bred. Cantril Farm would become one of the worst estates in Europe and be nicknamed Cannibal Farm by a television show, though the estate is now known as Stockbridge Village. It certainly used to be notorious for the scale of crime and unemployment in the 1970s and 80s. The public were scared by its reputation, and the community was forgotten. The end of an era.

CHAPTER 9
THE TALE OF THE CAGED BIRDS
1980

In 1969 when I was housed in St. George's, an approved school for a period of three years by the British government's policy, one of our joys was the love for pigeons. They would fly around the massive building and make their home, mostly on drainpipes or even air pockets that were attached to bathrooms. We could hear them early in the morning making their cooing noises. We would often climb up to the window to have a peak at them. Admiring their beauty took my mind off the abuse from the Beasts of England.

Being friends with Victor Steele, a little black boy, same age as me, from the south of Liverpool, was the first time I ever experienced racism. The so-called teachers would beat the shit out of him as well as the older kids in the home. However, he stood his ground, and he fought back like a little lion cub. He was my best little friend.

One day, we decided to feed the pigeons with bread and water, which we would smuggle in our pockets from the dining hall from our breakfast and evening meals. We would sneak out of the yard to the dormitory. I would give Victor some help to climb up the wall to place the bread and water in their nest. It gave us so much love and comfort. What did we care or know, we were 12 years old!

One morning, I looked into the nest and saw two eggs. We couldn't wait to see the baby pigeons. I got an idea. When the eggs hatched, we would raise the baby pigeons ourselves, especially Victor who adored them. This would give us joy and bring

79

enchanting peace for both of us, due to the umbrella of abuse we were under.

Then one morning, we noticed the eggs had hatched! Two beautiful baby pigeons sat cooing. This encounter had a profound effect on our lives. We could hear their joyous chirping in the early mornings that echoed through the bathroom and the dormitory instead of the loud voices from the Beasts of England. We decided to feed them with the same bread and water we stole from the kitchen when the mother and father were out looking for food.

When they got to a few weeks of age, just before Christmas in December 1970, we had taken the baby pigeons and placed them in a box in the fire exit adjourning the staircase of the building.

"I'm going to take them home, Victor."

"OK, Terry."

Each day we would feed them and change the box. We got empty boxes from the dining room staff who would tell us to put them in the bin. As winter was setting in, our Christmas leave was coming up, a time when all the children in the home got to go back to their families for the holidays. We were so excited to take them home.

"We can have one each," I said to him.

A couple of days before the 23rd of December, 1970, we were getting ready to go home for two weeks. We got escorted this morning and left the building with the rest of the boys. As we left, me and Victor turned back, went through the door, snuck up to the side of the fire escape and got the two pigeons. I was carrying them down the stairs in the box, when, all of a sudden, Headmaster Hickey was leaving his office and saw the both of us. We were escorted back to his office.

He took the pigeons off us and let them go. Next thing he said to me and Victor, "Take off your pants!" I knew what was coming next: the cane. The wicked Hickey Beast of England bent me over and viciously whacked my arse with six strokes of his cane. "Pull your pants up, boy. And wait outside like nothing happened."

I heard Victor screaming, "No, no, no!" Then it was over. He came out of the office, out of breath, sobbing his eyes out.

We were marched up to the dormitory and put in our beds with the door locked. There would be no home leave now for me and Victor. Our stay at St. George's was our Christmas, the year was 1970.

We would be monitored for two weeks, locked in a dormitory all day, only being let out to shower or scrub the corridors with a toothbrush. Our meals would be brought to us. I don't even remember what we had. We were locked into another world of abuse.

As I got older, I studied pigeons and birds: the blue tit, the red robin, the blackbird... One day I took a trip to Southport with my old friend John Lally. We were childhood friends. He was my partner in crime in Norris Green as children. It was a notorious part of Liverpool. He was the kind of guy if you were going to the guillotine he would sing his way through the darkest times with gallows humor and blunt wit and shout, "We are the mob!"

Our objective on that day was to observe some banks and post offices. Southport once was a wealthy community where nothing much ever went on. It was a tourist destination. We had a couple of drinks in the pubs then decided to walk along the pier, and settled down on a beautiful park bench where we fell asleep. A couple of hours later, we both woke up to the noise of the rush hour traffic and the sun shining on a beautiful spring day. People were strolling through the gardens and most of all it was peaceful.

"Let's go for a walk," John said as he inhaled his cigarette.

I nodded. "Yes, OK."

I had seen a sign that read: Botanical Gardens Aviaries Southport. We care for many animals from loud Macaws to Jumping Rabbits, Parrots and Peacocks.

"Let's go have a look at the Macaws, John. I wonder if they'd talk?"

We walked on. Then, emerging suddenly into view, was a massive aviary. We both stood at the end of the caged fence. You could hear the birds screaming at each other. Then, so swiftly you wouldn't know where it came from, a pink and white cockatoo landed on the cage next to me and John. He started to say hello.

"He's beautiful." I breathed out, "Hello." John just started laughing. Then an African Grey joined him, and another cockatoo, and one more African grey with his grey body and red striping.

The gears in my head began to spin.

"I'm going to take them home with me, John."

"You OK, Terry?" He was laughing.

"No really. Let's set them free, John."

He looked over at me. He could tell I was serious. We started to talk to them.

"Who's a pretty boy? Hello, hello!" Our conversations rang out.

"Let's come back tonight, John, get some wire cutters and make a net out of hangers. We'll capture the cockatoo, and two African greys. Maybe a macaw."

"Come on, Terry. Let's go." John said.

We walked back through the park. It started raining just slightly. We made our way through the town centre, stumbling into a store that sold houseware, called Argos. We walked in.

I asked the cashier, "Do you have a pair of pliers? Wire cutters?"

"Yes," she said.

John looked at me with a strange look. "Are you joking, Terry?"

"No. I'm going to cut the wire to the aviary tonight when the dark sets in, John. Also, I'm going to buy a bag to put the parrots in. But before we do anything else John, let's buy some biscuits and whiskey."

"Sure, they could use a snack."

"We can use the whiskey to put on the biscuits and feed them to the birds, so they'll get drunk. By then we'll just have to pick them up when they fall on the ground."

John was really laughing his head off now.

We got the wire cutters and two bags large enough to hold the birds. It was about six in the evening now, so we decided to stay till dark. We went to a local pub and had a few glasses of lager, then did a pub crawl around Southport. Around 8 o'clock we were pretty tipsy.

"Let's go and get them, John."

We both burst out laughing once again like little children. We made our trek over to the aviary. We took the biscuits out and whiskey. We threw some biscuits into the aviary. All of a sudden, the cockatoos and the African greys were having a party on digestive whole wheat biscuits. Then they all followed each other up to the cage where we were standing. Now they were hooked.

"Put that whiskey on the biscuit, John."

We began to feed them the laced biscuit, and they loved it.

"Fuck it, John. I'm going to cut the wires."

"Go on then."

I ripped the wire mesh apart and managed to grab two cockatoos and one African Grey from the sprawling branches of the tree, placing them carefully into the bag. One African Grey tried to fly away, so I pulled the mesh further open and crawled into the aviary. I ran after the African Grey, its tired wings flapping vigorously. I was fast enough and caught it. On the way out of the aviary I noticed a peacock running towards me. I didn't think anything of it at first. I was still a bit drunk, and my mind was calm, when all of a sudden it leapt from the floor and landed high on my shoulder. He started to attack me, then another one joined in.

By this time, the quiet home of the birds was awake and screaming. I kept hold of the African Grey, releasing myself from the attack of the peacocks. John was laughing so hard from outside the fence. I had to crawl my way back under the mesh to escape. As I handed the African Grey to John he put the bird in the bag, then he said, "Your neck is bleeding."

He was still laughing.

We left the aviary and walked to the car, placing the birds in the boot of the car then drove to Liverpool. It was hysterical. We could hear them moving around and talking in the back of the car,

"Where shall we go, Terry?" John asked.

"The Farmers Arms, mate."

It was a local pub we drank in. It was approximately 9 o'clock when we pulled up.

"Open the boot," I said to John.

"What for?"

"We're bringing them into the bar."

"No fucking way," he said.

"Ye, let's have some fun," I encouraged him.

Laughing, we grabbed the bags and walked into the bar. The place was packed with its usual customers; however, we knew everyone. I placed the bags on the floor. John ordered two beers. All our friends were saying hello to us. The moment was right, so I decided to take the cockatoo out of the bag and then placed it on the bar. Just then, an eruption of laughter filled the room. The bartender was in hysterics, laughing as the cockatoo kept saying "Hello, hello" and running along the bar. I asked the bartender for a small glass of beer. The cockatoo started to drink the beer. By this time, most of the bar was watching now.

They all asked, "Terry, where'd you get them from?"

"They were caged in the aviary in Southport," I told them, "so I set them free and took them with me."

I decided to take out the African Grey.

"Take them all out!" John was saying. "Put them on the bar!"

We put the two African Greys on the bar with the two cockatoos. The whole bar room was staring wide-eyed at them, laughing their fucking heads off. There must have been at least 60 people watching. The four birds were running along the bar now, drinking beer. It was the greatest show of any pub scene in the whole of Liverpool.

I decided to keep one cockatoo for myself. Me and John sold the African Greys and the other cockatoo for £150 each. The cockatoo brought me and Annette a sense of peace and tranquility into our home. His name was Joey. This encounter had a profound effect on the vocal bird. He did not have a cage, he had a box where he could go as he pleased, all by himself. The cockatoo's inability to communicate its plight effectively had led me to believe that they were content and joyous. Consequently, the cockatoo had adopted a facade of cheerful chirping and talking along with a love for chips.

The tale of the caged birds during the time of our young life brought peace upon us, served as a timeless parable, reminding us of the power of silence and patience. Just as the birds' songs were misinterpreted as happiness, we too often mask our pain and distress by embracing silence and patiently enduring our trials. We can find solace in the hope of eventual liberation. Like the cockatoo and birds, we must preserve and trust that one day our sorrows will fade away and we will soar freely towards a brighter future.

The caged bird story reminds me to listen to the silent messages hidden in the hearts of others. Take time to understand the unspoken language of those around us. Sometimes people may not express their true feelings openly, but their silence speaks volumes. By paying attention and offering supportive presence, we can provide solace and understanding to those who are silently struggling. Patience is a virtue that can help us navigate through difficult times.

The caged birds endured their captivity with silence and patience, knowing that freedom would come, similarly in my own life. We may face trials and challenges that require us to be patient and endure. Instead of complaining or becoming disheartened, embrace the power of patience. Trust in the process and have faith that hardships will eventually fade away, leading you to a better future and life.

Joey found a new home when my wife Annette joined me in California in 1981. Mick Cox, my dear friend, took Joey. He loved him, too. Now he gets to ride on Max the Doberman's back all day. The caged bird still sings all day now free as a bird, that oppression and injustice, all the dreams and aspirations that seem unattainable can be overcome. Amen.

CHAPTER 10
MARRIED AT THE HUYTON SUITES
1978

I had been dating Annette since 1975 when we met at a nightclub in the city entre called the Knightsbridge. I had just come out of prison, and it was love at first sight. Our relationship became strong. We travelled together everywhere. I even brought Annette onto the Queen Elizabeth II ocean liner.

We decided to get engaged. I bought a lovely diamond ring with the money I saved from my wages. We'd been engaged for one year when we decided to get married. I always wanted a family, given my nightmare childhood, and especially since losing my mother to that dreadful disease, cancer, and losing my father to numerous illnesses. I knew that Annette was the right one for me. We set the date: August 5, 1978. We chose the Huyton Suites, known for its class and wedding functions.

We went out one night near Huyton to a local pub on the Hillside estate. We discussed our plans for the wedding. We would have a sit-down dinner for 50 people, then in the evening we would invite whoever else we knew. I bought Annette a beautiful diamond wedding ring to match the engagement ring I had proposed to her with. She picked a beautiful white wedding gown. She made her choice of five bridesmaids who wore beautiful pink dresses. The girls were her best friends especially Susan Globe, a little Jewish girl.

I chose Alan to be my best man, my brother. We both wore blue velvet suits, blue shirts, and blue striped ties. All the expenses were paid from my wages and Annette's, even though we thought we didn't have much. It was more than enough. We booked the

Huyton Suite and the restaurant, as well as the main hall for the evening. At the time it was one of the best places to hold an impressive wedding. We had a head count, around 300-400 people attending in the evening. The ceremony was at Saint Agnes church, on the Blue Bell estate. All the expenses I paid for. Alan paid for all the cars. We had big posh Ford Granada cars all decorated with pink and white ribbons.

Everyone was so excited. The morning of August 5th arrived on a Saturday on a beautiful summer's day. I'd been out the night before with friends and got drunk, but I was fine. I would wear a blue velvet suit, and the pageboy, Anthony, would wear the same to match me. He was three years old.

I arrived at the packed church with Alan in a taxi. There must have been 300 people clapping and cheering as I exited the car. Annette's mom and dad were so excited. Alan was laughing all the time with the bridesmaids and all our friends were anxiously waiting. Annette would drive by herself, and her father, Alfie, would be waiting outside, eager to walk down the aisle to give her away.

Then, all of a sudden, there she was beside me, the priest waiting to give us our vows. The church was absolutely beautiful, decorated with pink and white ribbons. After we accepted our vows, a hymn was sung, Ava Maria, Annette's middle name. Everybody congratulated me and Annette, and we were off to our main destination, the Huyton Suites. We had a sit-down dinner which was filet mignon steak. The tables were decorated with beautiful pink silk tablecloths and bunches of flowers for centrepieces. Moët et Chandon champagne flowed like crazy on each table.

All the guests started to arrive at 7 p.m. with wedding gifts galore. There were probably a good 380 people that turned up. We danced until one in the morning, till the place closed, drinking our fill from the bottles of champagne all night, Moët et Chandon, once again. We listened to the greatest hits of the 1970s blaring from the DJ's speakers by the Beatles: "She loves you, yeah, yeah, yeah, with a love like that you know you should be glad."

It was amazing. People commented that it was the greatest wedding that they'd ever been to! One buddy of mine told me it looked like the Godfather's wedding. I just laughed. There were quite a few gangsters at the wedding.

The next day we woke up with massive hangovers, but we were fine. We boarded a train to London for our honeymoon and stayed at the Savoy Hotel where we toured the whole of London, Buckingham Palace, and all the beautiful shops such as Harrods. However, we could not afford anything as we did not have much money left. After one week we took a train to Brighton and stayed with my brother, John, and his wife, Denise, for a few days. After that we went to stay in a little cottage in Dorset in the countryside with Annette's friends, Maureen and Ronnie. We would take long walks, ride bicycles, and wait for Ronnie and Maureen to arrive home. Our evenings were spent together in the beautiful country pubs sharing our life stories. Sadly, Ronnie would be killed in the Falkland Islands war in 1982. Rest in peace, Ronnie.

We had a beautiful time. We were just kids really, 21 years of age. Annette and I would live together in my parents' old home till I made other plans for our own home or until the Council gave us a flat in the tenements in Cantril Farm.

That beautiful day of August 5, 1978 was one of the happiest days of our lives for me and Annette.

CHAPTER 11
HIJACKING SECURICOR: THE AMBUSH 1978

For a bit of history, the Securicor Company was founded by Edward Short, a former liberal Cabinet minister, in 1935. As Night Watch Services, its guards rode bicycles and wore old police uniforms. However, in 1939 it was taken over by Lord Willington and Henry Tiarks who developed it into a leading security business. It guarded and transported money and valuables and was targeted by armed bank robbers early in the 1960s. Now it was our turn in the 1970s and 80s due to the large amounts of cash they were delivering, ranging from £100,000 to £1 million.

After the wedding and honeymoon in 1978 I was walking one day through the city centre in the early morning. I was on my way to Water Street in the heart of Liverpool to take a look at some of the local banks in the financial district of Liverpool. Police patrol the banks with their specially trained German shepherd dogs. I would walk past the banks. They were massive old buildings that secured a lot of money and were always guarded with police and the dogs 24 hours a day. I noticed Securicor vans delivering the money to these banks. Nothing special, they were just regular men doing their job. It looked easy to me. I decided to find out where Group 4 Securicor was located. I went into a pub, the Crocodile, and ordered orange juice.

"Excuse me, love, do you have a yellow page phone book?"

The woman behind the counter pointed at the book, said it was next to the phone. I looked up Securicor Group 4. To my amazement it had a local office just off Lancashire Road, right outside Liverpool. I knew all the wages would be paid on a

Thursday morning to factories throughout Lancashire, Liverpool and Manchester, through information from an old friend.

I decided at 4 p.m. to go to the Lancashire office later at 4 o'clock in the morning to check them out. I got up at 3 a.m. and drove to Lancashire in my GT Cortina. I arrived at 3:50 a.m. I parked the car and turned the lights off on the industrial area outside Wigan. I watched. Got my thoughts together. I would follow the first van to see where it was going at that time in the morning. All of a sudden, I saw two high-beam lights in the distance coming towards me. I ducked down. As he went past I turned the engine on gently. I kept my lights off and followed him, slowly. He was heading towards Liverpool. At the sign to Kirby, he exited and drove around a roundabout.

I kept on his tail, following him or half a mile. Then he made a left into an industrial building. I parked my car on the corner a few hundred feet away and walked down slowly. I could see the Securicor van. I was wondering what kind of building this was. I entered the grounds and saw a building in the distance with its lights on. There was a group of men standing in line. I walked slowly and peeked through. The security guards were paying the wages to the group. I walked back slowly, trying to find the name of the building. Then there it was, the Liverpool Corporation Office, a government building. I noticed, across the street, a load of bin lorry's trash trucks. I walked back to my car and slowly drove home. If this was the bin yard it would cover the whole of Liverpool. There must be a lot of people working there. I got home and crawled back into bed. My wife, Annette, felt the weight of me shifting beside her.

"Where have you been?" she whispered,

"It's OK, go back to sleep."

I thought I'll get up at 8 o'clock and take my wife to work in the city centre. Annette worked in a corporate office as a manager's assistant.

I got up at 8 a.m. and made some tea for her.

"I'll take you to work, OK?"

We sat and talked about the future. I drove to the city centre and dropped Annette off. I gave her a kiss and told her I loved her, and that I'd see her tonight as she got out of the car, glancing back at me and waving. Then I headed through the city to my old friend Brian's house on Scotland Road.

The time was ten past nine. I went up to the flat and banged on the door. His grandmother, Maggie, answered, an older woman aged about 80 with grey hair and chubby cheeks but still as sharp as ever and beautiful.

"Come in, Terry. You're early this morning."

I smiled back. "Good morning, Maggie, nice to see you."

"Brian is in bed. Come in. You want a cup of tea?"

"Yes, sure."

Then Brian appeared, half asleep, rubbing his face,

"Don't you ever sleep, lad?" he said with a grin.

"I've got something."

That was a message in code. I told Brian the situation and he was delighted.

"Big money, Brian."

"Good, lad. We will take a look on Thursday. In the meantime, we need two good men."

"Don't worry, I'll sort that out this time, lad. Leave the other guys out of this one, we know who to bring in. Meet me Thursday morning."

"OK, lad. Pick me up here."

"OK. I'll be here at 4 a.m. OK, mate?"

Thursday morning, I arrived at Scotland Road. Brian came out on time at 4 o'clock.

"Get in, lad, here we go."

We arrived in Kirby at 4:30 a.m.

"That building, Brian, there. Group 4 security van will arrive soon."

At 5 a.m. on the dot, they arrived.

We gave them 15 minutes to set up and we slowly walked over. We both peered through the window. There they were, picking their wages up for the week.

"Let's go, Brian. Piece of cake, lad."

We drove home to his flat on Scotland Road in a car filled with smoke. Brian was a chain smoker.

"Come in, have a cuppa tea."

"OK."

"There's a few quid there, Terry. It's the whole of Liverpool. The men getting their wages for the week. Did ye see all the bin lorries? There's loads of them!"

"Yes, mate," I said. "What do you think? In a few weeks we'll have the lot!"

"All good, lad. I'm going to bring Eddie and Joe in, if that's alright?"

"Of course."

We had worked together a few times with Eddie and Joe. Trusted men. Hard cases.

"We can meet tomorrow, at the Throstle's Nest, OK?"

"OK, mate."

"See you tomorrow at 7. Make sure you bring them."

"I will, no problem."

Friday night I drove to Scotland Road to the Throstle's Nest, a crazy pub for gangsters and hard men. We would be safe in the back room of the pub and have privacy at the back door near the lounge.

Joe Marran walked in with Eddie H.

"Alright, lad? Brian will be here soon." "You want a pint?"

"Yes, sure."

I got four pints of lager, then Brian walked in. We discussed the whole operation with the four of us, Joe saying "Fucking love it, Terry!" Then he said, "How you doing, Rocky?" that was his famous line.

We enjoyed the night and arranged to meet at 4 a.m. on Thursday morning to take a look at the Binyard, as we called it.

Thursday morning, Joe popped up.

"Usual pickaxe handles, Terry?" with excitement in his voice.

"Yeah, mate."

"Without the hammer?" I laughed at him.

"We know what you carry, Terry!"

All of them were laughing. We all took a look and agreed we would have it the following week. These men were fit. Joe was 6ft. 4in. and had the look of John Wayne with his big, bulking shoulders and the sway in his walk. He was loved in Liverpool by the gangsters, especially in Huyton. Eddie was his old partner and was just as game and good. He was a quiet man and observed everything looking over his government spectacles. We were all friends from childhood, and we stuck together through thick and thin so we knew we could trust each other.

"Eddie, you drive, OK? Joe and Brian will do the business as soon as they enter the building. We'll come in front of them and block their exit to the building."

"That's easy. Let's stand outside and smoke a cigarette so they won't think nothing is wrong." It was absolutely freezing.

As usual, we'd put the men on the ground. Joe would take one, and I'd take the other, while Brian and Eddie would grab the boxes. Joe would get the stolen car the night before and park outside the back of the Green Man Pub just outside the city centre. Then we would all stay at Brian's flat at Tatlock Towers. I would sleep on the sofa, while Joe and Eddie took the floor.

It was Wednesday night; the rain was pelting down as usual, and the wind was howling. Joe was knocking on the flat door.

"Come in," Brian said.

"You get the car?"

"Yeah, I got a 3.5 Rover. Fast car that one, lad."

We all had a cup of tea, and it went quiet for the evening. My body could hardly relax. The old Victorian clock kept us all awake, ticking timelessly away on the mantelpiece. Eventually I dozed off and entered into a crazy dream that the police were chasing us.

We all awoke about 3:30 a.m. after Joe's snoring all night.

Joe got ready along with Eddie. We put our boiler suits on, black racing driver gloves, ski masks and parka jackets. As usual we were set. I put a claw hammer in the inside of my parka, just in case. We all had a hot cup of tea to warm us up with a piece of toast.

It was a cold morning in October when we walked down from the flat to the Green Man, pub. It was absolutely grim as the winter was setting in now.

"I'll drive," Joe offered.

"Sure, lad," I said.

He got in the driver's seat while Eddie and Brian hopped in the back, and we were off to Kirby. There were so many red lights we had to stop as the fog was blinding the view.

"Always remember," Joe told us, "fuck them up if they fight back."

You could tell the anxiety was starting to build now. Brian and Eddie stayed nice and calm. We arrived at Kirby around 4:35 a.m. and it was all quiet on the street.

"Soon as ye see the van come down the street head down into the toilets, OK?" Joe said.

The car was parked just outside the building, with the keys in the ignition for safety. All of a sudden the van made its way down the street. Joe led us to the toilet. My heart was pumping a little and my nerves were going. As we entered the toilet Joe took the lightbulbs out. It was dark now. We all put on our masks. Then suddenly Joe's voice cut through the darkness: "Get ready. They're here."

We all piled out and jumped on the two men as they were entering the building. Joe and Eddie were screaming "Get on the floor!" Then all of a sudden the guards were down; it happened so fast.

"Let go of the boxes, you fuckers!"

Within a few seconds they gave in. Brian and I grabbed the boxes. Joe and Eddie were still holding them down.

"Let's go!" Brian shouted.

We all went to the getaway car, threw the boxes in the boot, jumped into the car and headed out slowly to the old safe house.

"Fucking great, boys!" Joe said as he picked up the speed.

I shouted, "Keep it slow, don't go too fast!"

All was good. We were on our way now. Brian threw cigarettes around as usual to calm the nerves. We cut down the East Lancashire Road in the thick fog, the high beam guiding the car into Knowsley, then into Huyton to the safe house. We parked the car on the corner of the Blue Bell and walked a few hundred yards to the front door of the safe house and entered slowly. We were all shattered.

There we were, as safe as could be. Eddie was anxious as he put the two boxes on the kitchen floor. He took out a small hammer from his inside coat and banged the locks off them. I could see the sweat dripping from his forehead and his hands were shaking. I told him to relax. The two boxes contained brown envelopes of wages with all the names of the employees on them from the bin yard. Eddie and Brian counted the money, a grand total of £98,000. We paid the safe house owner £8,000 and shared £90,000 among ourselves. We changed all our clothes and left them in a pile for my friend to burn, plus the stolen Rover, and the empty boxes. We all left midday single handed. We had been successful once again.

Unfortunately, I would not see Joe again. He would pass away due to uncertain circumstances when the police chased him through the city centre. To this day, the details of his death are still unknown.

As for Eddie H, he was sentenced for fraud to three years in prison. However, the police visited him and told him "You are going away for 15 years."

As Eddie got back to his cell, his brain was so confused. The only way out was suicide. All his properties were to be seized by court order. That was the end of my childhood friends from Scotland Road, Joe Moran and Eddie H. As for Brian, he is still my friend today.

CHAPTER 12
LIVERPOOL MOTOR COMPANY ROBBERY 1979

We were standing all together at the funeral of Denny McGiven and his girlfriend Maria Molly. They had been killed on a busy Saturday night on London Road, Liverpool.

Denny had been in the Risley Remand Centre with me. We had struck up a nice friendly relationship. He expressed his innocence to me. He had been charged with a £4 million robbery of the docks in Liverpool, at 33 years of age. At the time he was 5ft. 9in. with light fair hair and a stocky build, with a beard and glasses. A true gentleman.

There was another nice man on the same charges for stealing £4 million worth of Travelers Checks off the docks in the city centre of Liverpool. He was ruthless but quiet. At the trial in 1979, Denny was found not guilty along with my other friend, Phillip Shields.

After Denny and Maria's funeral I drove with Michael, an underworld figure that would later become known as Britain's biggest drug dealer. I sat with him in his white Rolls Royce talking about how sad that lives can be taken away so easily. Michael was from African descent and a good- looking man. Later on, he would become a community leader who worked in the city council.

He used his reputation to mastermind a plot to load the streets with cannabis and heroin. Michael was dubbed the Godfather. His criminal exploits have been well documented. He is now well-retired from his role in the Merseyside underworld. An impeccably dressed man, his name is still remembered.

We made our way to a pub called the Hermitage in Walton. I was shocked to see all the Liverpool gangsters, especially the mob from Huyton. It was a scene right out of Peaky Blinders but the scousers were better looking than that lot. We had the pub all to ourselves. I glanced around the room and noticed a real tough guy from Huyton. His name was Tosh. He had moved to Huyton from Croxteth and was now catching my eye. I knew he was about to come over, then, all of a sudden, he did.

"Hello, Terry. How are you?"

"OK, lad."

"Sad day, lad, poor Denny and Maria. I didn't know you knew Denny."

"Yeah, I was in Risley with him. I didn't know his girlfriend; I believe she was a nice girl. What a waste of life."

"You had a good result, I heard, Terry. Not guilty, hey? ... Can we talk Terry?"

"Yes, sure."

"I can bend you in on a big job, Terry."

As we sipped on our glasses of lager I could see in his eyes he was excited to speak to me. Tosh was about 5ft. with a wiry body, deep green eyes, and black hair. He had a hell of a reputation in Croxteth.

"Go on, lad."

"There's five of us, Terry. We need another strong guy. My friend works at the Liverpool Motor Company; he told me they bring in the wages at six in the morning."

"Great that, lad. When are you thinking of having the place off?"

"Few weeks."

"Where do you get your information from?"

Tosh replied, "Inside, from a friend, Terry."

"That's great, Tosh."

"Meet tomorrow at 7 o'clock in the Dog and Gun pub in Croxteth? You can meet a few of the boys, they already know you, lad."

I finished my drink and left with Phillip Shields and Tommy Molloy. We went to the city centre for a drink, with the Liverpool Motor Company on my mind.

Halewood Body and Assembly is a transmission and manufacturing joint venue project owned by Liverpool Motor Company. The plant is located in an area of Liverpool, Merseyside. It began its operations in early 1960, an automobile production complex for cars. The company would eventually oversee the assembly of cars for the European market, the Ford Escort and Ford Capri. They also owned Jaguar and Land Rover Company. The company was on 44 acres of land. There were thousands of men that worked there on both the night and day shifts.

I met Tosh the next day, a Thursday night, at the Dog and Gun pub in the notorious Croxteth. The place was well known for armed robbers, and bred ruthless men. Later in life it got really bad when Norris Green and the Strand gangs started killing each other.

I walked into the bar. Tosh was sitting with three other men whom I recognized straight away. The bar was a filthy shitbox known throughout Liverpool as a place for tough bastards.

I calmly said "Alright!" to all of them.

"You want a pint, mate?" Dave said. "Go on, mate."

It was Dave Brown from Croxteth. I was in an approved school in the early 1970s with Dave. I knew he was a tough and crazy guy. Tosh's younger brother, Jimmy, who I didn't know, said hello to me. He was slim, with long black curly hair. Then there was Sonny Jenkins. I knew him from the city. He was a stocky man with black hair, while Dave was tall and slim with fair hair. They called him Welter because he was a boxer. You could see he was strong. Tosh leaned over to me and said he had the Liverpool motor company boxed off and sorted out.

"There will be £80,000 at least, Terry. Or more!"

"Sounds good, what's your plan?"

"Well, we always use shotguns. Sawn off."

I just listened, then said, "You the leader, Tosh?"

"Yes."

"Where'd you get your information from?"

"A local guy who works there told me. The Securicor van comes at six o'clock on Thursday morning. There's gates to the place, however there's a football field at the back of the company."

I asked Tosh a second time, "How do you get your information?" I could see he was being honest with me.

"From my friend, Terry, he works on the assembly line."

"Good. Who is making the moves?"

"We will, Terry."

"What about the safe house?"

"I know a guy in the outskirts of Liverpool very close to the motor company. He has a safe house there, too. Anything goes wrong, Terry, you come in as a heavy."

"OK. No problem."

"Let's go and look next week. Just me, you and Tosh. OK Terry?"

We arranged to meet at the Dog and Gun pub at 5 o'clock in the evening on a Monday night. In the meantime, I went to the Liverpool Motor Company and estimated the time to drive to my friend's house. He was a boxer who I used to train with. They called him Tony the Tiger; he was a boxing star before he was gunned down by a masked shooter. I knocked on the door.

"Alright, lad?"

"Come in, Terry! What are you doing up here?"

"Some business. Can we use your house for a safe house?"

"Let me think, Terry. My girlfriend's pregnant."

"OK."

"Hold on, though, I've got a mate around the corner. He lives on his own."

"OK, let's go and see him then."

We walked around the corner and knocked on the friend's door.

"Hello Jimmy! Cuppa tea, mate? Come in."

"Tony, this is my mate, Terry."

"Hello, Terry."

"Have you ever been in trouble, Jimmy?"

"No, mate. I haven't been in trouble. I'm all clean."

"Is it possible we could stop by early one morning for a few hours? There will be five or six of us. You working, mate?"

"No."

"OK, we'll give you a few quid, OK?"

He agreed. Anyone who was a friend of Tony Sinnott's had to be sound.

"I'll come see you soon, OK?"

"OK, Terry."

The distance from The Liverpool Motor Company to Jimmy's house was two miles. We would watch the van pull up at 6 a.m. That's all I needed to see.

The following week me and Tosh drove to the outskirts of Liverpool. It was a cold January night when we hopped the fence from the football field and onto the ground of the Liverpool Motor Company to stake the place out. We made our way to the front entrance where the van would enter. The place was a perfect getaway.

"Tosh, let's come back and hide behind the cars and watch the security van come in next Thursday when they deliver the wages."

OK, Terry," Tosh replied.

I met Tosh at the Dog and Gun as usual, this time Sonny was with him.

"Alright, Terry. Let's go, lad."

It was a frosty and freezing morning at 5 a.m. Sonny pulled a cigarette out, "You smoke, Terry?"

"No, mate."

We parked the car on a housing estate. Then jumped the field fence and went over the wall at The Liverpool Motor Company at 5:45 a.m. We hid behind the employees' cars, gathering our breath.

Six o'clock on the dot and suddenly the van entered the gates. Two security guards from Securicor got out of the van. They went to the back of the van, opened the door to get the four brown boxes out and closed the van door. We watched like hawks. We could have taken them right there and then. We drove back to Croxteth. All excited, we parked at the Dog and Gun and I sat in the car with Tosh and Sonny.

"Next week... we can have that," Tosh said.

"Let's all meet here Monday night," I said. They both agreed.

We all met on Monday evening at 7 p.m. Dave, Jimmy, Sonny, Tosh, and me. We were all ready, but there was a problem.

"I've got two shooters, sawn-off shotguns," Sonny said.

I looked at him. He was used to carrying shotguns and was successful at hijacking security vans in Britain.

"We don't need fucking guns, Sonny, how many times have I told you. The guards are not big fellas. Only medium height," I said.

The air was starting to get thick with palpable tension.

"Doesn't matter," Sonny retorted.

"OK, I'm out then," I said,

Tosh piped in, "I'll tell you what, let's use sledgehammers instead."

Sonny thought about it, the gears in his head turning. He agreed and so we arranged to meet once more that Thursday morning, just before dawn.

"Make sure you get the car, Dave."

"Already done, mate, a van, and don't forget the ski masks."

They all laughed at this.

"You know, they've done it before, Terry!"

I drove to see Tony the Tiger on the outskirts of Liverpool, and knocked on the door.

"Come in, mate."

"I need to speak to Jimmy."

"OK, let's go."

We walked to Jimmy's house.

"Hello, mate. We'll be here at about 6:15 or 6:30 on Thursday morning, OK?"

"Ye, OK, Terry?"

He had a habit of sating 'ye' instead of 'yes,' or 'you.'

"We'll stay only a few hours. I have a bag here, mate, with some clothes in if that's OK?"

"Ye, mate. Leave them in the bedroom, the first one on the right as you go up the stairs."

"OK, thanks." I went up, and threw the bag on the bed.

"See ye then, mate."

"OK."

We walked back to Tony's.

"He's OK."

"Yeah, sound, Terry."

"OK. You pick me up there, Tony, OK? About 10 o'clock in the morning on Thursday."

"OK, Terry."

I prepared my usual things. Boiler suit and mask, gloves, and a pickaxe handle. I woke up at 2 a.m. I couldn't sleep due to the anxiety and the sweats I was having. My wife just turned over, she didn't say a word.

Thursday morning at 5 o'clock I arrived at the Dog and Gun. It was cold, misty and miserable. It was perfect for a robbery. There it was: the white van.

"Hello, boys," Tosh said. "How are we?"

We all bailed into the van. They were dressed once again like army soldiers, like professionals, however, they were all tough men, trying to make a living for their families. They would have made great soldiers in the real world but were not meant to be.

Tosh took off slowly towards the outskirts of Liverpool. I placed the pickaxe handle on the floor.

Sonny piped up: "No fucking messing out of them?"

"Remember to keep your voice down," Tosh said.

"No violence," I said. "Just go for the boxes."

We arrived at the football field.at 5.30 a.m. and scaled the wall. I could see Sonny, Jimmy, and Dave all in their black uniforms, with their boiler suits and masks on, black leather gloves, and pickaxes over their shoulders. Jimmy was behind Tosh. We all arrived at the main building and stooped down at the side of the cars that were parked. Tosh would give the order to move. All of a sudden the gates opened, and in came the Securicor van. We could hear the engine. The two guards didn't get out; they must have decided to have a sandwich and tea.

"Up to you, Tosh."

"Sonny, do the front window screen in with the pickaxe handle, smash it to fucking pieces," Tosh said.

"Jimmy, you do the other window in," Sonny said. "OK, Terry, get ready."

Breaking the silence of the early morning of fog and mist there came an almighty crash. All the fucking windows went in at once, the glass shattering all over the place mainly inside the van.

I ran with Tosh and pulled the two guards to the ground. We did the pin-down move and held them on the ground with our knees pressing into their arms so they couldn't move, paralyzing them. They were frozen. I knew this would scare the fucking life out of anyone. Jimmy jumped in the back with Sonny and Dave and grabbed the boxes. They were all passed to me and Tosh.

"Stay down!" Sonny yelled at the height of his anxiety. "Don't move! Or I'll blow your fucking heads off!"

One of the guards was mumbling, "Please don't hurt us."

We all made our escape over the fence, crossed the field, and entered the van.

"Well done, lads!" Tosh said.

We drove slowly to Speke to Jimmy's place. Sonny took his mask off, I screamed at him to "keep it on, for Christ's sake! They all have to be burnt. Don't leave it there in the van, it will have forensics on it, lad."

He finally obliged. "I'm sorry, mate."

Jimmy had his front door open. We piled upstairs to the bedroom carrying the boxes and placing them on the floor.

"All OK, Terry?"

"Yeah, Jimmy."

"Cup of tea lad?"

"OK."

"Happy days, Terry."

"Job well done," I replied.

"Happy days, lad," Tosh replied.

Me and Tosh smashed the four boxes open, each one full of brown envelopes. Once again it would take hours to count the money that was mostly £20 notes totaling out to £125,000. We stayed till ten o'clock drinking tea and eating egg sandwiches provided by Jimmy.

Jimmy wanted to get the bus, but I told him, "No, we'll wait another minute. Jimmy will drive you all to the Dog and Gun. Make sure you burn the van tonight, Jimmy."

"I will, mate."

We settled with £25,000 each, the richest we'd been. We felt like millionaires. I asked each for £1,000 to give to the safe house owner and they agreed. I said my goodbyes and waited. Jimmy would also drive me to my mother's old house and drop me on the corner of the street. We waited till things settled down to see if the police would come in my direction. Thank God they never did.

That night I packed a suitcase and left for Brighton to see my brother, John. There I stayed for two weeks until everything died down.

My wife called me. "No, the police hadn't been to the house," she said.

The headlines read that night: Ambush at Dawn at the Liverpool Motor Company!

I never saw most of the men again - fate had something else for them. As for Dave, he'd later develop a heroin addiction and pass away. Tosh also passed away, he had the same problem. Soon after, Sonny would be arrested on the docks for armed robbery and given a seven-year sentence. Young Jimmy, Tosh's brother, well, I never heard from him again. He was to burn all the evidence in his fireplace at home, in the coal fire, eliminating any chance of our discovery from the forensics there, making it impossible to catch the band of thieves. The police didn't have a dog's chance of succeeding. We were victorious once again.

CHAPTER 13
WALTON JAIL
1979

I woke up at dawn one early morning in May to take a look out the window. It was bleak and snowy, which was unusual for May. The trees were full of snow. However, it was a magnificent view. I was staring out of the window as the snowflakes were falling to the ground. I noticed two beautiful red robins in the tree playing together.

I went downstairs to make a cup of tea to get my thoughts together, then made a cup of tea for Annette and boiled a few eggs for breakfast. We sat in the kitchen together talking about the day, she was so dedicated to her job at the local bank, Lloyds Bank. It was in the city entre. Her duty was as a receptionist. All seemed well. After breakfast, I told her, "I will drive you to work."

"Thanks, Terry."

The snow was pretty heavy. As we were driving into the city there were cars skidding off the road and a lot of congestion.

She asked, "What are you doing today?"

"I'm not sure."

As we approached the city entre onto Dale Street the traffic was jammed due to the heavy snow falling, I pulled up on the corner of Old Hall Street and let Annette out of the car. She gave me a kiss on the cheek.

"I'll see you tonight, OK?" I said.

"OK," she said, and gave me another kiss.

As I was driving home I thought I'd go and see my old friend John Jones in Risley Remand Centre. We were friends growing up together as children. He had blond hair, a slight dent in his nose, and a short stocky build, about 5ft.7in." They had charged him with burglary. The place was where I'd spent many months of my life but this time I was a visitor, not a prisoner.

I got home, read the morning paper, and relaxed the whole morning. At about 1p.m. I got ready and dressed up to go to Risley. John was on remand and could not get bail. The one thing that is customary is to visit childhood old friends, to give them moral support.

I stopped outside a local store to buy some local sandwiches and fruit. Most prisoners are allowed meals brought in from the outside. I headed up the East Lancashire Road in my Cortina, heading towards Warrington, then to Risley. I pulled up in the prison car park in my new GT Cortina and walked over to the office. I gave the name of the prisoner, John Jones, then my name.

My mind was racing. I had all the memories coming back to me from the years when I was a prisoner in Risley. This time I was immaculately dressed, with a gold Longines watch on one arm, and a diamond ring on my other hand. I observed the visitors with their little parcels of food for their loved ones because the food in Risley was atrocious. We stood in line waiting to enter the main prison.

We waited about 15 minutes, then got called into the visiting room with the rest of the visitors.

"Go to C6, Mr. Moogan."

There, the guard ushered me in.

"Hello, John. How are you?"

"Hello, Terry. Thank you for coming, mate."

He was behind a mesh glass window with an opening at the side which we spoke through.

He had confessed he was guilty; he was just one of many friends who had spent most of their life in institutions.

"Don't give in John." We talked about his case. "Just hang on in there."

He was facing three years' imprisonment.

"Some of the guys here know you, Terry."

We carried on with our conversation about life. All too soon the prison officer shouted, "Times up!"

"I'll see you, John, keep your head up, mate. All the best, OK? Keep your head up."

As I was leaving, one of the prison officers called my name, Mr. Moogan, in a loud tone, which was unusual.

"Can you just wait here for a moment?"

I thought this was also unusual.

All of a sudden six detectives walked through the waiting room door. It was evident that the law enforcement agencies were following me,

"Can you come in here, Terry, to a private room?" one of them said, "we just want to ask a few questions at the police station on St. Ann Street in Liverpool. You're under arrest, Terry."

Keep quiet, Terry, the whispered voice said in my mind.

"What about my car? You've got the key."

"Yes, that will be coming with us to St. Ann's police station."

I was taken away in handcuffs, tied to a detective, a small guy but stocky. I could see him looking at the diamond ring on my hand and the gold watch. I knew what he was thinking. "This bastard got away with so much."

They took me into an interview room. It was dim. The lights were probably only turned on when they were interviewing someone. I noticed the light bulb hanging over the table from a wire. It reminded me of the approved schools when they left a small light on at night. Here, the light was also dimmed when the detective walked in.

"My name is Detective Sergeant McAtter."

As the detective interrogated me I felt a rising tide of panic as my heart pounded. I felt like saying, "So what? Fuck off, you cunt!"

I kept calm as usual.

"Where were you this morning at 11a.m?"

"I was at home."

"Well, there was a robbery at Ogden's Tobacco Company in Liverpool. You were involved.

"Not me" I said. "You got the wrong person."

"We know you have gotten away with a few, Terry."

I ignored him. Again, he said, "You were involved, tell us about the robbery this morning."

"I don't know anything," I replied. I used my patience, silence, and power.

"I'll tell you one more time, I was at home and got ready to leave at 12 o'clock. I arrived at Risley at 1 p.m. so that's impossible."

They couldn't pin me for anything.

"Well, you went shoplifting in Warrington, we found two leather coats in your car."

"No, they are not mine," I replied.

"You will be charged with theft for two stolen leather coats from a Marks and Spencer store. You will appear at the Liverpool Magistrate's Court tomorrow morning."

"How did they get in my car?" I protested.

I knew it: they had no evidence on me. But now I would be framed for shoplifting. They forgot all about the robbery and focused on getting me one way or another. I thought, OK, I'll get out on bail the next morning. It's no big deal.

I slept on a hard board in the police station called the Bridewell, in the city centre. I didn't get much sleep. The sound of the door unlocking woke me up early. An orderly passed me a cup of tea and a jam butty. Annette was on my mind. She wouldn't know where I was. It seemed like a day had gone by.

A few hours later I was called up to the Magistrate. The packed courtroom room buzzed, oh no! It's Woolton, the same Magistrate I had been in front of before. I plead Not Guilty and was denied bail and put into custody for the theft of two leather coats. I was escorted to Risley Remand Centre that evening. Risley, still a fucking dumping ground for the poor souls who were committing crimes, had not changed. It took me back to the time when I was 14 years old. I must have been the youngest prisoner in 1971. The place still stunk. In fact, now it was worse than ever.

Part of the prison housed sex offenders beyond repair, with a lack of rehabilitation. There were unannounced prison inspections to Her Majesty's Prison, Risley. It had not changed for decades there. In the reports it was an astonishing failure, up until April, 2023. It had high levels of violence, self-harm and suicide among the inmates.

I got the social services to call my wife to explain the situation and pass the word on to get me a solicitor. The next day I got a visit from Annette. I told her the situation. She couldn't believe it.

"I will fight the case, Annette, don't worry, love."

"I got you Paul Rooney, the solicitor, he will come up to see you," Annette said.

Then the prison officer shouted, "Time's up!"

"OK, love, I'll see you at the weekend."

I arrived at the courthouse the following week, the magistrates' eyes slowly staring at me,. After spending a miserable seven days in Risley I plead Not Guilty. The Magistrate set a trial date for two weeks out. I was sent back to Grizzly Risley. I spent two horrible weeks in a cell by myself there. It was diabolical. I knew all the guys in Risley and I coached them with their cases, some innocent, most guilty. The place was full of real tough guys, psychos and killers. The two weeks did seem to go by fast, though, thanks to Annette's daily visits. I thought there was something strange, though, I told

I arrived at the courthouse d and waited in their dungeon cells. Next thing I knew my name was being called up for the trial that was all set up by the police to frame me, I told my lawyer. There were 12 jurors in the court that would listen to my case. Paul Rooney, my lawyer, had told the jury I had never been into that store, or stolen leather coats, as they had claimed. He also mentioned how I didn't know how the coats got into my car. The jury went out for half an hour and found me Guilty due to my past convictions. The Magistrate, Wooten, was a bald guy with a twisted mouth. He looked at me from his desk with a disapproving, scowling, frowning look. He ordered me to stand up.

"Mr. Moogan, you have been in trouble since you were ten years old. I have no alternative but to send you to prison for six months."

I got the shock of my life. The detectives had smiles all over their faces, expressing joy. They had their man in custody, and I was sent to the dungeon below the court once again, then on to Walton Prison in Liverpool. My memory of Walton prison came back to haunt my mind once again.

I arrived at the prison at seven p.m. that night with a police escort. I was once again back in the same prison I had been in for two years when I was 16 years old. After a week of settling down I got a visit from the Serious Crime Squad to be interviewed. I was escorted and placed in a room just like a cell. There were four detectives, the lead detective was McAtter.

"Terry, we want to talk to you about some armed robberies."

"I don't wish to talk." The other three detectives stared right through me,

"We have you down for quite a few," he said, staring at his paperwork. "You need to come clean. If you don't, we'll arrest you again when you're released in a few months outside Walton prison."

My mind said, fuck off the lot of you. I kept my mouth shut.

"I am not answering any questions," I said.

This went on for hours. Eventually they left with fuck-all. I carried on with my sentence and was visited by Annette every month.

"Don't worry, love." I said to her, "I'll be out soon."

I got a job serving all the prisoners their food, work that would serve me well in the future although I didn't know it then, of course. Time went by fast. Before I knew it I would be released on appeal after serving one month. My solicitor had made an appeal on my behalf, but he quietly mentioned to me that I might be arrested upon my release. For robbery.

"You might be arrested for the hush-hush police probe, so be careful, Terry."

He told me my case went to the Magistrate's board. They made an order that there was no evidence, and I would be released straight away. I had served one month, then I was released on a Friday night from Walton Prison. I walked out the gates scanning once again for the detectives in waiting,

Annette picked me up. We went to a local pub to celebrate. Thank God there were no police detectives waiting outside the prison. The wall of silence was unbroken once again.

CHAPTER 14
A HUSH-HUSH POLICE PROBE
1980

There was a new article in the local paper, *The Liverpool Echo*. The headline read: Hush Hush Police Probe. Today resulted in a man being questioned over an armed robbery of £77,000 in Liverpool. Detectives from the Serious Crime Squad have been working on a string of robberies in the North of Liverpool. They called their investigation Operation Transit. Most of the cash was never recovered, one of the cases being a holdup in Bootle. A gang armed with pickaxe handles confronted post office van drivers, broke in the back, and put the men on the floor. Another Securicor van was also hijacked at Ford's Motor Company. The men made off with quite a lot of money in getaway vehicles. Despite extensive inquiries, the cash was never found. Officers from the Crime Squad based in St. Ann Street revealed that a man is now being questioned in connection with these robberies. He is being held on a shoplifting charge at a top Security Prison in the city of Liverpool. The investigation is ongoing. We hope there will be an arrest in the next couple of days to bring the culprit to justice.

There was no arrest of any kind. Their plan was to plant the leather coats in the car outside Risley to have me arrested. There was also a conspiracy with the Magistrate to have me put in jail so they could hold me. My solicitor was Paul Rooney whose father was a retired police officer. Carrying out inquiries, Paul found there was no evidence about me whatsoever.

Every time there was an arrest in the city or some of our friends were arrested we knew who to turn to: Paul Rooney and his dear friends Bernie Feilding and Jimmy Mullen. We would pay them for the intelligence, to see what information the police had. Unfortunately for them, they never had anything. Only once when they got an old woman to frame and identify me in a police station, and even then I was still found Not Guilty by the jury at one of the biggest trials of a robbery in Liverpool.

CHAPTER 15
CATCH THE MIDNIGHT EXPRESS
1980

I decided one day to go to the Farmers Arms pub in Clubmoor, Walton. It was famous for the graffiti on the walls from all the local gangs where everyone knew each other. I pulled up into the parking lot in my Cortina. I noticed a car behind me but didn't give it much thought. I walked into the bar. My old friend, Anto Garvey, was waiting for me, along with Terry Finnigan. We were close friends. Anto would mind all my belongings from his house, the money, etc. He passed me an envelope with £1,000.

"What do you want to drink?" I said.

I bought Anto and Terry a drink, then told them that I had to leave.

"I'll see you later."

I left the bar and got into the Cortina. As I took off towards the north of Liverpool, I scanned the mirror to see if there was anyone following me. And there was, the same car, a green Ford Granada. I leaned over to the glove compartment and pulled out a pair of leather gloves. They would help secure my grip on the steering wheel. I knew I was in for a chase.

As I entered the Queen's Drive area, I was heading towards the M62 motorway. I took it towards Manchester. Here he comes… the green Ford Granada

I knew who they were. They were detectives. I put my foot down on the accelerator and got the car up to eighty miles an hour, then ninety, then a hundred. He kept close to me. I headed towards the M6 to Birmingham. OK, I thought, this is it. The Cortina GT is going to move now. I picked it up to 120 miles an hour. I'd seen that they were lagging behind me.

A service station was coming up, called Knutsford, only eight miles away. I pulled off the exit to the service station to confuse them, then right back out the exit back to Birmingham. It worked; I'd lost them. I got to Birmingham and pulled over in a country lane to the nearest pub.

The pub was called the Hen and Chickens. I walked in. A few eyes peered at me.

"Can I have a Britvic Orange please?"

The bartender, a nice young lady, obliged.

"You have a public phone here?" I asked her.

"Yes, in the back room."

"Thank you."

I sat in the back room. I'll call Bernie Fielding, I thought. At his home. He was Paul Rooney's assistant. I dialed the number, he answered. I pushed the 50-pence coin into the phone box.

"Hi, Bernie."

"Hi, Terry."

"I'm being followed."

"You need to come and see me tomorrow morning. I have an idea of who that might be."

"OK, I'll come see you tomorrow."

I drank the Britvic Orange, used the toilet, and headed out back to Liverpool, keeping my eyes on the rearview mirror. All was good. I slowly exited from the M6 to the M62 then onto the M57. I entered Queen's Drive and kept the car going slowly. It was approximately 10:30 p.m. when I arrived home. I put the key in the door.

"Annette? Are you here?"

"Yes! I'm upstairs."

All was good. Fuck. If they want me, they can come and get me. That was my mindset at the time. Me and Annette had a cup of tea and went to bed.

"Oh, I'll take you to work in the morning. I've got to go and see Paul Rooney, the solicitor."

We woke up in the morning. I made Annette her breakfast

and we both sat there, finishing our tea. We got ready. At 8:30 a.m., we left the house and got into the Cortina. I took off slowly. The same car came up behind me, a different color, a red Cortina this time. I knew I was under surveillance from the Serious Crime Squad. I slowly drove into the city centre. I kept quiet and didn't mention a word to Annette. I dropped her off as usual. I parked the car in Dale Street in a car park and walked to Paul Rooney's office. I rang the bell.

"Oh hi, Mr. Moogan." The receptionist said. "Bernie is waiting for you in his office."

He didn't say a word.

"Let's go and have coffee."

"OK" I replied.

We walked down to Dale Street to a little shitty cafe. He still hadn't said a word. We entered the cafe. A little lady with a thick Scouse accent reached out.

"Can I help you?"

"Yes, two teas," Bernie replied.

I was a bit nervous to say the least. Bernie had told me he was also an ex-detective. I just looked at him as he was drinking his tea.

"Terry, we have some intelligence. My friends in the Serious Crime Squad told me they want you, mate."

"Carry on," I said.

"They said you've been doing some heavy shit."

What came out of his mouth next blew my mind.

" Do you know the Friday Night Gunmen, Terry?"

"No," I replied.

I just looked at him and nodded. My head said no once again.

"Well, the Serious Crime Squad is after them. If I was you, Terry, I would take the midnight express train to London."

The evidence was mounting, and I knew my life was about to change forever.

"Thanks, Bernie." I slid him £300 across the table.

We finished our tea and left. I would never see Bernie again.

I should have taken that midnight express. I was arrested at gunpoint only a few weeks later. I was the luckiest man alive when that prison strike got put into effect. I was released and put on a 24-hour bail. I was meant to report back to the same police station one day later. However, I knew the Serious Crime Squad was going to frame me, as they had done before. I could not take the chance.

Instead, I took the early morning express, by car, to London. I was desperately shattered and anxious about a Pan Am flight to Los Angeles out of Heathrow Airport. That was my midnight express.it was December 12th, 1980.

CHAPTER 16
A MAN ON THE RUN IN HOLLYWOOD BEVERLY HILLS 1981

After getting to Hollywood, just as Elizabeth Taylor had advised me, and after my experiences being a butler with Clint Eastwood, George Segal, and billionaires, I would encounter the famous Max Factor, the makeup mogul to the stars. After starting a whole new life, I decided I'd venture out to even farther horizons.

After World War II the film studios began to move outside Hollywood, and the practice of filming on location emptied many of the famous lots and sound stages, or turned them over to television show productions. With the growth of the TV industry Hollywood began to change. By the early 1990s it had become the home of much of network television entertainment.

Many stars, past and present, lived in communities such as Beverly Hills, Bel Air, and the Hollywood Hills. Among the features of Hollywood, aside from its working studios, are the Hollywood Bowl, a natural amphitheater used since 1922 for summertime concerts held under the stars. I got to experience seeing Shirley Bassey and Rod Stewart at The Greek Theatre in Griffith Park, also a concert venue where I had the honor to watch Tony Bennett and Barry Manilow as well.

The Chinese Theater is decorated in concrete with the foot and handprints of many stars, also the Hollywood wax museum with its numerous wax figures of celebrities. The Hollywood Walk of Fame pays tribute to many celebrities of the entertainment industry. The most visible symbol of the district is the Hollywood sign that overlooks the area. The new sign was erected in 1978. The sign originally said: HOLLYWOODLAND to advertise new homes being developed in the area. But the sign fell into despair and the "Land" section was removed in the 1940s when the sign was refurbished.

And here I was, the urchin child from Liverpool, arriving there with my various skills. Which star would I encounter next? I knew Dora from the world's best International Agency had some great ideas for me. Many present stars lived in these great communities, such as Beverly Hills, Bel Air, and Mulholland Drive.

Then one morning the phone rang in my Santa Monica apartment.

"Good morning, Terry."

"Good morning, Dora."

Dora was a beautiful woman who had pleased all the stars in Hollywood by placing domestic couples in their homes. She was of Italian descent and had built up the largest international agency in the world to the elite in Hollywood: producers, directors, and actors. You had to love this plump little woman, sitting behind her desk calling the shots to the Hollywood stars. With her long, black Italian hair, and her round face and deep brown eyes, you would never know she was filling the needs of all the A-listers in Beverly Hills on a domestic level.

"I need you to come in today."

I was a man on the run once again, in Hollywood and Beverly Hills.

CHAPTER 17
FARRAH FAWCETT THE BEAUTIFUL ANGEL
1986

I drove, as directed by Dora, to Beverly Drive. It was about ten o'clock on a Monday morning. I pulled my Mustang into the parking lot. It was a beautiful sunny day. I paid a valet a couple of dollars and walked up the Boulevard to the Beverly Wilshire Hotel to stroll around. I decided to pop in for a cup of tea. Beverly Boulevard sat at the intersection of Wilshire Boulevard and Rodeo Drive. The hotel itself has been a shooting location for film and television scenes. I sat at a table on the street, observing one of the most beautiful places in the world. A young waitress came to serve me.

"Do you have a cup of tea, please?"

"Yes, sir."

I was pondering, who could Dora have waiting for me next? Which movie star name? They had made movies in the hotel, *The Planet of the Apes*, *Clueless Sex and the City*, and most famous of all, *Pretty Woman*. I sat there, once again dreaming and observing the most beautiful cars going by. What do you expect in Tinsel Town?

The waitress appeared, what a beautiful soft voice she had.

"Sir, here is your cup of tea."

Ah, I'll let Dora wait a little while. I'm always on the ball. Within ten minutes I walked up the stairs to her office. I was dressed in gray slacks and a blue shirt to pair with my shiny black moccasin shoes. I opened the door.

"Good morning Terry." She couldn't wait to tell me. "Terry, you look like you're going out for an interview!" I just smiled. "I have a position for a few months for you. The couple I had placed in this home had to leave for the UK. He was an English butler, and his wife was the maid and personal assistant."

I nodded and listened.

"I'm going to make a phone call right now," she said.

I didn't pay much attention; however, I had an idea. Dora was raising her voice suddenly.

"He's my first choice! He has worked with many stars. How about tomorrow morning at ten o'clock?" Her eyes lit up.

I raised my hand as if to signal, OK. She hung up the phone and wrote all the details down for my interview, then asked,

"How are you doing, Terry?"

"I'm fine."

"You look good."

My eyes were focused on all the stars on her office wall including Frank Sinatra, Dean Martin, Jerry Lewis, and Marlon Brando. The list went on and on. I joked, with my Liverpool sense of humor,

"You should put my photo up there."

"You look great, Terry, once again." She handed me all the information. "Be there at ten o'clock in the morning, OK?"

As I was leaving I said goodbye.

"I'll call you tomorrow afternoon," I said, and waved.

As I was making my way down the stairs, I read the profile of the person on the paper. Farrah Fawcett! The address was Mulholland Drive with the directions showing how to get there. I got into my Mustang and left the lot. I drove through Beverly Hills, staring at the most beautiful homes in the world, and down the windy Sunset Boulevard towards the beach to Santa Monica. I was a man on the run.

I arrived at my apartment in Santa Monica. Annette was on the phone. I put the paper with all the details on the table. Annette was just getting off the phone with her mother in the U.K.

"Take a look at that paperwork."

"That's very nice. She is going to love you."

I just laughed.

Farrah Fawcett was born in 1947 in the coastal town of Corpus Christi. She was the second daughter of Pauline and Jim Fawcett, an oil field contractor. She had attended John J. Pershing Middle School in Houston, Texas, a school which is now the Magnet Program for Fine Arts. From 1962 to 1965 Fawcett attended W.B. Ray High School where she held the title of Most Beautiful student. In the fall of 1965, Fawcett enrolled at the University of Texas at Austin and joined the Delta Sorority.

The following year, a Hollywood publicist saw her photograph and asked her to come to California to work as a model. Initially her parents had forbidden her to go. However, in the summer of 1968, they conceded and accompanied her on her trip out West. Within two weeks she had landed a modeling job and a modeling contract. She remained in Hollywood and began a relationship with actor Lee Majors. The couple married that same year, July, 1973. She made guest appearances in September 1976 on the "Six Million Dollar Man," and on the television series, "Charlie's Angels," also starring the beauties Kate Jackson and Jaclyn Smith. The Aaron Spelling drama premiered to high ratings. The public loved it. The three women were an overnight sensation.

Shortly after the show's debut, a poster of Farrah dressed in a seemingly innocent red bathing suit sold 12 million copies. It was a combination of the girl next door kind of innocence and blonde bombshell sexuality.

On Tuesday morning I woke up early and had a cup of tea with Annette. She had prepared me a gray suit, white shirt, and a red tie. I got dressed, making sure to take all my references.

"You look beautiful, Terry."

"Thank you Annette. I'll see you later."

"Good luck today, love. You'll do well."

Mulholland Drive is a street and road in the Eastern Santa Monica Mountains named after a pioneering civil engineer, William Mulholland. I drove it one day with Annette. It was along the 405 Los Angeles freeway.

I drove my Mustang on to the 10 freeway in the congested traffic and connected to the 405 north, getting off at Mulholland Drive. I looked again at the address. It was in the 1500 block of Mulholland Drive. I drove, zigzagging for a few miles, till I reached 1500. There it was. I pulled up outside, fixed my tie and put my jacket on. I ran my fingers through my hair and wiped my loafer shoes with a clean cloth. I grabbed my briefcase. My mind was wandering as I approached the house. Was her boyfriend going to be there? Ryan O'Neal, the actor? I approached the gates, pressing the intercom. A voice answered.

"Hello. Good morning, Mr. Moogan. I'll open the gate," a soft voice answered.

As I walked to the front door, Farrah was waiting for me. Her long blonde hair was draped across her white jumpsuit. I would say she was petite, a lovely woman with lovely green eyes. Or maybe they were contacts? She reached her hand out.

"Hello, I'm Farrah."

"Hello, I'm Terry Moogan."

"Yes! Come into the lounge Terry."

I followed her in and then stood where I was until directed to sit down.

"Thank you."

She proceeded to tell me the same thing, about the English couple leaving for home. The position would be for three months. I kept eye contact the whole time.

"I presume you have your references?"

"Yes." I reached into my briefcase, pulled a file out, and passed it over to her.

"Beautiful references Terry. Would you like a tour of the home?"

"Yes, please."

The house was overlooking the canyon. There was a large pool adjourning the living room. The living room itself was full of beautiful furniture, sheltered by large windows viewing the canyon. We walked outside to the garden. There was a large lawn, then steps going down to the tennis court. We went back to the office.

"You love to cook Terry?"

"Yes."

"What's your favorite meal?"

"English roast dinner."

"Can you plan for a dinner party?

"Yes."

Her eyes really were a lovely green as she looked into mine.

"Oh, Terry, let me show you to your little apartment."

It was at the back of the garage. As we walked she asked me,

"Do you prefer to live in or out Terry?"

"Living out if possible."

"That will work."

"I'll write a curriculum for your home."

"Thank you," she replied.

I noticed a beautiful painting over the fireplace. It was the one and only Andy Warhol portrait of Farrah. We made our way back to the office.

"Well, when would you like to start?"

"Next Monday morning? Ten o'clock, I can be here at the gate."

"OK, Terry, I'll call the Agency today, then."

Farrah shook my hand.

"See you next Monday," I said.

"Thank you, Terry."

I arrived the following Monday at 10 a.m. and rang the intercom.

"Hello, Terry," she said in her nice, soft voice.

I told her I would be writing the curriculum for the home. I wore my nice, neatly pressed white shirt, black pants, with a butler's waistcoat, and a grey tie.

Farrah commented, "You look very sharp. I'll leave you to take care of the home, then."

I got to work on each room. The home was already immaculate.

I noticed the chandeliers could have used a bit of dusting. I also went to the garage. There were two Mercedes convertibles, one a 450 SL, and a green Rolls Royce Corniche – also dusty. I noticed Farrah was getting ready to leave.

"Would you like me to pull the car up to the door, Miss?"

"Yes please, Terry. The Rolls Royce," she replied.

I opened the door for her then closed it. Within two minutes she was gone. I decided to start with the chandeliers to keep occupied. I stripped it down and placed all the crystal in a bucket of hot water with vinegar. It was immaculate by the time I finished, right upon her arrival. She noticed me putting the finishing touches together. She chimed in, looking beautiful, "Terry, thank you."

At this point, the chandeliers were gleaming.

I asked Farrah towards the end of the day if she would like me to prepare some food for her evening meal.

"Oh no, thanks, Terry."

"I'll see you tomorrow then, Miss."

"Thank you, Terry."

I could see the house was needing attention, even though it looked beautiful. Throughout the next few weeks, I carried on from room to room, giving each a deep cleaning.

One of the joys was driving down Sunset Boulevard to the carwash in Brentwood. I would have them detail the green Corniche. When Farrah drove it she would always comment on how nice things were. I would leave beautiful salads in the fridge for her each day, she would not indulge in heavy meals, seeing as she was a model.

I had been under her employment approximately six weeks, and never had I seen Ryan O'Neal, the movie star, her boyfriend. Ryan was born in Los Angeles. He started his career in the late 1960s. His career took off on *Peyton Place*. It was an instant hit and boosted O'Neal's career. He later found success in films, most notably in the romantic drama, *Love Story* in 1970, for which he was nominated for the Academy award for best actor, and the Golden Globe award for best actor.

Peter Bogdanovich and Stanley Kubrick promoted him. He was also portrayed in *Titular*, and a character in Richard Attenborough's *A Bridge Too Far*. I had heard so much about O'Neal in Hollywood, his negligence over his family and the rest of the gossip, especially regarding Farrah. She, however, had never once mentioned his name to me.

Finally, he arrived one morning. Farrah let him into the home. He said a brief hello and offered little small talk. I sensed the jealousy of this man. I went into the garage to give them some privacy. Then I heard a loud voice screaming. He was engaged in a sudden screaming match. Then as quickly as he'd come in, he was gone. That was the only time I'd ever seen him.

One morning Farrah approached me.

"Terry, we will be having some friends over. Can you prepare lunch at the pool?"

"What would you like?" I asked.

"Some nice fish dishes."

"OK, Miss. Do you mind me taking the Rolls?"

"No, go right ahead Terry." That was my joy.

I went to the Santa Monica Seafood Company and bought six pieces of fresh swordfish. I cooked it and served it at the pool for all the guests with a Caesar salad, fruity melody, and a bottle of white wine from the cellar. One of the guests was Alana Stewart Rod's wife, and was close to Farrah.

I would clean the tennis courts and get the home up to standards, especially the kitchen cupboards. All the plates and cutlery were beautiful. All the colors in the home blended well against the white carpet.

Farrah commented one morning, "the house has never looked so beautiful, Terry!"

I just smiled. One evening, Farrah asked me to drive her to a Japanese restaurant in downtown Los Angeles for dinner with her.

"When do you want me to drive?"

"This Friday night, OK, Terry? I know you finish at six, I can pay you!"

"No." I interrupted her. "It's my pleasure."

My duties carried on, the easiest job I had ever experienced in my life. Farrah was peaceful but I knew she was secretly in turmoil with Hollywood, and with Ryan O'Neal.

When Friday arrived, I took a special change of clothing just for the occasion. About 5:30 p.m. Farrah told me we would leave for downtown Los Angeles to her favorite Japanese restaurant. I pulled the green Rolls Royce Corniche to the door of the house. I was dressed in a pale blue suit with a Gucci shirt, and a red tie. I waited at the front door of the Rolls. As she exited the house to the car she looked as beautiful as ever, nothing short of a stunning angel with her heightened, toned figure paired perfectly with her sheer red shoes and dress. Her long, voluminous blonde hair waves cascaded perfectly over her shoulders, framing her radiant smile. To my surprise, she sat in the front with me. I took off slowly from Mulholland to the 405, then to the 10 freeway, all the way downtown.

"Exit on Fourth Street, Terry. It's called the Red Dragon.'"

"OK," I replied.

We arrived at the Red Dragon. I valeted the car, and we both entered the restaurant. All of a sudden the manager began to make a fuss of her, like she was royalty. He must have thought I was her boyfriend. We were seated close to the window overlooking the main street on a beautiful summer evening. I noticed the lovely pink tablecloths and expensive silverware. The tables were set immaculately, with fresh red roses for the centrepiece.

"Have you ever been to a Japanese restaurant before?"

"No, Miss."

The manager came up to us at the table.

"The same as usual, Miss Fawcett?"

She just nodded, and a bottle of crystal champagne arrived.

"With two glasses please. You like it, Terry?"

"Oh, no thank you, a glass of orange juice, please."

Japanese egg rolls appeared on the table within a few minutes. I must say, the whole place seemed to have their eyes on the table and on both of us, especially Farrah.

"Terry, would you like some Shabu Shabu?"

"What is that?"

"Raw beef in hot broth. You dip the beef in the hot bowl of water Terry."

"I will try it, thank you."

A plate of raw sushi arrived. I'd never had anything like that in my life. I tried a few pieces. Our conversation centred around England and Europe, and people's lives. As the night went on I noticed her getting a bit tipsy.

"Did you hear anything back from the couple in the U.K., Miss?"

"Oh yes, Terry, they'll be back in a few weeks."

All I was thinking to myself was I have two weeks left after a beautiful meal. The manager brought the bill, Farrah passed him a black American Express gold card, then we carried on the conversation talking about London and how she loved the city.

Farrah said, "I just wanted to get out for the evening, Terry."

We exited the restaurant. The valet pulled up the Rolls Royce. I opened the passenger door for her; she stepped in and we were on our way home. She spoke little in the car as she seemed to be tired now and tipsy.

We arrived at her residence, I pulled in.to the driveway at approximately 9:30 p.m. I opened the door to the house. As we both walked inside Farrah kicked off her beautiful red shoes and watched them sliding across the Italian tile, ending up with her beautiful bare feet walking across the Italian marble.

"Oh, thank God, Terry. Such a relief to get those shoes off." I bid her good night.

"Good night Terry," she replied, "thank you once again for a beautiful evening. Thank you for driving me."

The following Monday I returned to her home and did my usual thing. I made sure the home was well kept, clean and tidy. I made lunch for Farrah, salmon and salad with orange juice and set it on the patio. She was a private woman, and my time was coming to an end. I always wondered if the relationship with Ryan O'Neal was deteriorating, and if they broke up.

Eight years later Farrah appeared in *Playboy* magazine at the age of 50. She suffered injuries when she appeared in a movie, *Man of the House*. I watched her on David Letterman when she was rambling in an interview. That started rumors about drug abuse. The new millennium had brought her problems. O'Neal suffered from leukemia, to which he would pass away in December, 2023 at the age of 82, after struggling a long time.

Her son, Redmond, also suffered drug abuse and was always in and out of jail. She lost her only sister, Diane, to cancer. She was devastated a couple of years later when her mother, Pauline, passed away to cancer in 2006. Arron Spelling also died. Farrah would be diagnosed with anal cancer. On June 25th, 2009, she'd lost her own battle with cancer at 62. Farrah Fawcett was a 20th century goddess. She had a fine bone structure, white teeth, and an incredible mane of leonine blonde hair, the perfect complement to her blazing green eyes.

It was my pleasure to have served her, such a beautiful woman, going through so much turmoil emotionally, while also pregnant with Redmond in 1985, when I was her butler. As for Ryan O'Neal, what he didn't realize in life and in his dreams was the real Farrah Fawcett, his beautiful fiancé. That was the true story of his life.

I have kept Farrah Fawcett's private world private. May she rest in peace. Her picture is displayed on my Instagram, The Hollywood Butler. It reads, "Terry, love Farrah."

CHAPTER 18
JOAN RIVERS - LAURENCE OLIVER
1985

Within two days my phone was ringing. I had an answering machine and people always left messages if they were important, especially Dora. I was downtown with Annette in Santa Monica. We went for a walk along the beach, drank a few beers in a big Dean's pub overlooking the beautiful blue ocean, and then strolled along the pier. It was a lovely summer evening watching the sun go down. We took a ride on the carousel that was in the film *The Sting*, with Paul Newman and Robert Redford.

Malibu beach was to the north of us, and Venice beach to the south. We walked and cut up to Ocean Park where we had our house a couple blocks from the beach. We arrived home early in the evening just in time for a barbecue. I was sitting on the patio when I asked Annette to check the machine.

"Yes, a couple of friends have called. There's a call from Dora, Terry. Sounds important."

"What do you mean it sounds important?"

"Isn't it always important when she calls?"

"I'll call her in the morning."

At 9 a.m. the next morning I called and left a message. Within ten minutes Dora returned the phone call.

"Terry! Top job, good money."

That's her favorite line. You had to love Dora; she was magic.

"I'll come in this afternoon, OK, Dora?"

"OK, Terry."

At 1:30 p.m. I did the usual thing. I drove along the Santa Monica freeway, off the exit to Santa Monica Boulevard, then

131

down to Beverly Drive, parked the car and ran up the stairs to Dora's office.

"Hi, Terry."

"Hi, Dora."

She said, "This is important. My client is a bigshot, and she is demanding you can handle this, there's nobody that can do silver service like Terry. The job for you is in Bel Air on Sunset Boulevard. Let me call her right now."

I was able to hear some of the conversation as Dora said, "He will be there in the morning at 10 a.m. OK, Terry?"

"Yes, Dora."

She passed the description order to me.

"Her name's on the top of the work order. Let me know."

I took a glance at the order. It read, Edgar Rosenberg - Joan Rivers, Bellagio Blvd, Bel Air, Los Angeles.

I arrived at Sunset Boulevard at 8:30 a.m. in the morning in my beautiful red Cadillac going towards Beverly Hills. I turned into Bel Air off Sunset, then into Bellagio Blvd. The house was on the right-hand side. I found the house number and parked outside and sat for a while as I was too early. So, I decided to drive around Bel Air and take in the sights of the beautiful homes. I drove to the top of Bellagio and parked the car. It was breathtaking seeing the homes and the views of Los Angeles. This was freedom I was in, or was it a dream? I said to myself.

I was dressed immaculately. Dark blue suit, blue tie, a beautiful white Armani shirt, and black loafers. I looked at the home from the outside. Beautiful colonial house with large iron gates, nestled in the hillside of Bel Air. I parked the car outside and walked towards the house. I rang the bell to the intercom.

"Hello, Mr. Moogan." The voice on the intercom answered. "I'll be right there."

A man of about 50 years of age greeted me.

"Hello. I'm Edgar Rosenberg," he said. "It's so nice to meet you with your beautiful English accent. I'm Joan's husband."

"My name is Terry Moogan, sir. I've heard all about you."

"Come, follow me."

We entered the front door of a French contemporary house with dark wooden floors creaking as I walked along beside him.

"In here, Terry, to the kitchen."

We sat at a glass table. I could see the beautiful breathtaking rose garden from the kitchen. It looked so peaceful. I made a comment to Edgar.

"I've never seen so many magnificent colored roses. I will use them for centrepiece decoration when you have a formal dinner party, sir."

"That will be beautiful. My wife will be here soon, wait just a minute, she is always late, Terry. I'll go fetch her."

In a minute I could hear Joan's voice approaching, louder and louder with each step she took coming down the corridor from the bedroom. Then she appeared.

"Hello, Terry." She stared right through me. "Oh my God, you have beautiful blue eyes."

I just gave a light smile back. I actually didn't know what to say. I knew she had a blunt, often controversial comedic persona that was heavily self-deprecating and acerbic, especially towards celebrities and politicians, all delivered in her thick New York accent.

She commented, "It will be lovely to have a Liverpudlian in our home. We would have a fifth Beatle!"

Wow I thought, what a compliment. I automatically liked her, then a young Melissa Rosenberg walked into the kitchen.

"This is Terry Moogan. Say hello, Melissa.

She reached out to shake my hand softly.

"My pleasure to meet you," I said.

Joan Rivers was an American TV show host, comedian, writer, and actress from Brooklyn, New York. She was married to Edgar Rosenberg until his suicide in 1987. Her daughter, Melissa, was just 15 when I met her, a beautiful young lady,

"Let me just quickly explain the position here, Terry, as I have to run to the studios in Hollywood, then my husband can finish the interview. Do you do formal service, Terry? For eight people?"

"Yes, Miss."

"Can you do English Trifle, Terry?"

"Yes, Miss."

"Well, the rest is easy. Sir Laurence Olivier will be coming for a few months to stay, and we want the best service for him, Terry. Can you work Thursdays through Mondays?"

"Yes."

She had requested from Dora at the agency for an English butler to take care of Sir Laurence Olivier and drive him to his appointments and give him personal attention. Laurence Olivier was an English actor and director. He dominated the world stage. He also worked in films throughout his career, playing more than 50 cinema roles. He was also a theater actor and played in a much-celebrated production of *Romeo and Juliet*.

I had to say yes to everything after Joan left. I spent an hour with Edgar, talking about my life and experiences. Edgar himself was originally from Germany but had acquired an English accent. He was also a producer for Fox studios.

"The job's yours Terry."

"OK, Mr. Rosenberg. I'll start next Thursday."

"Splendid. Oh, and one last request Terry, please take extra good care of Sir Olivier when he arrives."

"Of course, Sir. I will."

He smiled, a comforting sort of smile.

"Come then, Terry, I will show you the guest house on the grounds."

There was a little cottage at the back of the house. It was neatly decorated, a large bedroom with a king-size bed. The linen was Laura Ashley, I noticed.

"Your job is to maintain the cottage and the kitchen, as well as drive Mr. Olivier when he needs driving,"

"Let me ask one question. When would you like me to start?"

"Monday morning?" He smiled again. The position was a live out position. I noticed a beautiful Rolls Royce in the garage and a new blue Cadillac Seville.

"You may drive any one of these, Terry."

He showed me where the keys were kept hanging in the garage. "Mr. Olivier will arrive on Monday evening, if you could prepare a little bit of a light snack for him?"

"Which store would you like me to shop at?"

"The Gelson's nearby, OK, Terry? Here's a card for you. So stock the fridge up on Monday with whatever you need."

I arrived Monday morning and pressed the intercom. Edgar let me through the secured gates.

"Good morning, Terry, lovely to see you, welcome aboard. Do your thing. I'm going to be very busy today in my office."

"Thank you, sir."

I went straight to work cleaning the bungalow. Afterwards I worked my way to the kitchen, which took me all morning. In the afternoon I drove over to Gelson's in Century City and bought the finest food that catered to Beverly Hills stars and its many millionaires.

One of the light meals I would prepare was a walnut salad, salmon, a hollandaise sauce and tropical fruit. I would cover the plate up and place it in the refrigerator for the evening. Edgar had told me they would serve themselves.

I left at 6 p.m. Edgar told me to arrive the next morning, when they would have a meeting overlooking the lush, green, mani-cured lawn and rose garden. On Tuesday morning, I was greeted by Joan, Edgar, and the one and only Sir Laurence Olivier.

Laurence Oliver was an English actor, playing more than fifty cinema roles in his career, and had considerable success in his roles on television as well. His most celebrated plays included Shakespeare in *Richard the Third* and *Hamlet*. He received two Academy Awards, five British Academy Film Awards, and three Golden Globe Awards. He was married three times.

I actually couldn't wait. And there he was, 5ft. 5in., small frame, a nice gentle smile on his face, greying hair, and a white shirt with black corduroy pants and slippers to match. I made coffee and small fruit bowls for all of them and rye toast and marmalade while they sat in the dining room. Edgar introduced me.

"This is Terry, Laurence. He is also from England. He is an English butler."

"Nice to meet you, Terry." he said, reaching out with his hand. He gave me a warm handshake, and a gentle smile. He had a beautiful accent. Rather posh.

I left them in privacy and checked in on them every ten or so minutes and poured them coffee.

"We have to go to the office soon." Joan would say with her rough New York accent.

"Which car would you prefer, Ms. Rivers?"

"We'll take the Cadillac."

I pulled the car up to the door of the house and opened the driver's door for her, closing it after she got in. Joan drove out the secure gates down Bellagio Blvd.

I unpacked Mr. Olivier's suitcase and hung his clothes up. I noticed his suits were immaculate, a special brand from London. I ironed his stunning Yves St Laurent shirts, made his bed carefully, and washed all the towels. Most days consisted of organizing the house and making the evening meals for them. I would turn the covers of his bed down at night and leave fresh water with a couple of chocolates at the side of the bed.

Joan, Edgar and Sir Laurence would sit on the patio at night overlooking the rose garden. I knew it was their peace away from the hectic Hollywood scene. I would make shepherd's pie some-times, and steak and kidney pie on the weekends. Mr. Olivier always appreciated it. Occasionally, I would drive him to the Hilton Hotel on Santa Monica Boulevard to have lunch for his appointments. They really embraced me like royalty. Edgar would say to me, "it's so grand to have you, Terry."

Sometimes I had to pinch myself. Life was so good now, and yet there was always a dark cloud hovering over me, because of my troubles back home. After my midnight express from London, I knew there'd be no getting rid of what was on the back of my mind at all times. Even if they had no charges on me, it was always there'd.

Edgar approached me mid-morning on Monday.

"Terry, do you think that you could stay a bit late tonight?"

"Yes."

"We have four people coming for dinner. What could you cook?"

"Pork chop stuffed with apple filling?"

"Wow, that sounds great! And perhaps maybe a Caesar salad to start."

I set the table beautifully, white linen cloth, the fanciest china and silver, and Waterford glasses. My skills always kicked in from my years of experience aboard the Queen Elizabeth. About 7 p.m. when Joan, Edgar, and Sir Laurence were sitting in the main living room which overlooked the prestigious rose garden, I served them a special bottle of red wine, Opus 2.

"Another guest will be joining soon, Terry."

"Alright, I'll be in the kitchen."

"I'll answer the door while you're busy." Edger said.

I heard the noise from the door shutting, and some voices coming from the kitchen. I better go and get the guest a drink, I thought. I walked into the room and couldn't be more mistaken: it was the one and only Marlon Brando, just sitting there.

"Would you like a drink, sir?"

"Yes, the same as my fellow guests!"

Within 15 minutes the evening's meal was ready. They all sat at the table. I served a walnut salad, then a pork chop with apple stuffing for the main course. It was quite a sight, serving some of the greatest actors in the world. For dessert, I brought out an English trifle, topped with white cream with chocolate flakes, and Irish coffee.

At the end of the evening, I cleaned up the dining room and Marlon Brando left. I thought, I will go and turn the bed down for Sir Laurence and get him some fresh water for his bedside table. All of a sudden, the door opened and there was Sir Laurence standing there.

"Ah, thank you Terry. Beautiful meal!"

My mind was racing; I wanted to ask him a question.

"Good night sir... Oh sir? May I ask you a question?"

"Go ahead, Terry."

"Who do you think is the best stage actor?"

He thought for a moment, then muttered quietly, "Marlon Brando."

I knew it!

My time was coming to an end. Sir. Laurence would be leaving in two days. I carried on with my duties for a few more days. They were really busy and there didn't seem to be any more requests. Finally, I served one more lunch on the patio.

Edgar approached me.

"Where do you go from here, Terry?"

"I don't know sir. Dora will call me for another position."

"Well, Marlon Brando needs help, Terry, at his home."

"Tell him to call Dora at the agency sir,"

"I will, Terry. We'd like to thank you for your services."

"You too, sir, thank you."

I said goodbye. I got into my Cadillac, drove down Sunset Boulevard towards Santa Monica, listening to Frank Sinatra's "I Did It My Way." What a beautiful summer's evening, zig zagging along the bends and the turns towards the ocean.

The public ending to a private life, the suicide of Joan Rivers' husband, came without warning on August 14, 1987.

No one had any idea that the 62-year-old film producer would swallow a fatal amount of Valium in his room of the downtown Four Seasons Hotel in Philadelphia. He recorded three cassette tapes. One was for his wife, one for his 19-year-old daughter Melissa, and one for his business partner, Thomas Peleggi.

Joan Rivers was a gifted comedian and actress. Unfortunately, Joan would pass away on September 4th, 2014. She was 81years of age when she died of cerebral hypoxia.

I'd had the pleasure of meeting these three beautiful people in my life, and I am forever grateful.

Laurence Oliver would also pass away. It would be July 11,

1989. What a marvelous man. Thank you for giving me the pleasure of serving you.

CHAPTER 19
MARLON BRANDO THE WILD ONE
1986

I had taken a little drive up the coast to Malibu and gone for lunch most days with my wife, Annette. It was a mild afternoon in October, 1985. I would drive to Gladstone's, a restaurant in Malibu famous for its fish and chips. Just the thought of it would remind me of jolly old England. Then we would stroll down to the shore, and watch the sun descend over the perfect Malibu beach, in time for the sunset.

I knew that the phone would be ringing again. The last time I spoke to Dora in her office I'd told her I wanted to go freelancing, to work only on weekends or only take a job for a few months. The salary I made in three months was far greater, almost closer to nine months' worth of pay.

After about four days, the phone rang in the morning after 9 a.m. Annette answered it this time.

"Hello, Dora."

"Hi, Annette. Is Terry available?"

"Yes he is. He's right here." She passed the phone to me.

"Good morning."

"Terry, Edgar Rosenberg had a guest at his home recently. He says he's interested in you."

I knew it was Marlon Brando.

"OK," I said.

"Can you come in today?"

"OK, I'll get ready and drive over."

"Thank you."

I had a cup of tea with Annette. Who would not love driving

to Beverly Hills? It was a good excuse for a day out. The morning was a lovely spring day.

"You want to come with me, Annette?"

"OK."

"We'll drive around in Beverly Hills."

"Get the keys to the Mustang then. We can go up Wilshire Boulevard, take a slow drive."

As we approached Beverly Hills, the traffic became hectic. I knew I was running late at this point. I turned on Beverly Drive and arrived at the parking lot.

"Come inside with me, Annette."

"OK, Terry."

As usual Dora was on the phone when we walked in. We sat down, and she waved to acknowledge the both of us. Then she hung up the phone.

"Hi, Annette." Dora blurted out. "You know who was calling for you, Terry?"

I didn't answer.

"Are you listening, Terry?" I didn't really fucking care, the torment my mind was going through. Then all of a sudden I snapped out of the torment.

"Yes, I am Dora. Go on."

"Marlon Brando!" she said, raising her right hand in the air.

I just gave her a slight smile.

"Next Monday, can you make it at 12 o'clock? To his home? Edgar gave you the most beautiful reference. You are a lucky man, Terry."

"Thank you," I said.

Dora wrote all the particulars down for me, and directions to Marlon Brando's home, along with the time and date. Here I was the little kid from Liverpool who was thrown on the slag heaps of Britain's institutions going to meet Marlon Brando, the Godfather.

"I'll call him right now," Dora said with excitement. "Terry, he is the greatest actor in the world!" I smiled. "Then I'll call you to confirm, OK? He made a comment to Edgar that he was delighted with your service, Terry."

I looked at the address. Once again, it was on Mulholland Drive. This was where the Wild One lived. We would probably make a good match in our youth, and I thought he wouldn't make it into our gang because he wasn't tough enough. However, I agreed with Dora that he was the best actor in the world.

We enjoyed the day in Beverly Hills and decided to visit the Polo Lounge at the Beverly Hills Hotel. The Beverly Hills Polo lounge was famous to the Hollywood elite. We sat on the patio, watching and observing all the people coming and going. The place was amazing.

I said, "Could you imagine, in the 1940s and 1950s, all the great stars that once dined here right where we are sitting? I must say, Annette, we are very fortunate to be sitting where the elites of Hollywood had their lunch and dinner and not to mention all the beautiful women."

By the time I got home in the evening there was already a message in the answering machine. After hitting the button on the machine, I could hear the voice of Dora: "Twelve o'clock Monday morning, Terry! You've got to be at Marlon Brando's house on Mulholland Drive!"

I said to Annette, "She's gotta be careful she doesn't have a stroke," and we laughed together.

Marlon Brando was famous for this role in *The Godfather*. However, before that movie was even released he was already a star. In *A Streetcar Named Desire* he played Terry Malloy and in *On the Waterfront* a retired boxer working on the docks.

I set off at 11 a.m. on Monday morning. I was dressed in a black suit with a white shirt and blue tie, my maroon loafers tying everything together. I entered Mulholland off the 405 in my red Cadillac. I was looking for the 129 blocks, going around all its bends. Finally, I arrived at the top of Santa Monica Mountain. The street view at the hilltop home had razor wire atop the gate, blocking the driveway, along with a sharp pointed perimeter iron fence. There was nowhere to park the car, so I pulled up to the gate and rang the bell. A lady answered on the intercom. I felt like saying this looks like a fucking prison.

"Mr. Moogan," I announced.

"Oh, come in," she answered back to me with her unusual voice.

I drove the Cadillac into the compound. The front of the house had so much green foliage that you couldn't recognize what the actual house looked like.

The maid came to the front door to greet me, dressed in a black and white uniform that looked like it had never been ironed. Her hair was black, and she had beautiful deep brown eyes and olive skin.

"Hello, Terry. My name is Helen. Mr. Brando is waiting for you."

I thanked her and walked through the door. The whole place was dark inside, with dim lights and dark paneled old wood on the walls. The floors were wooden with old carpets on each walkway. The smell was musty, I thought, as I walked through.

"Come into the office, Terry."

I walked in. Mr. Brando was sitting on a leather chair with his maroon gown that looked too big on him in hindsight, but that maroon gown suited him. I noticed he was unshaven, and his grey hair was unkempt, long, and down to his neck. As he raised his eyes ton me his big heavy shoulders relaxed, coming forward.

"Hi, Terry!"

Clutching his hands together in a soft gentle voice, he rose from his seat. "A pleasure. My old friend Edgar recommended you wholeheartedly. Here, take a seat."

I sat on a red leather chair facing him.

"This is my home, Terry. Helen will give you the tour."

He explained to me that he did not entertain much and that he stayed home more often than not.

"What would you like me to do sir?"

"I want you to organize my home Terry."

"OK, Sir. I'll take the tour with Helen then."

Then he shouted in a loud voice.

"Helen!"

I looked at him, I couldn't believe what I was hearing, just like the movies, the way he shouted for her. You'd think he was acting. Just then, Helen emerged.

"Right this way, Terry," she said.

Marlon ordered Helen to give me a tour of the home, and we were off to the kitchen and the pool. The place was approximately two and a half acres and unkempt. The kitchen was old. Helen marched me through the living room. The furniture was old green leather sofas, with old paintings hanging on the walls. It reminded me of the headmaster's office in the approved schools in the 1970s and my mind started to flash back to the abuse I had suffered. Snap out of it, Terry, come on, lad, I thought to myself. Get your thoughts together,

"As long as it's clean, that's all he wants, Terry."

We walked through the untidy gardens. They weren't anything too special, just a simplistic style with lots of greenery and dry foliage with a few rose beds dying in the corner.

"The gardeners come twice a week. You can let them in and out," Helen said. I nodded.

We made our way back to the kitchen; the place was in disarray.

"Will you help me, Helen? To organize the home? Where are you from?"

"I'm from South America,"

"Venezuela?"

"Yes. How did you know?"

"I just guessed."

She started to laugh, "You are very funny. Of course I will help you."

"I'll show you the English way."

Helen smiled. "I'll only be coming over two days a week, Terry, I'm going to be semi-retired soon, you see."

"Ah, OK."

We made our way back to the office. Marlon looked up from his desk, combing his fingers through his hair and pushing it behind his left ear, he was reading a book or some kind of a script, I noticed,

"What do you think, Terry?"

"It's rather fine, Sir."

Dora told me that money was no object. I could do this for a few months, make a nice few bucks then relax for a few months. That was my plan.

"When would you like to come on board, Terry?"

"Monday morning sir."

"That's fine, Terry, see you then."

"Is nine to five OK, sir? I can write a curriculum for your home. That is my job description, sir."

"OK," he replied.

I knew his home was dull and miserable, but I really liked him.

I drove home; my mind was racing. I knew his life had to be tumultuous, and he had had a large number of partners in his life. I wondered if they would be coming and going. Or if I would remember any of their faces from the big screen? I arrived home. I couldn't wait to tell Annette about Marlon. Well, she just smiled.

"I'm going to work for the one and only Godfather, Annette!"

I arrived the following Monday. Helen opened the gate for me. Mr. Brando was in bed. I went to work in the kitchen with Helen. Within a few days it was all organized and the chandeliers were glowing. Mr. Brando had his lunch on the patio, sitting in his maroon gown which I thought was odd. Helen cooked scrambled eggs and wheat toast – his favorite lunch – with tons of ketchup. He ate overlooking the pool, in silence, all by himself. Helen served him while I wrote the curriculum. I left him a light salad and some lamb chops with mint sauce and mixed greens for his dinner in the evening. He was a man of few words isolated in his bedroom away from the Hollywood scene.

That day I was about to leave at 5 p.m. He walked into the kitchen and said to me,

"Thank you, Terry. The kitchen is beautiful."

I would carry on doing just that, making his home clean and beautiful. I had taught Helen more skills in one month than she'd come to know in ten years.

The home had beautiful wooden floors. Me and Helen would strip them down with sandpaper, then redcoat them. They came out stunning and shiny. One evening, when I was leaving, he told me he would be having a guest for lunch the next day.

"Could you set the table on the patio? I have a business meeting, Terry."

Then I heard him say Mr. Evans would be arriving around 11 a.m.

I couldn't believe it: he was the producer of *The Godfather* and *Chinatown* movies. I told Marlon, "Sir, I have met him. He interviewed me at his home in Beverly Hills. However, he had chosen a French chef over me."

"Well," Marlon said, "say hello to him when he arrives."

"Thank you, sir."

Here I was the next day, serving Marlon Brando and Robert Evans, the head of Paramount Pictures, in the hills of Santa Monica.

The lunch consisted of baked trout with a lemon sauce, an array of assorted vegetables, a green salad, and fruit for dessert, and mineral water with lemon. There they were, the two most powerful men in Hollywood, sitting having lunch overlooking the mountains in Santa Monica. They were being served by a man on the run, a Liverpool bank robber on this spectacular afternoon. What a show this was. It would read well in a movie screenplay.

In the early 1980s, Evans' career and life took a downturn after he pled guilty to cocaine trafficking. He only produced two films after that. *The Colton Club*, and the *Chinatown* sequel. Both movies had flopped, as did *Jade* in 1995.

Helen came up to me one morning.

"Marlon is going to Tahiti. We need to pack his suitcase. And he might want you to drive him to Los Angeles."

Marlon was busy having his breakfast that Helen had prepared for him once again.

"Come on, Terry," she said. "Come with me to the master bedroom."

Helen took two large suitcases from the closet. We went into Marlon's dressing room and neatly packed two of the suitcases with proper Tahiti attire. Helen mentioned to me that Marlon owns an island.

"You know, Terry, some of his children live there."

"Oh, how nice."

"He doesn't see much of his children." She began to say.

"What's the island like?"

"It's called Tetiora. He loves it there."

Helen and I carried on with our duties. I pulled the car out of the garage, a Lincoln Continental. I wiped the beautiful car down with a soft cloth and cleaned the windows. At about 5 o'clock Helen and I loaded the suitcases into the car.

"He will be leaving at 6 p.m. Terry. His flight is at 9 o'clock on Tahitian Airlines."

I watched patiently in the kitchen at the counter where I was writing the duties we had achieved that day. Marlon appeared. He looked so totally different. He was shaven, with a bright blue flowered shirt and a fedora to match his black pants, and dark brown shoes, so different from the mindset from when I first had the interview with him in his office. Just like the movies, the transformation was mind-blowing.

"Hi, Terry, I'm ready to leave."

"The car is ready sir."

I opened the passenger side door of the car to let him in.

"All good, Terry," he muttered sliding inside, puffing his breath a little.

The gates opened. I drove down Mulholland to the 405 free-way to Los Angeles Airport. He engaged in some small talk on the way.

"What's Liverpool like, Terry?"

"It's about as small as New York Sir."

If I'd really told the Godfather about my life in Liverpool, he probably would have loved my story. He would have started a screenplay. The Liverpool bank robber to Hollywood butler starring Marlon Brando as Terry. I told him Albert Finney had done a movie there called *Gumshoe*.

"Oh?" he replied.

I decided to ask him a question.

"Where did you grow up, sir?"

"You know, Terry, I spent a good amount of my life in Newport Beach when I was a kid."

"A beautiful place, sir."

We were about ten minutes from Los Angeles airport.

"How is Tahiti?" I asked him.

"Oh beautiful, Terry. I'll be there for a week. I'll call the house to let you know when I'm back. Probably the same day next week. It'll be later at night, is that OK, Terry?"

"Yes Sir."

I dropped him off at the curb side and got his luggage from the trunk.

"I'll take that now, Terry."

"Have a nice trip sir."

He waved his hand slightly in the air. I took the Lincoln home that night, parked it on the street in Santa Monica. As I entered our apartment Annette was waiting for me. We sat and had a light snack.

"You like the job, Terry?"

"OK." I said. "Marlon is quite an interesting man, and he is paying me good money. I might do one more month even though the job itself is so boring."

The following day me and Helen cleaned all the bedrooms and deep-cleaned the rest of the house. Each night I went home early and arrived late the next morning at the house. I also had the weekends off, before Marlon would arrive home.

Monday night after a short day I headed to the Los Angeles

airport, driving the Lincoln. I waited at the curb for Marlon to walk out. He appeared from the airport. I was surprised to see he wasn't recognized.

"How are you, Terry?"

"Fine, thanks, sir. Did you have a nice trip?"

"Beautiful," he replied.

I put his two suitcases in the trunk of the car. He looked so tanned in his blue flowered shirt and white pants. His large straw hat and sunglasses were disguising him. I opened the passenger door, and he hopped in.

"It's good to see you, Terry. How's the home?"

"All's fine, sir."

"How's Helen?"

"Oh, she's great."

"You should go to Tahiti someday," he said as I was driving along the 405 freeway. "You would love the place, Terry."

After we entered the compound and parked I opened the passenger door for Marlon. He walked straight to the front door of the house. I took his suitcases upstairs. With his soft voice he uttered,

"It's good to be home, Terry," his breathing shallow.

"Helen made you a small meal, lamb chops and pasta, it's in the fridge."

"OK." Marlon said, "thank you. Can I get a bottle of wine, Terry?"

"Of course, sir."

"Would you like to join me?"

My mind started to race. Why would a man like this need my company? Was he lonely? However, I did decide to join him.

I suppose I'll be polite and take a glass of wine. Just a quick one. It's getting late. I have to get home to my wife. I thought this to be unusual, though. We sat drinking a glass of Chardonnay for about half an hour, talking about life, and the way it is. I told him "That his children are important." he seemed to go quiet all of a sudden, my heart was really racing.

"My wife is not well at the moment; I will need to get back home, sir," I said.

He agreed. Perhaps he was disappointed. Or was this just part of the Hollywood scene?

"I have to go now, sir."

I took my glass and put it in the sink.

"Good night sir."

He softly wished me "goodnight" in return. He walked towards the front door by my side. I thought I was in a movie,

I got in my Cadillac and headed down Mulholland Drive. Did he really just say what I thought he said? No, he didn't mean that. Did I take that the wrong way? There's no way he could have meant something like that. My mind was racing as I drove along the L.A. freeway. He had told me I was perfect.

I decided to let Brando get on with his life, with the reputation he had as a rebel and a recluse. I'll call Dora tomorrow and ask for another position. I salute his brilliant mind and extraordinary life and acting career, he was one of the greatest actors of the 20th century,

The next day I called Dora and told her I was sick. I stayed home for a week and decided I would not go back to Marlon Brando's home, even though I would miss Helen. When Brando passed away he had promised Helen he would leave the home to her. He ended up leaving the bulk of his estate to his producer, forgetting to even put her in the will. She would eventually sue for $627,000. However, since the promise had never been written down or recorded, the court was restrained by what was only contained in Brando's will, on the assumption that he had made all of his wishes known. Helen would eventually settle the case for $125,000, and she was lucky to have even received that.

Marlon Brando would die in July, 2004 a broken man. Throughout his life he was one of the best actors of all time. It was my pleasure to have interacted with him and served him.

In interviews, Miko, Brando's son, told how the screen superstar's spirit was broken when his son, Christian, killed his daughter Cheyenne's boyfriend, Dag Drollet, in 1990 at Marlon's own home on Mulholland Drive.

What an honor it had been to be in the presence of the Godfather.

CHAPTER 20
AMERICAN EXPRESS HEIST, LIVERPOOL 1986

I got a call from a friend who had been involved with a £4 million heist at the docks in Liverpool. It sent shivers through the series of police departments in the North of England. I met the man in Risley Prison Remand Centre. He had been charged with the crime in1979 when I had been awaiting trial for robbery with force. The news had gone haywire in the city of Liverpool in 1979. It read, "American Express Heist, £4 million stolen off the Liverpool Docks."

There was a manhunt for the culprits. Jerry would eventually be the only one ever convicted as a scapegoat for the heist. I felt so sorry for him, even though I knew the other men. One was Phillip Shields, my dear friend who I had also been close to in Risley.

I told Phillip, "Stay calm, don't say a word at your trial, the only words you say are Not Guilty, mate."

That worked perfectly in November 1979, as I sat in the gallery of the court. There was no evidence on this man whatsoever, the only evidence was that he was friends with Gerry Connor. We were the only two men that year to walk free from that courthouse because we kept our fucking mouths shut. Most of the men in that jail convicted themselves by not keeping their mouths shut, not to mention that the jury was on Phillip's side. Gerry Connor was found Guilty and sentenced to five years in prison. He finally moved to New York after his release. He had met an old friend of mine, Ronnie Gibbons, who was also my best friend from childhood. Ronnie gave Gerry my telephone number and he was quick to call me. We made arrangements to meet.

"I can fly to California to see you, Terry."

"OK, Gerry."

"I have some business."

I knew he had something going on.

I called Dora and told her I would be taking a break for a month.

"What happened to Marlon Brando?" she inquired.

"Oh, it was boring," I told her.

"Alright then. I'll have something for you soon though, Terry, OK?"

"Thanks, Dora, let me know."

I knew Gerry well. He was much respected in the underworld of Liverpool. He called me again a few days later.

"Terry, I'll be flying out to Los Angeles in two days. I'll be staying in a motel on Wilshire Boulevard in Santa Monica."

"Which one?" I asked.

"The Motel 6."

"OK, Gerry. Call me when you get here."

I had a funny feeling. Gerry would not trust many men. We were close together in the Risley Remand Centre, waiting for our trials. I often visited him when I was out on bail. He was a tough guy from the rough and notorious estate on the outskirts of Liverpool, Kirby. Within a few days, he called me one morning.

"Hi, Terry."

"All good?"

"Yes, Terry."

"OK, I'll come over to pick you up."

I jumped into the Cadillac and headed up the coast, towards Malibu, all the way up Wilshire Boulevard to 26th street, and to Motel 6. Gerry was waiting outside. There he was with his large thick frame, chiseled jaw, and black hair. He was 6ft. and stood out a mile away.

"Alright Gerry, lad?"

"Terry! Lovely to see you."

We hugged each other then got in the car.

I headed west towards the beach in Santa Monica.

"Do you want some fish and chips?"

"Yes, mate."

"OK."

I stopped at the King's Head Pub on 2nd Street and Ocean Avenue, Santa Monica,

We entered the pub.

"Nice place," he commented.

We sat in the back room. It was quiet at that time, with beautiful red sofas just like an English country cottage, an aesthetic design that evokes a sense of warmth and comfort and timeless elegance. Nobody could listen to our conversation.

Sipping on a nice pint of Guinness,

I said, "Cheers, Gerry!"

"Cheers, Terry. God bless ye, lad. Lovely place, California is, Terry."

"Yeah, nice, Gerry."

"Are you still a butler?"

"Yeah. I'm just taking a break."

All of a sudden, Gerry was switching topics.

"Do you still have your English driver's license?"

"Yes, I still got that, mate."

"Terry, remember the American Express checks?"

"Yes?"

"Well… I've brought thousands of them with me."

"How many?"

"Thousands, mate."

"Lovely," I replied.

"You want to come in with me?"

I was buzzing with excitement.

"OK, lad."

"I'll give you 50%."

"I think the best thing to do is fly to San Francisco, get rid of most of them in the city, then work our way down the coast."

"Great idea, Terry."

"OK then, we'll leave tomorrow."

We booked the flights. Gerry stayed with me and Annette for the night. Next morning, we flew from Los Angeles airport to San Francisco. We booked into the Hilton hotel on O'Farrell Street and made our plan to go the next day to work, spending ten dollars out of the hundred-dollar check in the little stores in San Francisco. The plan was I would watch Jerry cash them, and make sure no one was suspicious of him. I had his back.

We went all over San Francisco, working ten hours a day. We went out in the evenings and do a few more hours. He would sign the check, buying something for five to ten dollars, usually cigarettes, then he would be give $95 back in cash. Traveler's checks were in denominations of hundreds.

We would wine and dine at some of the finest places in n Saint Francisco, overlooking Union Square, eating filet mignon and drinking red wines. We would talk about our times in Risley Remand Centre when we were awaiting our fate at Liverpool Crown Court. We spoke about men that went to jail for long sentences.

"You know, Gerry, there were only two men in that jail that walked out and were found Not Guilty. That was me and your co-accused, Phillip Shields."

Gerry smiled at me. "You know why, Terry? Because the two of you kept your fucking mouths shut. I wish I would have been in the same position. You know I did five years for fuck-all, mate."

We also took a day trip to Alcatraz, comparing it to the jails in England. There were no comparisons to be had, England was so bad, but these poor bastards that had been sent to Alcatraz, some of them for robbing a liquor store, were sent to live out the rest of their lives in prison for 40 years. What a horrible place. Alcatraz is the worst.

I told Gerry. "What a fucking mess, indeed." He replied, "Let's go get a car and drive down the coast."

I hired a beautiful red convertible Mustang, and headed to Monterey Bay, Carmel, Santa Barbara, and Ventura. The background music from the tape was ringing out, "This is My Life, and I Don't Give a Damn!" by Frank Sinatra, while me and Gerry just smiled at each other driving down California's gold coast. We passed the vibrant beaches, dramatic cliffs, and bustling towns, all bathed in the golden light of the Pacific Ocean, a far cry from grizzly Risley, the most hated prison in the U.K.

From there we'd eventually make our way back to Santa Monica. We kept all the money in a small brown suitcase. Then I would deposit it into my bank account. Our first stop was Monterey, where they had all the little gift shops, then on to Carmel. Within one week we had cashed in around $45,000. Everybody thought we were on vacation as we handed them our identification, a green English driver's license with no picture identification. It worked perfectly.

We got to Santa Barbara, headed down Main Street, and got to work at around 4 p.m. Then on to Ventura. Everything was going so sweetly. Gerry informed me, "I got to send some of this money home, Terry. To my wife and kids."

Now here was a man that already served five years in prison, risking his life once again, all for his family.

Eventually we reached Santa Monica and took a rest for a day. The next day we left Santa Monica Mall, and West Los Angeles down to muscle beach in Venice Beach. Then Malibu. Gerry informed me he only had about $1,000 left. The next day we went to Beverly Hills. We had accomplished our mission, sitting in the Polo Lounge at the Beverly Hills hotel, sipping on a glass of champagne while watching the guests.

We ended up in the King's Head Pub once again. Our mission was complete, getting rid of the $100,000. Jerry thanked me.

"$25,000 OK, Terry?"

"That's good, Gerry."

I had made $25,000 in approximately three weeks.

In the midst of our conversation over a pint of Guinness I leaned in towards him.

"I want to tell you something, Jerry. Your co-accused, who was found Not Guilty, gave me $30,000 in traveler's checks."

"Really, Terry? Wow," Gerry said.

"Yes. Gerry, I still have them."

We spent a few more days together in Malibu on a variety of beaches, swimming, sunbathing and surfing, and most of all watching the beautiful sunsets of Malibu, which were magical. I drove Gerry to Los Angeles airport, where he flew back to New York. That was the last time I would ever see Gerry Connor.

In 1993 I decided one morning in early April that I would take the rest of the checks to Disneyland and quickly disperse them throughout the registers. But this day would be one of the biggest mistakes I'd ever make during my life in the United States. An elderly woman had noticed one of the checks wasn't signed properly and called the security police on me immediately. I thought I was okay and scot-free, but all of a sudden I was pounced on by eight security guards on Main Street, Disneyland. I must have given the kids quite a show that day. What the fuck is happening to me? You idiot.

The three felonies for fraud added up to a four-year prison sentence. But through my attorney, John Barnett, who defended the police in the Rodney King trial in East Los Angeles, which was infamous all over the world, I was able to strike a deal with the judge. He said if I gave the $25,000 back in restitution he'd only give me 18 months instead of four years. I took the deal, serving only 12 months. I was eventually released in 1994. Thank God I was not a suspect in the £4 million heist of the docks in Liverpool.

CHAPTER 21
JAVA JOINT CD HEIST, SAN FRANCISCO
1991

After leaving Santa Monica in the late 1980s, Annette and I settled down in Santa Ana, California, where I'd put my skills to use. I had worked for some high profile people, which included the famous Terry Giles, a criminal lawyer who had worked on the Hillside Strangler case along with the $100,000 million child abuse settlement against the Catholic Church in Orange County, which was coincidental with my case also against the Catholic Church, and included the Bishop of Orange County. I also hired out my catering business for clients like Buzz Aldrin, the second man to have walked on the moon.

We moved to a residential area of Irvine. Kelly, our beautiful daughter, was four years old. A good move from Santa Ana, as the Irvine schools were ranked number one in the country. Annette and I had purchased a little two-bedroom house. Here we'd be able to lay down roots and give Kelly the best education, even with me still being on Dora's radar for jobs.

I met a young gentleman by the name of Mark one evening. Mark was young and good-looking, tall, and handsome with cropped fair hair and brown eyes. He told me his mother was English and lived in the U.K. We became close. He was the manager of a Java Joint Coffee Shop in Irvine.

He was a charming man, and he was honest. He would shoot the breeze all the time. I opened up one night about my life in Liverpool, careful not to say too much, but enough to where he became interested. He informed me he would be relocating to San Francisco as a manager of Java Joint there. They had offered him a good compensation package.

"When are you leaving, Mark?"

"Next month, Terry."

"I'll come and visit you."

"OK. Great."

The following week Mark informed me that Java Joint was getting into the CD business. They would be flooding the whole of San Francisco and California with CDs for sale.

I mentioned to him jokingly, "imagine taking the lot from the store, Mark. You could buy a little house for the wife in Irvine."

He nodded and what he said next astonished me.

"We can do that, Terry. You just come in and help yourself."

He then went on to tell me that the CDs sold for $25 each.

"No one gets these CDs, Terry, they're straight from market to Java Joint only."

"I'll tell you what, Mark, when you move, me and Annette love San Francisco, so we'll take a trip up there at Thanksgiving."

"Be great, Terry."

"I'll take a look at the CDs as well."

Mark nodded.

December and the temperature in the city by the bay, San Francisco, hovered around 40 degrees. The sky was moist but there was not a drop of rain in sight, which was unusual for this time of year. What was more unusual was the heavy fog floating overhead like an elevated carpet outside my small window. I listened to the traffic honking and the cable cars with their horns bursting out as they climbed into the sky. As I sat and watched from the Hilton Hotel on O'Farrell Street, Annette approached me.

"Let's have some breakfast."

We sat with Kelly, watching her enjoy her beans on toast. I listened to the traffic honking once again with its usual chaos. Mark was on my mind. I knew where he was, in Union Square. We cleaned up a bit, got Kelly ready, and entered the hustle and bustle of the streets of San Francisco. It was beautiful, decorated everywhere with lights all aglow, the large Macy's sign being the brightest in Union Square. We walked slowly, taking in all the sights. And there it was, at the corner of Union Square and Mission. The words announced "Java Joint.'"

"You want a cup of tea, Annette?"

"Yes, please."

"I'll get you a hot chocolate, Kelly."

"Yes, Daddy."

The place was packed. I stood in line. I could see Mark in the background directing the employees. I glanced down, noticing all the CDs in front of the register. I nodded to Mark.

"Hi ya, Terry! You made it."

"Yes, I'm with Annette and Kelly."

Mark gave us our drinks complementary.

"I'm off for lunch at one o'clock, Terry, I'll meet you in the Square, OK, mate?"

Union Square was a beautiful place. You had all the Christmas shoppers and there were sales going on all over the place.

Mark sat down while Annette took Kelly to Macy's. I didn't waste any time. I got straight to it.

"What do you think, Mark?"

"I'm the operations manager, Terry. I fill all the Java Joints with CDs. There are hundreds of thousands, Terry. Our newest one is Kenny Loggins. I'm working till ten tonight."

"Alright, I'll come in then. I'll take twenty."

I had a massive coat with me so I could store them all in my deep pockets. When I ordered my tea I kept my eyes on everyone, slowly grabbing ten CDs. Then another ten, sliding them into my large pockets. They all read "Kenny G's Greatest Hits."

I got a total of 40 on my first go. I walked to the door and stood there putting milk in my tea. I scanned the whole place. I knew I was safe. The girl behind the counter carried on, serving the next customer. I walked out, my anxiety level starting to rise dramatically. I knew I could get $15 a piece for them, but where would I sell them? That's 40 CDs, they would net around a good $600. I met Mark at Union Square the next day.

"Hi, Terry. Come in tonight, OK? It's all stocked up."

I bought a special little hold-all bag to carry the CDs in, so I could take them on the plane when a friend picked me up at Long Beach Airport.

I did the same thing later that night, another 40. I worked out that if I could get 600 a night for one month that would get me $18,000 a month! We discussed this together in Union Square.

"Listen, Mark, we could make at least $20,000 a month. If we do this for one year, that's around $200,000-$250,000. You just tell me the best CDs, Mark, when they're stocking up."

"OK, Terry."

After we finished our few days in San Francisco, we boarded the plane, JetBlue, to Long Beach. My mind was going crazy. Then an idea came into my head, where to sell them. Bingo! A swap meet in California.

We arrived home that Sunday evening. I couldn't wait to go to the swap meet in Orange County next Saturday. I had a total of 140 CDs and had done all my research on the swap meets in California. They were everywhere. The next week, I packed a bag, put the CDs inside, and began my drive. I arrived at the Costa Mesa Fairgrounds, took five CDs out of the bag and headed into the swap meet. Before long there was an older man selling CDs. I browsed through his options.

"Can I help you, sir?"

"Just looking." I blurted out. "Do you have any Kenny G CDs?"

"No, I wish." The old man responded.

I went quiet for a few minutes. As I was walking away, I said to him, "I could get you 100 of them for $15 apiece."

"Really?"

"Would you like them?"

"Of course."

"You got the cash?"

"$1,500, OK?"

"Yeah, OK. What's your name?"

"John."

"My name is Mark. You should sell them all in one day. You

could sell them for $25 each, make yourself $10 a piece off the back end. You could make a good $1,000."

"Great!"

"OK, I'll be back in an hour then, John."

I walked around the rest of the swap meet. I saw another man selling CDs.

"Hi, how are you? Do you have any Kenny G?"

"No, hard to come by."

"I hav40, they are $15 a piece if you'd like them? You could sell them at $25 each, make yourself a quick $400."

"OK, yeah."

"OK, I'll be back in an hour."

I collected $1,500 from John, and another $600 from the second man. All together that was $2,100. I told them I'd be back to visit them.

This was better than robbing banks. If anybody stopped me in Java Joints I told Mark I would pay for them to keep things clean. If you pay before you leave the shop, there's no crime.

Mark called me on Sunday night.

"Bingo, Mark, all sold."

"How much Terry?"

"$2,100."

"That's great!" he said with a laugh in his voice. "We need to go to work at Java Joints."

"Let me sort something out. I'll come back to San Francisco for five or so days again. It'll take me around ten hours a day, five days a week, going all over each area to Java Joints in San Francisco."

"OK, Terry."

There was a reason Java Joints got into the music business. The way the higher-ups saw it, it was a perfect opportunity. You step into your local Java Joint and you're likely to be greeted with gentle music, the sounds of whirring coffee machines, and the tapping of laptop keys. Most notably recognizable is the signature soundtrack that always plays in every establishment. For the Seattle-based company, music has served as much more than mere background noise. It's also been a way for Java Joints to expand its brand and ensure an immersive experience of coffee house culture.

When customers began arriving in the 1990s store owner Timothy Jones became a Java Joint manager and started experimenting with his own mixes of music within the store. When customers began asking to purchase the music played in the cafe, Jones had an idea. Thus, he began the Java Joints foray into the music business. CDs hit Java Joint counters nationwide. The next year, Java Joint released its first compilation album called, Blue Note Blend.

The album featured a jazzy collection of tunes from artists including Nat King Cole, Louis Armstrong, and Duke Ellington. The response from the customers was overwhelming. Java Joints sold 500,000 copies of the Blue Note Blend CD in just a few weeks. The CDs became as much of a Java Joint staple as the coffee. Clearly something had struck a chord with customers. And also, with me and Mark.

I arrived in San Francisco on a Sunday evening and booked into my favorite hotel, the Hilton on O'Farrell Street. I told Mark I could see him on Monday at lunch in Union Square. I got showered, put my clothes on, and my large coat over my shoulder. Its big, lined pockets were perfect inside the coat. I took O'Farrell Street to Union Square and, jumping on a cable car which was absolutely packed with all kinds of people from around the world. It took off toward Powell Street. It was quite an experience as the cable car started climbing the hill. I thought about the song automatically, "I left my heart in San Francisco where little cable cars reach halfway to the sky."

A storm was coming in from the Pacific. I held tightly on to the railing as the rain started to come down heavily. As I looked up towards the sky, I thought of my mother who had been lying in the hospital for months suffering from cancer and my father, who had suffered all the time. I missed out on their lives. I lost my mother when I was 16 years old and my father when I was 18.

I looked out at Alcatraz in the distance where I once visited it out in the ocean and couldn't help myself. It brought me back to thinking about all the jails and prisons I was in as a young man and were probably part of the PTSD getting to me. The rain was pelting on my face now. Amidst the water from the storm, I felt tears start to stream down my cheeks. For a minute I was in a sort of trance and a battle went on in my mind. I was at war with myself on the cable car. An old lady came out of the blue and approached me.

"You OK, son?" She passed me a napkin.

I tried to sound tough when I said, "I'm fine, thank you."

She put her hand on my shoulder and tapped me with her fingers. That's all she said. I wondered later if she could have been an angel coming through my mother's spirit. The little old lady got off at the next stop on Lombard Street, turning her head and giving me a quick wave to say goodbye.

I suppose that little child had just swept over me, had engulfed me. It felt like the trauma had all surfaced at once that night.

I jumped off at Fisherman's Wharf. There weren't many people in sight. I thought I'll hike back to Union Square and hit a few Java Joints. I headed towards Knob Hill. Right there on the corner was a Java Joint. I entered. Thank God the place was empty. I was dressed incognito, glasses and a hat both concealing my face.

"Cup of tea please. Earl Grey."

The young girl turned her back. I placed a handful of the CDs by the register into my pocket. She was slow. I reached out again, putting another handful into my pocket. Eventually she passed me my tea.

"91 cents, please."

I gave her $1.50 and walked over to the little counter where the milk was available. I took a look around. I was in the clear. I left and kept walking up to Knob Hill and threw the tea in an alleyway. I counted the CDs, a total of 21.

OK, where's the next Java Joint? I headed towards Chinatown.

There it was again, on the corner. I repeated the same act, this time grabbing a total of 17. Right then I had a total of 38. I arrived back at the Hilton, placing the CDs in a cupboard. They all read "Kenny G." I went to bed early; the excitement was on. The following day, I met Mark at Union Square.

"Mark, I got 38 last night."

"Good, brother."

"I'll start tonight when it gets dark."

Mark explained to me how there were hundreds of stores. I estimated that our goal then should be $5,000 a week.

"Easy," I said.

I zigzagged through the streets of San Francisco. Each night I would get as many as I could. On Friday night, I had a count. I had a total of 480 CDs. At $15 a pop the total I could net was $7,200.

I flew back to Orange County the next morning on Jet Blue Airlines. I took my hold-all bag it on the plane as carry-on luggage. A friend picked me up from the airport.

"Where to, Terry?"

"The Orange County swap meet," I told him.

I went back to see John. He was delighted. I sold him another 200 Kenny G CDs for $3,000. I moved on to the other man whom I'd sold to before, Adam.

"Hi, Adam. I got another 280 Kenny Gs."

"I'll take them. Come back in two hours, I'll run to the bank."

"The total, Adam, is $4,200. OK?"

The total we got that week was $7,200. Mark called me Sunday evening.

"All good, brother?"

"Yes. I got $7,200," I told him.

He was laughing, and we chatted for a bit. I told him the part about me using his name and he got a real kick out of that. Who would have thought we'd make it here when we first met all those years ago in Irvine?

I concluded our conversation: "I'll take a little out for expenses Mark, OK?"

"Sure, Terry."

I thought I'll put Hollywood on hold for a year. The following week I would repeat the same dummy run, however this time it would be at different Java Joints at different locations. This time around I even removed the lining from my pockets so I could fit more CDs into them. I started on Monday morning. Fuck, I'll just blend in with the customers, take my chance when ordering my tea. I walked towards Mission Street, on the corner was St. Patrick's church.

I was born a Catholic. I decided to go into the church and light a candle for my mother and father, then all of a sudden it took me back to Israel when I went to Bethlehem in 1976. I got on my hands and knees and started to pray; my mind was in turmoil once again wondering which way to go. This was the way I went: I got back up and carried on with an expanded hand at a Java Joint on Lombard Street, grabbing as many as I could and sliding them into my pockets. Out of the corner of my eye, I saw an old man watching me. He was sipping on his coffee, and he had a smile on his face, his eyes fixated on me. I kept my eye on him. I just smiled back.

I worked all the way between Lombard Street, Castro Street, Height Street, Ghirardelli Square, Broadway and Filbert Street. By Tuesday Morning I did a count. I had a total of 640. I met Mark that day, the same place as always in the Square. I told him the 640 would net us $9,600. I could do $50,000 a week. Mark then began to tell me:

"They will release a new C.D. The Blue Note Blend, with several artists."

The following week it took me approximately ten hours a day, for five days a week to collect the CDs. The next Friday, I counted 3,175,000 of them. For the next few weeks, I would concentrate on the Blue Note Blend. I told Mark after about six weeks I'd start concentrating on Orange County and leave San Francisco alone in case the heat started to come on. We picked all of the swap meets in Orange County, two of which were at the Rose

Bowl in Pasadena, the Orange County Fairgrounds, and one in Anaheim.

Those were the main three we would sell at, wholesale, for $15 each. We had all the contacts, just like John and Adam. Then we concentrated on all the flea markets in California. Mark would fly down to Orange County for his share of the money. I told him I had put it in a safe deposit box in the bank.

Orange County at the time was flooded with Java Joints. I would work the north, central, and south at night when things were quiet. Between 1996 and 2006, Starbucks was growing fast, going from just 1,000 stores to a hefty 3,000. They were seemingly everywhere, all of them distributing new CDs such as the likes of Paul McCartney, a classic, "Live at Shea Stadium," Elvis Presley's greatest hits, and Frank Sinatra. The last CD we targeted was Andrea Bocelli's "My Christmas Album." It was a massive hit; no one could get hold of it. Me and Mark would target Orange County when it was released. Java Joints had been suspicious of Mark's substance abuse and negligence in his job. Eventually, they let him go for denying the drug test. He was spending all his gains from our expeditions on white powder.

The Andrea Bocelli's CD was passed throughout the swap meets and flea markets of California. It took many years of this operation, off and on. Our goal was to collect around $250,000. We well-exceeded this goal. We decided to call it a day after an employee in Newport Beach would not keep her eyes off me in the store. I left quickly, walked up the street, and moved my car to another location to wait. Ten minutes later, a police car passed by. Another few minutes, backup arrived. The three police cars swiftly surrounded the Java Joint; one officer had his gun drawn as he entered the store. I slowly took off towards Laguna Beach in my Mercedes with no sign of the police.

We ended our arrangement. I helped Mark get clean from all substances. He finally got married. Kelly, my daughter, was the little bridesmaid at his wedding. Eventually he would move to England to be closer to his mother and father for a better life. His mind and my mind were blinded; we had to open our eyes to the pleasures of life.

In March, 2015, music fans, people who stood in line for $5 caffeinated drinks, were gathered to bid farewell to another idea from Java Joints. Goodbye, Java Joint CDs.

CHAPTER 22
THE BEAUTIFUL AND THE BAD
1974

I woke up in a darkened room at the Walton Neurological Hospital Centre in Liverpool. There was a dim light attached to the ceiling over my head. I was sort of in a trance, not aware where I was. The nurse lightly tapped me on the shoulder to awaken me.

"Terence, the doctor is here to see you,"

I was at the Royal Infirmary Hospital. I winced in agony as the doctor inspected my wounds. He was the doctor who had performed the emergency surgery on my arm. The tendons and nerves had been cut to pieces, plus an artery had burst.

The night before, I was arrested by three policemen who set me up for not complying with their orders. As I was leaving the Hermitage Pub, they grabbed hold of me. One of them pushed me deliberately, and my right hand went straight through the glass door window, bursting an artery and chopping off two fingers on my right hand.

They had reattached part of my fingers separately. The doctor, in his report, said the wound was a jagged laceration across the hand and into the lower arm.

"It hurts, doctor!" I complained, moaning. "They threw me through a window, doctor!"

The police officer did his best to mitigate the situation, telling the doctor I had fainted and that I fell through the pub door.

"He was drunk, doctor," said the, lying bastard policeman.

The story seemed too far-fetched for some cynical reason. When the doctor asked me what had happened, I told him otherwise, that I in fact did not faint and wasn't drunk. Then the voice of the policemen interrupted.

"He's been a bad boy."

"That's ridiculous!

"You bastard!" I blurted out.

The doctor left and I stayed laying there, the handcuffs locked onto my left hand. The adjourning handcuff was also locked to the bed, preventing me from escaping. There were 83 stitches on the inside of my arm, and 43 on the outside. The tubes were horrifying coming out of my arm as I lay there motionless. I was helpless, to say the least. To make matters worse, the cops had me on a 24-hour watch for the next two weeks. Was it that serious? The whole episode was ridiculous.

I was eventually released to the main police station, Bridewell, in Liverpool's city centre, escorted by three police officers The Sergeant informed me I would be getting a police escort to Brighton, in the south of England. I lay on that cold floor all night in the cell with a blanket over me. The place stank; all I heard was drunken men screaming all night. The next morning, the door opened, and I felt confused. I was given a cup of tea and a boiled egg for breakfast. In the next hour, three detectives would arrive from Brighton, I was informed, and told to be ready. I dozed off to sleep, then all sudden the door flung open.

"Come on out, Moogan."

I used my left hand to get myself up off the floor and up the stairs to the Sergeant's desk where the three detectives sat waiting for me, staring me down. I don't remember what they looked like. I didn't give a fuck. All I heard was, "we don't want any trouble out of you, boy."

"OK," said the Sergeant. "He's in your custody now."

One cuff was still holding onto my left hand; the other was attached to the detective's right hand.

"We're taking you to Brighton, Terry. You will be charged with stealing two shirts from a clothing store, Debenhams, in Brighton, a few months ago."

I was actually relieved, not knowing I would be arrested for a night safe snatch in Liverpool a week before where we had escaped with £245. Thank God.

I was eventually paraded into the Magistrate's court.

"You will be put into custody," that's all I heard, "in prison for two weeks in Lewes Prison, on remand."

Her Majesty's Prison, Lewes t was a top security prison. My charges were shoplifting. My court date was set for two weeks' time.

My fate, two weeks later as described in that courtroom that day in 1973 by the Judge, was a two-year prison sentence.

"I have no choice but to send you to prison for two years." The words were from the judge.

My brain was numb once again. I was then transferred from Lewes to a high security prison in London called Wormwood Scrubs. The judge labeled me a "bad boy."

I realized bad boys have more fun because rules don't apply to us. If it's naughty, count me in. Behind every bad boy is someone who made him that way. I am a bad boy with a good heart. Trust me, it's a deadly combination. Every villain is a hero in their own mind. A villain is simply a victim whose story hasn't been told. Behind every villain lies a broken heart. Having beauty, possessing great qualities that give great pleasure or satisfaction, are to see, to hear, to think about, delighting the senses or the mind. Beauty is subjective, and what one person finds beautiful may not seem the same to another.

That said, there are certain traits that tend to be considered attractive, such as symmetry, averages, and simplicity. However, the best beauty comes from your mother. Mine came to visit me in that prison in 1973. The bus took nine hours to get to the establishment. When she laid her eyes on me, she hugged me and said, "You are beautiful."

The visit was only for an hour or so, though it seemed like only a minute had gone by, and then she was gone. I would never see her again. When I was released for a short period of time as she passed away, it was November, 1973. In my mother's eyes, I was beautiful.

What have you done to be called a good person? I fed the

homeless. Have you done any good to someone this year? I have mentored a child. When did you donate to a charity cause? I cleared my wardrobe out and donated the clothes. Did you ever give advice that improved someone's life? Make sure you don't use drugs, and always make sure to get a good education. When was the last time you performed or did something good? I helped a young girl, and I donated to her college fund. Did you ever comfort an audience? Yes, at a funeral. I gave a speech, telling them how beautiful their daughter really was. Amen.

What truly makes a villain? Intelligence, charisma, ruthlessness in the pursuit of power. What is a good villain motivation? Get revenge for past trauma, saving a loved one, gaining acceptance in a specific community, gaining status, or punishment in a cruel world. That's the beauty in me compared to the bad. Looking back, I can see how my naivety led me into danger.

CHAPTER 23
INSTITUTIONAL BANK ROBBERY

It was a beautiful summer evening on Balboa Island in June 1994, in Newport Beach. As I sat watching the sun set, in the background was the famous actor John Wayne's house, and Shirley Temple's. Their homes towered over the yachts that were berthed in their moorings. Annette, along with our daughter Kelly, and I were bearing witness to beauty. The evening was unusual as the sun was descending, with a bright orange, yellow and red background, as it slowly sank into the ocean.

I had been watching a program that was interesting and would eventually get me haywire and ready to go again.

"Come on, Annette, I want to get home to watch *60 Minutes*."

We all jumped into my Mercedes and drove slowly off Balboa onto the ferry to Newport Beach, Kelly saying, "Let's stop in the pub, dad, for fish and chips!"

"Next time, honey."

This was my favorite TV program. Everything was real life stories.

After we arrived home in Irvine, California, I settled down while Annette got Kelly ready for bed. I switched on the T.V. *60 Minutes* would air in the next 30 seconds, Mike Wallace being there to announce the show's introduction:

"Tonight we will be investigating high school children committing suicide."

I watched the screen closely, my ears shifting to another level of listening and focus.

"The institutions have been going to high schools, offering low interest rates on credit cards. When the children could not pay the credit card companies, they targeted parents for co-signing. Also,

173

when the children defaulted, the credit card institutions hounded them with threats. These poor high school children had no means of paying it back. The reason was the high interest rates. And the threats of harsh punishments were made with bombarding calls to the home to persecute the parents. The only way out was suicide for these poor souls. This was happening all over the country."

My head was in a rage. I thought of my own daughter. Eventually, I turned the T.V. off. It made me sick. You bastards!

I called Mark. He had moved back to Orange County from San Francisco as he had been fired from Starbucks, and his life was in disarray.

"Come over tomorrow, OK? Let's have a cup of tea."

The following morning, Mark arrived around ten o'clock.

"Everything OK, Terry?"

"No, it's fucking not. Have you seen what these institutions are doing? These bastards are giving credit cards to kids. When they can't pay, the kids kill themselves. I have an idea. What I heard on *60 Minutes* last night really got my head going."

"What is it, Terry?"

"When the high school children defaulted, there's a law, just like insurance that pays the credit card company."

"What's your idea, Terry?" His eyes began to widen.

"Do you have any credit cards, Mark?"

"Yes, Terry. About t eight, why?"

"What's the balance?"

"Very low."

"Well, we need a plan to increase all credit cards with high balances. I want you to phone all of them tomorrow and increase your balance."

"I have about 80,000 credits, Terry."

"How much cash?"

"About $60,000."

"Good, I have about $50,000 too. Let's make a plan, Mark. Let me think it through. You in?"

"Yes, Terry."

And so, we would concoct a plan. A plan to increase all credit cards,' savings accounts, and checking accounts, and then deposit all the proceeds of the CD money into the institutions. The law states that when you lose a credit card that is tied to a savings bank or checking account or an institution, you are not responsible for that loss. Each bank will deposit funds that have been taken illegally on a lost or stolen card.

By the end of August we had

deposited $750,000 into all these accounts. Now, the task was to get it back out, and for the banks and institutions to refund that loss. Where would this happen?

I told Mark one morning to make a pattern and withdraw some of the money, then replace it at the end of the month. It worked out just fine. Our destination was London. Mark was so excited, he would finally get to see some of his cousins and distant relatives again. The following week Annette would drive me and Mark to the Los Angeles Airport with Kelly.

"Daddy! Will you bring me something nice back from London?"

"You better believe I will, my little dear."

I sat in the silent hall, waiting for that final call: L.A. International Airport to Heathrow Airport. I couldn't wait.

I watched the captain with his silver wings on his coat, and his co-pilot. He looked to the left and took a glance at me. I just smiled. We were on our way. I didn't say much to Mark, but I knew he was over the moon. We slept much of that night after a light meal. Then the captain awakened us.

"Good morning! We will be descending into Heathrow Airport in 45 minutes."

As we disembarked the plane we were a little groggy. We had used our British passports to enter the U.K.

"Welcome, sir." The young immigration lady said to us with a smile.

"Come on, Mark."

We headed to the taxi rank and jumped in a cab.

"Hilton Hotel, Park Lane, please."

"Yes, sir."

We booked ourselves into Hilton Park Lane and put the bags into the room. We both had a double bed. The room looked over a beautiful park, and was decorated like an English cottage in pastel colors.

"Put all these cards onto the table, Mark."

"OK, Terry."

Now Mark knew I meant business. My mind started racing.

"Let's go, Mark."

We headed down to the receptionist. "Excuse me Miss. How far is the Financial District?"

"One mile down the street, to the left, sir, when you get out the door of the hotel."

We strolled through the London streets, admiring its historic architecture, and breathing in the beautiful crisp fresh air. The hustle and bustle of the city was nostalgic. We arrived at the Financial District. I took a look. H.S.B.C, Holdings, Lloyds Banking Group.

"Sit on that bench, Mark. I'll be back in 15 minutes."

It was a beautiful late September afternoon. I watched all the educated gentlemen pass by, with their bowler hats and pinstriped suits. I sat and stared, as I had all the little children in my mind that had taken their own life. I waited in line for the teller at the bank. A young blonde lady with a beautiful London accent said, "Can I help you sir?"

I pulled out a credit card and an English driver's license.

"Could you please give me £5,000?"

"Yes, sir."

She swiped the card through her banking system and took a look at the driver's license and said, "Would you like an envelope sir?"

"Yes, please."

She passed the envelope to me containing all £50 notes. I walked out of the bank, taking my glasses and hat off.

"There you go, Mark. The first £5,000. Now go over there to Barclays Bank. Use your I.D. and act normal. Here, put your glasses and hat on. Use your baseball cap, mate.

Before 15 minutes has passed Mark came out.

"There you go, Terry, £5,000."

Within two hours we withdrew a total of £60,000. We walked back to the Hilton and called it a day. That evening we sat in the bar and had a nice pint of Guinness together and a lovely meal followed by a bottle of champagne, Moet et Chandon. The jet lag was beginning to catch up to us so we had an early night. My mind floated back to watching *60 Minutes* and the poor little souls who had committed suicide. I was on my mission now for those dirty financial bastards and their institutions.

The next day me and Mark were back at the Banking District. We repeated our transactions, going from bank to bank. The total was around £120,000. On these cards there were no available balances left. Now came the task, to report our claim. The next day we had to report our cards lost, not stolen. We called, one by one.

"Did you make any recent transactions sir?" The answer was no. After completing a claim on each card, we heard the claims adjuster on each of them.

"You will not be responsible for these charges. And the funds will be put back onto your card within the next ten days. There will be new cards sent to your home."

And there we were, off the very next day with more cards to the Banking District. We took it easy the following day and reduced the withdrawal down to £3,000. Mark couldn't believe his luck; he was already planning on buying his first home in Irvine.

We toured London, went to Buckingham Palace, Westminster, and toured on an open bus through the streets. It was a far cry from my youth when I was in prison in London, at just 17 years old.

We were out of the jurisdiction of the law. The loss occurred in London, not the United States. So there was no investigation. By the time we had completed all our transactions on the cards, our total was £480,000. This was just the tester.

I finally went to Harrods, making sure to keep my promise to my daughter Kelly when she'd asked me to bring her back something nice. I really did, a purple bear, the name read: Princess Diana.

We arrived at Los Angeles Airport at five o'clock in the evening on the 747 Virgin Atlantic flight £480,000 richer. It was only the beginning.

CHAPTER 24
BRITAIN'S INSTITUTIONS: THE BEASTS OF ENGLAND

This is a story that has no precise starting point, nor does it have an ending. But it does have a few moments which are so significant that they mark turning points in my life, especially in the tragic history of abuse in children's Homes. One of these happened in Main Street, Widnes in 1993. It was our time to claim victory.

Jim, a former resident of the children's Home, saw a man walking along the road, his arm resting protectively around a little boy whom he was leading into the local Magistrate's court building in the town centre. An unremarkable scene in any high street on any day. But Jim saw the man's face and blanched. It was Alan Langshaw, a Beast of England, the housemaster at Greystone Heath, the children's Home and former approved school in Warrington where Jim had spent three unhappy years between 12 to 15 years old in the 1970s.

One cause of his unhappiness was quite simple. During all that time that Langshaw had abused him. Jim's experience at the hand of Langshaw was described at the trial held in November, 1994, which resulted from that last chance sighting. Jim had told the police how he had run away from the Home, and when he was caught, he was befriended by Langshaw and taken to his house. There he was bullied, and Langshaw performed oral sex on him, then buggered him.

The pain was so intense that he screamed. He was also made to watch another boy being buggered. As a result of Jim's testimony, and that of the several other former children Home residents including myself giving evidence to the police operation care, Langshaw was sentenced to ten years imprisonment for nine buggery offences, 17 indecent assaults, and four other offences over a period between 1971 and 1983. The punishment would have been much greater had he not pleaded Guilty, unlike many of the other abusers. Langshaw expressed remorse and regret, saying he realized he had to reform his sexuality completely. For Jim, my friend, though, there was no escape. He is now a currently convicted murderer in prison, blaming much of his predicament on Langshaw.

Langshaw was one of that group of abusers who are described as charismatic. He was a star who appeared to get results in a world where there are few. Working in children's Homes was an unglamorous task. Neglected not only by society at large, and even by the social services departments which were supposed to be responsible for them, it was a lot of work.

One day he played heavy mind games with me, I told my solicitor, Peter Garsden, a Stockport solicitor who acts for many of the victims in their attempts for justice. Thank God I was not his victim.

Jim's allegations enabled the police to launch "Operation Granite" which involved questioning more than two former residents of St. Aidans and Greystone Heath. There had been a remarkable culture of abuse there, stretching back to the 1970s. These institutions were closed in 1985. They became community homes with education when approved schools were abolished in the early 1980s.

The Liverpool Merseyside Police were drawn into the investigation. Because of St. George's, where I had spent three years, and St. Vincent's, the Merseyside enquiry was to dwarf even the Cheshire enquiry which eventually involved tracing 5,000 potential victims.

Indeed, the Merseyside investigation, given the name "Operation Care," is the biggest investigation undertaken by the police force in history. The way the Merseyside investigation snowballed is well illustrated by three whiteboards on the wall in the small office of Detective Superintendent John Robbins, the man who heads "Operation Care." Each of the boards is divided into a grid of twenty-six entries. The first column shows the name of the Home, next, the name of the alleged perpetrator, and the remainder given to the state of the case. When the investigation had started, Robbins clearly had thought that there would be plenty of space on his three whiteboards to compile all his information. But when they got to 59 children's Homes they ran out of space. The others added up to 76. By January, 1999 it had been listed in the adjourning room.

A year later, when I met John Robbins, the total had reached 84. Robbins reckoned that there would not be anymore, though he expected the operation to continue until 2002. In one Home alone, St. George's in the Formby area, allegations had been made against 91 people.

I had listed all the men who had abused me. I called them Beasts of England:

Mathews, Durkin, Carroll McKey, the headmaster McCarelle, and the rest who had stolen my life and damaged my brain. From all the beatings I had endured my emotional life was destroyed, which led me to develop PTSD: Post Traumatic Stress Disorder.

On a cold, bright February morning an old man sat on the corner of a Liverpool Crown Court, a grim 1980s building which a senior police officer confided was much less intimidating than the now-abandoned Victorian courthouse. The prisoner looked deathly pale. He had, in fact, suffered several strokes since his arrest a year or so ago. He looked unlikely to survive a year in jail, his probable sentence. John Carroll, the abuser, did not appear to have been a particularly nasty or violent abuser. On the scale of the abuse when I described what Caroll did to me, it seemed pretty mild. He liked to fondle boys' genitals in his office, to which he brought them when his wife, who also worked at the home, was not around to check. Or perhaps she knew. But as she died several years ago, she was saved from the indignity of watching her husband go to trial.

He was quite a large man, with thick cropped black and grey hair, and glasses. He wore his Sunday best, a blue suit, brown shoes, a white shirt, and a striped tie, which looked like it was his only one. He spent a long time consulting his notebook, a little diary perhaps, and writing extra notes outside the courtroom. There were the usual conclaves of barristers discussing cases with their clients. There were doubts about how Carroll, the ailing man, would plead. He has brought his bag with him.

"You don't do that for the first day of a trial if you have been remanded," said John Robbins, who liked to attend all the trials of the perpetrators. He hoped Carroll would plead Guilty to save the three witnesses having to give evidence. But he was not enormously bothered otherwise. We had the evidence. And the witnesses were OK and if he doesn't plead, he might go down for a longer sentence. Despite years of denial and subterfuge, the majority of Operation Care abusers had pleaded Guilty. It is a traumatic experience to get up in court and testify to the horrid actions of the man standing in the dock. My anonymity was guaranteed. I waited tensely in a special room, smoking a lot. An hour later Carroll went off with his defense barristers. A few minutes later the prosecution barrister, a large man who wore his wig more naturally than most, told the judge that Carroll will plead Guilty.

Carroll walked in with me and two other witnesses behind him. Judge Temple ruled that Carroll, a Beast of England, should serve 12 months in prison, despite his age. As he was led down, looking white and ill, it was clear that he might die in prison.

The victims refused to talk to the press. We seemed satisfied, despite the shortness of the sentence. However, there would be 41 cases left on file for John Carroll, who pleaded Guilty later on to 35 offenses stretching over nearly 20 years since 1964, involving boys mostly aged between ten and 15. Carroll's case had all the hallmarks of missed opportunities, bureaucratic errors, and managed sloppiness which characterized many of these cases. Carroll had been brought up in children's Homes himself and claimed that his life had been ruined by a priest who ran the children's Home with a cruel and brutal regime. However, Carroll was a Beast of England, a charmer, who was liked by many of the children he was looking after. The vulnerability of his victims was well demonstrated by one, me, who told the police.

He was brought back to the court for his new sentence. He pleaded guilty for the 35 offenses. Judge Temple told him, "You ruined many lives, and you are a wicked man. Your modus operandi was to take your victim by surprise. I hereby sentence you to ten years in prison."

He would die a couple of years later in prison. Our case had been proven. For me, it was just an ugly chapter in my life. I left the court and said goodbye, the same court, in 1979, where I'd been found Not Guilty of armed robbery.

CHAPTER 25
THE BIGGEST LAWSUIT IN BRITISH HISTORY
1997

One of the largest-running legal cases in the U.K. history centered on systemic sexual abuse at children's Homes in the North West of England. It was poised to end after a judge found in favor of two men who claimed they had been sexually assaulted while in care.

I got a call from my brother, Alan, in 1996.

"Hello, Terry. Alan here."

It was unusual for Alan to call. I felt his discomfort. I don't think he knew how to tell me one of the reasons he felt guilty. Alan would take me back to this home, St. George's, in 1971, when I ran away. It was on the outskirts of Liverpool.

I had been sentenced to a total of 12 years as a young adult and placed in three different Homes. There was a massive police investigation, one of the biggest of its kind in British history. The police's "Operation Care" would inquire at my family home one day, looking for me in Liverpool.

"Please tell Terry we need his help with this investigation."

Alan passed the information on to me, and informed me that there was a group of solicitors involved and that I should call them. The news had hit the local stations in the U.K. especially the BBC, with the major headlines in London. I thought to myself, I'll call my old friend Rob Brody, a solicitor in Liverpool.

He gave me all the information and told me it was a class action lawsuit. He said the lawyers taking care of the cases were Canter Jackson, in the centre of Liverpool. I made the connection and spoke to Mr. Whitelaw.

"Hi, Mr. Moogan, we believe you were involved in these Homes for a long period of time."

"Yes, I was."

"I suggest you join the class action lawsuit."

"Mr. Whitelaw, they ruined my life," I said.

"So come and get justice, Terry. They want to interview you for "Operation Care."

"OK, give me time."

"You have our number, Terry."

On Monday morning I called "Operation Care." A young lady answered the phone.

"Can I help you?"

"Yes, Mr. Moogan calling from the U.S.A."

She wasn't surprised. She knew my name straight away. "I'll put you on hold for just a second, Terry."

Within a minute, investigator John Robbins was on the line.

"Hello, Terry. We have been trying to reach you about the investigations into these Homes."

"I know, John. My brother Alan told me everything. I live in the U.S.A. now."

"OK, Terry. Would you be coming home in the near future, then?"

"I'll think about it, John. Which Homes are the ones under investigation?"

"Well, there were three that you were in. They are all under investigation."

"Any arrests yet?"

"Oh yes, Terry, lot of them. That's why we need to see you."

"OK, John. Give me time to plan a trip home."

"Thanks, Terry."

"I'll call you in the near future."

I pondered for many weeks. I was taken back to my childhood; the memories came flooding back. All those years I spent in St. George's, St. Aidan's, and St. Joseph's. They were all run by the Catholic Church, the Beasts of England.

A few weeks later I got a letter from Canter Jackson Lawyers in Liverpool. The courts gave me the go ahead to join the class action lawsuits which consisted of over 360 claimants in the U.K.'s biggest sex abuse suit. However, more than that had already died or committed suicide due to this abuse, which was heartbreaking for their families.

The Roman Catholic Church of England has advanced today. An English high court ruled that the North West Diocese was responsible for a residential care Home where 142 former pupils were suing for abuse. The Diocese faced over £12 million in child abuse claims. I signed the documents and joined the lawsuit on the three Homes.

The next month I flew to London, then to Manchester. The following morning I had an open appointment with Mr. Whitelaw for over three hours. He called "Operation Care" and set up an appointment at his office for a meeting in the next few days. I wondered how they would treat me.

Well, as it turned out, John Robbins had made me out to be somewhat of a hero during the interview. He said a lot of children had passed away due to suicide, and that I was a strong man for even coming forward to provide evidence against the Homes. Of course I would. I gave my testimony. It was recorded, and it was powerful. John Carroll and John Durkin would be arrested, the Beasts of England, along with another number of Beasts of England. There were 93 in total, all at St. George's, I was informed.

"You people haven't seen each other in over 30 years, since you were kids, yet you all share the same stories."

There were different kinds of abuse charges against the men. The worst was statutory rape with force. My mind was going crazy, to think that at last there was actually someone to believe us for once in our lives. Most of the teachers would be arrested at St. Aidan's. The priests at St. Joseph's would also be arrested. The ones with less serious charges would be dismissed, because their level of abuse was not as significant seeing as most of the children involved with them were now deceased.

There was a series of events to go through, seeing doctors in the mental field. In my case, I had already been under care for this situation. I had recorded it in St. John's hospital in 1981 with Doctor Messina. When I was tested for pains in the head and bleeding ulcers, I had recorded the abuse with him. He sent me to a psychiatrist, Doctor Obler. My case was well recorded, to say the least, though that's not to say that I would still carry on with the case for many years.

The trauma was causing me to take more medication for my anxiety and depression. It was a constant dance, shuffling back and forth for over ten years. There were times I wanted to give up. Some of the teachers and priests would pass away during this time. The ex-pupils and the cases would become weak. Some ex-pupils would accept a small payment of £2,000, instead of going through the harrowing trauma. In my case, I had three Homes I would sue. The value of my case was well over £80,000. However, the lawyers in London wanted us to keep it going so they could change the law so that no child should ever experience abuse in care again.

CHAPTER 26
RAMPTON HOSPITAL FOR THE CRIMINALLY INSANE 2001

Rampton Hospital is a high-security psychiatric hospital near the village of Woodbeck between Redford and Rampton in Nottinghamshire, England. It is one of three high security psychiatric hospitals in England alongside Ashworth Hospital in Merseyside and Broadmoor Hospital in Berkshire.

My attorneys in London received a letter from the British government assigning an appointment that had been made for me as an outpatient. The date was set in June, 2000. I knew it was serious. However, I figured I had a similar experience from interviewing with previous doctors in Beverly Hills. The consultation would be with Doctor Miline, a forensics doctor, and two other psychiatrists. Mr. Whitelaw briefed me and told me everything would be fine. However, I should be careful of Doctor Miline, who had been appointed by the court.

"They are not on your side, Terry. They are all on the defense side."

I arrived in the U.K. a week before and stayed in the city centre hotel, close to Canter and Jackson, so I'd be ready for my appointment with Mr. Whitelaw. He briefed me. There would be a six-hour interview. On the day, I woke early, at seven, had a cup of tea, and walked through the city centre of Liverpool. I was ready and prepared. I wasn't the little baby ten years of age. I was going to throw them back in time. I was so confident in myself that I had all the evidence of abuse documented. This was going to be my day,

I drove to Rampton. The rain was pelting down on this June

morning. I set off on the M6 motorway. My mind was in a terrible spin, thinking about the past and those fucking Homes I was in, and mostly, what would Dr. Miline be asking me? I was all alone in my mind driving to this nuthouse. But I kept calm. God was on my side. I knew it. He was guiding me all the way back and delivering my message for all of them to know.

It took me approximately three and a half hours. I knew that Rampton had an outpatient department. I quickly found it. My anxiety level was out of control, but I told myself to be calm. I could see the main hospital in the distance. It had two main columns, with two large birds as representations on the top of the columns. I had finally reached the monster house. I looked at the grounds. It was set on hundreds of acres of green countryside. Beautiful. Something that you would dream of. Rampton held some of the most violent men in history, the Kray twins. Charles Bronson and Frank Mitchell escaped in the late 1950s, though were later killed. The suspects were the Kray twins.

I read the sign, Outpatient Department, and pulled into the car park. I sat for a moment. I said my prayers. Here I was, all these years of my life, what I had been through, the things I'd endured for so long, all the emotions were rushing back to me at once, here at Rampton Hospital for the Criminally Insane.

The buildings were regular although the gardens were kept immaculate. I entered a door with a closed glass window. On the side was a bell which read, Please Ring. I rang, and a receptionist, a young dark-haired woman with a beautiful southern accent, quickly pushed the glass partition aside.

"Can I help you?"

"Mr. Moogan here to see Doctor Miline."

"Ah yes. Would you like a cup of tea?"

"Yes, please. That is very kind of you."

"You're a little early, Mr. Moogan. I'll let the doctor know you are waiting for him."

I drank my tea slowly. A locked secure door opened. A tall man, heavy set, with dark hair and black rimmed glasses, stared at me.

"Hello, Mr. Moogan," he said in his thick Scottish accent. "Come in, please."

I followed him to his office.

"Take a seat, Terry."

The office was large, with two luxurious blue leather sofas and a collection of diplomas displayed on the wall. I didn't know what to expect.

"I have two fellow doctors that will be joining the interview, Terry. Is that OK, Terry?"

"Yes, sir."

As he sat behind his desk I noticed him looking through my file, then the two other doctors appeared.

"Hello, Terry. I'm Doctor Smith, and this is Doctor Cohen."

"Nice to meet you."

"You know why you are here, Terry?" Doctor Miline said.

"Yes, sir."

"The courts want us to do an examination, Terry. The whole process should take about six hours."

"Yes, sir. I wonder, might I inquire, do you have my file there, doctor? Could you tell me the reports you have been given and their dates, please?"

"Doctor Alex Messina 1981, St. John's Hospital, Santa Monica, California, United States of America. Doctor Obler, a psychiatrist, Beverly Hills, 1981. Doctor Nelson, a neurosurgeon, 1982, Beverly Hills." He went on, "Doctor Carol, Ann Way, Orange County, 1986. Sounds about right?"

"Thank you, sir. I just want you to know, Doctor Miline, in these reports I documented my life."

He nodded at this. The other two Doctors stared in amazement.

The interview was a psychiatric report. It started with an introduction of all the doctors' reports. My background, my family, my schooling. All the reports then would be sent to London to their barristers for examination and evidence including "Mr. Moogan's recollection of St. George's Home, of his time at St. Aidans, of his days in St. Joseph's. Mr. Moogan did not take any public examinations. Also included is Moogan's employment, Mr. Moogan's account of his mental health, and his mental problems."

These were the general practitioner's notes from all the doctors, and psychological reports from Dr. Carol in the U.S.

"In an interview with Mr. Moogan in June, 2000. Mr. Moogan was appropriate in presentation and manner. His conversation was rational and to the point. Mr. Moogan did not report any psychotic symptoms. Mr. Moogan did describe how he tried to block out the images of his abuse. Mr. Moogan described abnormal sensations. He could still hear the clapping sound by the staff at the Homes which, as he reported, would wake the children in the middle of the night. Mr. Moogan expressed a great deal of anger towards the individuals who allegedly abused him. Mr. Moogan would suffer from low mood swings, and depression for a great deal of his life. Mr. Moogan revealed to me that he experienced pain in his head, neck, and arms, as well as his back, chest, and legs. These symptoms have been present most of his life. He also reported to have suffered nightmares as a consequence of the abuse. Opinion: post-traumatic stress disorder. In the International Classification of Diseases, edition 10 (ICD), published by the World Health Organization in Geneva, according to ICD 10: P.T.S.D."

The interview took only three hours due to all the documents they had from various doctors. Doctor Miline would ask me a question. Examples:

"Has anybody ever raped you, Terry?" In a soft voice,

My answer was, "There are many different kinds of rape. Which one are you referring to?"

"Sexual rape."

"No." I answered, "but the most important rape I ever experienced was of my mind."

Dr. Miline looked over his glasses and acknowledged my answer. He made several notes on his writing pad. Dr. Cohen and Dr. Smith were observing closely.

"Dr. Cohen-"

"Yes, Terry?"

"I have a question. Have you ever felt angry?"

"Yes, of course."

"I had thought later on in my life of killing the Beasts of England: Mr. Mathews, Mr. Dirkin, Mr. Hickey, and John McCardele, and the rest of them."

"Do you still have those thoughts, Terry?" Dr. Smith asked me.

"No. I got counseling from Dr. Carroll Ann Way. She told me justice would prevail. She told me to let go of those thoughts. I no longer have them, thank God, Dr. Smith."

The following question came from Dr. Miline.

"How is your mood today, Terry?"

"It all depends on my emotions, how I feel, and my thoughts."

All three doctors were exploring the patient's and my overall well-being. They were trying to identify any changes that may indicate the presence of a mental disorder such as a personality disorder, which did not exist. The last question after a grueling three-hour interview was,

"Have you ever thought of killing yourself, Terry?"

"It did cross my mind a few times but I'm OK now."

"Thank you for coming today, Terry."

Dr. Miline's report was the only report to go against their own lawyers who represented the court. I felt I had finally done justice to myself. Now the hard work was up to the barristers in London to fight the case, to bring everyone else the justice they deserved. I said my goodbyes to Dr. Miline, got in my car, and drove slowly out the gate. Looking in my rear mirror at Rampton Hospital behind me, I felt a sigh of relief. Thank God. I was driving out now, away from the monster house. I still felt anguish and despair and the memories lingered but most of the Beasts of England would die before their arrest. What a shame.

CHAPTER 27
SEXUAL POLITICS AND THE ZEITGEIST

The role and function of children's Homes transformed drastically between the mid 1960s and early 1970s. This was a direct result of the institutional changes set in place, such as the implementation of the government report, and also because of developments in society at large. One by-product of these developments was the employment of more men in the Homes. And this new trend was to have a profound effect on the services. As late as 1967 the service was female-dominated and the staff largely lived within the Homes as well. The Williams committee reported on staffing of residential homes as single women and one third of all staff were over 50 years of age. All but 7% of workers in the survey lived on the premises, which provided an important but barely noticeable safeguard for the children.

John Smith, a convicted but repentant abuser, recalls the change in the atmosphere.

"I joined in 1967 and worked until 1974. At the beginning I was the only male other than the head of the Home from the ratio of one man to twelve women at the start. By the end, it was one to three."

Enter the pedophiles, the Beasts of England,

There was also a more insidious influence at work, more than the mere political correctness and misplaced idealism. The social work profession was forced to work out a way to respond to the liberal mores brought in by the sexual revolution in the 1960s and 1970s. Social workers were having to cope with this new sexual climate, which obviously posed many challenges for those running the Homes.

The sexual revolution came in stages, each wave being initiated in the United States and quickly travelling across the Atlantic. In October, 1974, a group of pedophiles who defined themselves as child lovers not necessarily interested in sex with children, formed the Pedophile Information Exchange, the PIE, to provide the means for pedophiles to feel less isolated and gain a sense of community. The aim was also to alleviate suffering of many adults and children by campaigning against laws on the age of consent, by allowing adults to have sex with children.

But knowing this was an unpalatable message, they did not word it as such. Instead, they talked of the right of children to have sex at any age. If the gay liberation front represented homosexuals and the feminist movement was supported by women, then pedophilic activists were for children's rights. When the PIE suggested that a homosexual had become gay, pedophiles should be called a kind person. They realized that supporting the right of men to bugger children was unpalatable, but giving young people the right to express themselves sexually was a message that could have a resonance in the newly liberated sexual climate of the times.

Then came the influencers at the top.

Peter Righton worked vigorously as a probation officer, a teacher, and then lecturer in social work. In the mid-1970s he became a director of education for the National Institute of Social Work and a consultant for the National Children's Bureau. He also taught social services managers at the Open University, and was widely regarded as an expert on residential care. In the late 1980s he became a consultant for the new Barne's School in Gloucestershire for emotionally disturbed children sent by local authorities. His lover, Richard Alston, ran the school with Righton and was openly gay when being "out" was considered brave, and "right on" in liberal circles.

After 30 years of building this successful career in social work the police intercepted some child pornography that had been sent to him from Amsterdam. Righton claimed it was for research purposes, as had been his one-time membership of PIE.

But he was later prosecuted for possession of the material and fined, although the police launched a large investigation, and were convinced that Righton was in fact an active pedophile who had committed several offenses over a long period of time. In the end, they were unable to bring any further charges. Several staff from New Barns were arrested and the Home was quickly closed. A regime not unlike Pindown was uncovered with children being locked in a cupboard for hours.

The Home had been difficult for social workers and parents to get into as they were not allowed past the front hall under the rules set by the headmaster, which were clearly a cover for allowing abuse to take place. Righton was so well-connected in child-care circles that he knew many people who worked in the field, some of whom were later convicted of abuse themselves, too. For example, there was Rod Rydall, with whom Righton had sat on various committees. Rydall was director of social services at Calderdale Council in West Yorkshire, and was sentenced to six years in prison for indecent assault on two boys.

As Peter Garsden, my solicitor put it, "I'm glad we're having these trials in the 2000s rather than the 1960s, because we would never have got the convictions then."

It was the failure of the supporters for greater sexual freedom to distinguish between openness and exploitation, which meant that for the time pedophiles almost became respectable.

It is significant that more aware people like Roy Parker and Ray Wayne realized immediately that PIE was different from other liberation groups and should not be given any leeway. But the more humble care workers in Islington and in other places where the door was shut when sexual activity was discovered were unable to make the distinction as they were faced with an institutional ethos that left them unsure about the boundaries they were supposed to patrol.

CHAPTER 28
HELL TOWN

It is only natural for offenders like the Beasts of England to claim their innocence. When it comes to child abusers there is even more temptation to avoid confronting their crimes, as the very essence of child abuse is denial. Many pedophiles who abuse their victims deny that such sexual acts with children are coercive or harmful to their victims. There is a good chance to get away with such a crime. Convincing victims to testify in court is an uphill struggle for the police. The victims have often led difficult and unconventional lives, weakening their credibility in the witness box. They are aware that they could face devastating cross examination from the defense.

Invariably, they are reluctant to relive their awful experiences. In their efforts to get their stories believed the odds are therefore stacked against them. This makes denial a good bet for perpetrators, with the only downside being the widespread policy of judges to give lighter sentences to those pleading Guilty. Therefore, it is hardly surprising that many of the abusers protest and plead for their innocence right into jail and beyond.

The late Frank Beck from Hell Town was convicted of widespread abuse. In Leicestershire Homes he retained his coterie of supporters right to the end, despite overwhelming evidence against him. He even attracted the likes of Lord Longford to his cause, although Longford's support weakened as he got to know more about the case. Peter Howarth, one of the abusers in North Wales, and Ralph Morries who ran Castle Hill, also proclaimed their innocence and died in prison.

The stakes are high. A conviction can result in 10-14 years in jail, condemning many middle-aged men like Beck Howarth and Morris to the rest of their lives in prison.

The result of Webster's extensive investigation was a small book called "The Great Children's Home Panic," which was published early in the year 1998. Most of the book's text was also published in The Guardian newspaper at the time. Moreover, they say the children's Homes were not really children's homes, but institutions to which young offenders and other difficult adolescents were sent. Nor, of course, were these children making complaints, but by the time the allegations were made, they were adults mostly in their twenties and thirties. Therefore, a bunch of criminally motivated young men have been given a chance to get their own back on a society which had failed them.

Webster concludes that all in all, if a deliberate attempt was made to encourage false allegations, it would be difficult to better the conditions which resulted from the setting up of any large-scale retrospective inquiry. What has happened in the northwest of Liverpool is that large numbers of young men, many of whom belong to a culture in which financial gain traditionally goes hand in hand with some form of crime or dishonesty, have been presented with a hitherto undreamed-of opportunity. They have found themselves in a position where allegations against their former careers were being actively solicited by police officers, and, where any false allegations were provided, it is made against an individual who attracts other allegations and is likely to be given massive professional and institutional support. In summary, everything is distorted and not normal.

Peter Garsden had sat through trials at which you see some thug, a man who has committed some awful crimes. One, at 6ft.4in. Completely opened up in public and burst into tears. That is an amazing experience. It's a cruel way for these men who have spent their whole lives dodging the police to find that there is another side to them. It gives the abused victim a completely different view of the system, and I am pleased to say that while some are angry and make poor witnesses, others are fantastic, and it is moving watching them.

All the victims are given a hard time by the lawyers. The relief, the feeling of having unburdened themselves of their suffering, means that some victims are able to live happily for the first time after their abusers have been convicted. Donald, for example, told of how he never showered or even undressed in front of other men after playing sports. But now he could do just that, knowing his abuser had been sent to jail and gone to counseling.

This was an active issue by the summer of 2000. Well over 100 care workers (the precise number is impossible to obtain because of the failure to collect these figures centrally) had been prosecuted. However, there may be up to ten times that number of cases in the pipeline. According to evidence given by Robbins at a trial in June, 2000 there have been allegations against 91 care workers at St. George's alone, where I had spent three years of my life getting abused by the care workers from beatings to mental torture. A very British scandal, perhaps the most surprising finding of the research, has been the discovery that so little energy has been directed towards finding the real causes of these events at the national level. There has been only the second enquiry, and as we have seen, many of its recommendations were not acted on until quite recently, and even that failed to look at the size of the problem, or wider causes and implications.

In July, 2000, the newspaper decided to start outlining all those on a list of what claimed to be 110,000 sex offenders. The newspaper unleashed forces which were beyond its control, and those of the police and other authorities in response. Exposed pedophiles found themselves under siege from rampaging mobs seeking retribution by throwing stones and burning overturned cars.

No more sitting on the alley court bench. No more walks to the office for the headmaster's cane. When the abuser Beasts of England ring the bell, grab your coat and get out of Hell Town. I had no intention of being confined.

CHAPTER 29
SOCIETY'S PAYBACK: JUSTICE FOR ALL

One of the lasting legacies of these affairs will be the battle over compensation for victims of the abuse in children's Homes. It would take me 14 years of more abuse, depression, anxiety, and brutal anguish. They would drag me through the courts for the first decade of the 21st century, especially given that several of the major investigations are still going on and will not end for several more years. Early complaints faced a series of insuperable barriers in their claims for compensation. It was completely uncharted, as the abuse we had suffered had occurred such a long time ago. There was no legal right to access files before 1987, and even those who had legal rights and who received their files often found large sections missing.

"Terry Moogan's case raises many of the questions which will ensure that the compensation continues for years through the courts. Mr. Moogan was seeking to get to see his files to obtain an apology and to be compensated for his suffering, as he puts it, 'For the ten years of my life, which they wasted." Moogan even managed to track down the man who abused him, Mr. Hickey, the headmaster, a Beast of England, but the Crown Prosecution services decided it would not be in the public interest to pursue the case. The insurance company revealed the complexity of the compensation issue. Pursuing the Catholic Church has been no easier. Terry Moogan was outlined to the courts. He was advised by the Prosecution Barrister after the conviction of John Carroll, another Beast of England after his conviction. Terry Moogan's barrister explained to the court that he was getting appalling marks and indeed that he could barely read or write, and of course he did tell one of the house masters about his abuse. The case against the church should, on the face of it, be simple. Its priest was responsible for the appalling abuse suffered by Mr. Moogan. During the prosecution of Father McCarthy, another Beast of England, it was revealed that there had been previous convictions and that there had been warnings about the priest's behavior.

However, the church's solicitors have argued that the archdiocese does not employ its priests because they are self-employed, and has even tried to suggest that their trustees of Father McCarthy are not responsible for the abuse. And since then, Father McCarthy was now dead. Overcoming adversity. Criminal injuries. Compensation authority. The other source of compensation for victims is the Criminal Injuries Compensation Authority (CICA), formerly known as the Criminal Compensation Injuries Board was set up to compensate people who suffer from crimes of violence, and makes awards according to a fixed tariff based on the severity of the offense. Although there are a number of obstacles for claimants, the process is much easier and more transparent than civil claims through the courts. But the sums which are paid to victims are smaller, typically a non-penetrative act, would attract £1,000. The minimum payable under the scheme while a pattern of severe abuse over a period of three years would qualify the applicant for £6,000. Repeated rape, whether anal or vaginal, attracts up to £17,500.

There is a similar tariff for purely physical abuse, ranging from £1,000-£6,000. This tariff is less generous. This was partly recognized in one case where five men who had been sexually and physically abused in Homes in Liverpool won an appeal against CICA for refusal of the compensation because of their later criminal activities. All five were granted awards, three in full and two who had committed more serious offenses, with a reduction of 50%. However, the government says that on the whole, those with criminal records continue to receive only a fraction of their theoretical entitlement. They have taken on board this issue to some extent, but only in a very limited way.

CHAPTER 30
NEVER AGAIN

The impact of the children's Homes' scandals extended way beyond the realm of residential care and social services. The ramifications of the disaster, which largely occurred in the 1970s to 1980s, will continue long into the early decades of the 21st century because of the damage done to individuals like me.

The extent of the damage is, as we have seen, difficult to estimate. The police have provided figures and added in others which they have managed to find in their research. By early 2000 there were allegations of abuse reaching 10,000. There was an average of around three allegations per victim. Extrapolating from police figures, it suggested that at a conservative estimate, the number of alleged victims will reach 15,000 by the time the investigation ends. Many of the victims were already damaged children when they came into the care, having been abused physically or sexually.

Others, however, were just children. Many were hovering on the brink of delinquency and criminality, or at least still had the potential of turning out as net contributors to society and as functioning, balanced human beings, only for their experiences in care to put paid to those hopes instead of the mistrust and resentment caused by that failure. The psychological damage resulting from the abuse ensured that they would spend their lives on the margins, in and out of prison and relationships. The figures for the proportion of prisoners who have been in care show extraordinary correlation and represent an indictment of the failure of the concept of social work.

The national prison survey conducted in 1991 showed that 23% of adult prisoners and 38% of juveniles said they had been in care. These figures may underreport the true situation because of respondents failing to understand the question in the survey. A survey by Nottinghamshire probation service of 915 prisoners discharged from detention centres in 1981 showed that 61% had a care history. Of course, part of the explanation for these high figures is that care orders are made when juveniles offend, in order to try to prevent them from re-offending. But there is a converse argument. Children who are already in care before they have offended cannot be made the subject of a care order. This is because it would not represent a change in their situation and so they immediately go higher up the sentence tariff, meaning they are more likely to end up being incarcerated, moreover.

Why did it happen? As I would put it, we have always been cruel to children.

Institutions are particularly unsafe environments, and the British are particularly bad at looking after kids. But it does point a finger in the right direction to the British care Homes.

The factors underlying the scandals in children's Homes include the history of the status of children's Homes, changes to social services, cutbacks in spending, disengagement of government, poor quality staff, lack of training, insufficient regulations, and monitoring bad management changes in sexual mores. Also, an absence of whistleblowing and complaints systems targeting children's Homes by abusers, the failure to empower children, and a lack of understanding of the nature of the abuse. In other words, naivety, arrogance, carelessness, hubris, laziness, and thoughtlessness on the part of those responsible for the welfare of the children, both at the bottom and top of the system. There was so much risk included in the system that abuse was arguably inevitable.

As a police officer who spent four years investigating cases in Liverpool put it, "if you were the man on the Clapham omnibus looking down at these children's Homes over the past 40 years you would be able to see the hot spots where trouble was developing. And those hot spots spread out as staff moved on, slapping about too much mal-treatment, perhaps starting with small things but then escalating into physical abuse and often later into sexual abuse. It was in the culture of the places."

In the past there was no such thing as good Homes. Maybe in the future. As we have seen, children's Homes are a residual sector, with just a quarter of the number of residents now as there were in the 1970s. There will never be a return to the days of the large numbers of Homes which existed at the time, because of the prohibitive cost of running them. They have been made more expensive, of course. Closing all Homes has not been a successful policy as shown by the experience of those councils which did so in the 1980s. In Ireland, the hasty closure of care Homes in response to abuse revelations like Madonna House in Dublin led to a shortage of places and many vulnerable children ending up in bed and breakfast hotels, while there is an overall decline in some areas. For example, Clarence House in Freshfield, originally St. George's, has been empty for three years. Funny to think that I resided there just as long as it was vacant.

Many victims that the government talked to during the research wanted some kind of royal commission to look at the whale truth and issue, while accepting that what happened needs a thorough investigation, and that those who have suffered need to see that awful lessons of their experience have been learned. I am not sure that a purely retrospective look at a series of scandals is appropriate. In many ways, they do not have much relevance to the future because of the way that children's Homes are now completely different, and much-reduced welfare provision. The last thing we need is another inquiry, training and keeping pedophile Beasts of England out of children's Homes, as demonstrated above. Most of the solutions are known. It is a matter of implementing them. Amen.

We give ourselves so much pain when we are abused. The only deliverance in these institutions was dying.

CHAPTER 31
VICTIMS OF SEX ABUSE SET TO WIN DAMAGES
CATHOLIC CHURCH
2010

One of the longest running cases in U.K. history centered on systemic sexual abuse at children's Homes in the northwest of England and was poised to end after the judge found in favor of two men who claimed they had been sexually assaulted in care. A judgment handed down in the High Court in May, 2010 determining that the men had been abused while in the care of the Nugent Care Society Catholic Social Services in Liverpool. It also cast doubt on the testimony by two former Catholic social staff members at the Homes who had denied the men's claims. The allegations centered on sexual abuse between 1968 and 1982, at two children's Homes for juvenile offenders, St. Aidan's and St. Vincent's, both in Liverpool, both of which have now been demolished due to the nature of the abuse.

The Homes became notorious following high profile court cases in the mid-1990s that resulted in criminal convictions for a number of pedophiles who had worked there. One member of the staff, Alan Langshaw, a Beast of England, was jailed for ten years, while Colin Dick, a care worker, received four years. Following the criminal cases in action, four damage claims were started that originally featured more than 100. The claimants have settled, and some have since died while others killed themselves. But following many judgements, lawyers appointed by insurers acting on behalf of the former operator of the care Homes announced that they will now seek to settle 24 outstanding claims.

"The defendants have indicated they are going to settle this group action which has been going on for 13 years," said Paul Durkin, a solicitor with Aubrey Garsden McDonald, who represented the two men.

Durkin said the defendants had engaged in attributional litigation and had fought tooth and nail to deny the men's claims.

"They threw a lot of money at their defense." Durkin said, who acknowledged that the case could offer guidance to the other sexual abuse victims.

The two men received £12,000 and £45,000 respectively, in damages. This, plus interest, but Durkin added that the action was not about the money. It was about their need for someone to recognize that as children they had been wronged.

Legal wrangling over whether the men could bring their claims more than 21years after the abuse complicated proceedings. Durkin paid tribute to one of his clients, me, Terry Moogan, a man known only as T.M. whose case had been heard three times in the high court and twice in the Court of Appeal, without any weakness on his behalf.

"He is a strong man who had problems dealing with his abuse. As a child, no one believed what he said. But he stuck with this and has shown incredible endurance," said Durkin. "These men suffered the most horrendous abuse, physically and sexually. It was systemic and widespread. This will provide them with closure. For Terry Moogan, he fought with all his might against the Beasts of England and represented the victims who were too weak over a period of 14 years of his life. The compensation he received was a total of £17,500 for the abuse at St. Aidan's, and £2,000 for the abuse at St. George's. It was a childhood that was lost for most children. We pray for the survivors of this tragedy, and hope their spirits never die."

Amen. I'm still alive, you bastards.

CHAPTER 32
GANG WARFARE ONCE AGAIN
1990S

Tony Sinnott was a friend of mine in the late 1970s. We met at a local pub in Scotland Road called the Throstles Nest. We had decided to train with each other in Bates Boxing Club in the city entre and would often end up in most of the clubs there at the weekends such as the likes of the She Club and the Grafton Rooms. Even then, Tony was known for his ferocious punching power. Jackie, his father, was always present and looked out for Tony. He knew he was a promising boxer. With his jet-black hair and thick, wiry body, he stood 5ft.8in. He wasn't a tall man for his age, you could say, but he was sturdy, both in stature and physique. He was a beautiful specimen, although underneath he possessed symptoms and a thirst for violence.

I would teach him to strengthen his stomach. In the gym in those days, I was 22, Tony was 21. He was well respected in the city. We kept in touch when I moved to the United States. His boxing career was on a high roll. He told me he would fight for the British title soon. I was delighted for him. A dear friend, Anto Garvey, had mentioned to Tony about my life, and he seemed to be fascinated.

One morning, I got a call from Anto. He told me, "Tony Sinnott is dead, Terry."

My heart sank through the floor. I couldn't believe it. Oh no, not again. He was following in the footsteps of Ronnie Gibbons and many more of the underworld figures.

"What a lovely man," I said.

I had read in the news that Tony the Tiger was a boxing star before he was gunned down by a masked shooter. Tony had been involved as a security boss and was successful, both in boxing and security. They had sprayed 18 rounds from a machine gun pistol into his body, just like in the movie, *St. Valentine's Day Massacre.*

He had fought Terry Marsh during his five-year career. Marsh was the undefeated World Champion. Marsh won the fight. After retiring from boxing in 1985 Tony Sinnott moved into security and was a regular face on the doors around the South of Liverpool and Speke, a suburb of Liverpool known for its toughness.

However, Tony was executed in the most brutal of ways when the unknown killer sprayed Tony from a 9mm automatic weapon with 18 shots. It happened on an industrial estate in Speke in April, 1999. What a fucking dangerous game.

Tony was just 40 years old when he was killed in cold blood. Two men stood trial for the murder but were found Not Guilty. The news has revisited the murder many times. It is an unsolved crime. They have made a series about the matter to try and bring justice to his devastated family.

Me and Tony played football together on a Sunday morning for a local pub's football team, the Hermitage, in Walton, Liverpool. He was outstanding in his youth. He had told me he was leaving for Southampton for trials; however, he quit after three months when he became homesick and moved back to Liverpool during the 1980s.

Tony was rated one of Britain's top boxers. He made his debut at the stadium in Liverpool where he forced Dave Sullivan to retire. We all celebrated at the She Club in the city entre once again and with most of the bouncers on the doors including Tommy Malloy and Mickey Bennett, just to name a few. The champagne would be flowing, Moët et Chandon, with Robbie Davie's, the Birkenhead Bomber, after the success of his victory.

Tony chalked up six straight wins and victories before he was disqualified in a match against Dennis Pryce in the north of England, Morecombe, then he lost on points to Terry Marsh in Bradford. When the boxing career finished he expanded into the security business and worked as a consultant.

This is where the door wars started in Liverpool. However, I must say, Tony turned into a violent man. He was well known throughout Liverpool on the doors. He had a bad reputation with nasty individuals and gangs that didn't like him. I have my suspicions as to who these men were. Tony had stepped on the underworld's manners. He thought he could muscle in, however, he paid the consequences.

Tony had turned from boxer to slasher. He had become handy with a knife and was greatly feared around his neighborhood. He also attacked a former boxing champion, Alan Rudkin, whom I knew well, along with his two sons. The weapons were a spiked knuckleduster and a knife in 1995, which shocked me. Rudkin suffered face and chest injuries. He claimed Mr. Sinnott was behind the attack. However, three witnesses said Tony was on a fishing trip in Wales. Local sources told the news that weeks before Mr. Sinnott was murdered, he met the owner of a rival security firm at a local cafe, which resulted in an altercation between the two. There were also claims that Mr. Sinnott spent time in Blackpool in the weeks leading up to the murder, due to a security feud in South Liverpool.

Tony arrived at a small garage unit and scrapyard on the Shaw Road Industrial estate at around 5:30 a.m. However, what the Crown later submitted was a preplanned and clinical attack. A gunman with a scarf wrapped around his head ran into the unit firing an Uzi submachine gun. Tony was discovered on his knees covered in blood. The masked gunman threatened two workers at the garage before stealing a grey Ford XR2 which belonged to one of them, to escape the scene. Two men were charged and went before the Liverpool Crown Court. In 1999, Prosecutor Charles Garside told the Court that Mr. Sinott was executed by a man using a 9mm submachine gun, firing 22 shots. The man knew his target and intended to kill him. The question in the case is still, who is responsible for the murder?

A garage worker who witnessed the attack said that Mr. Sinott was hit 18 times in a concerted burst of gunfire by a man whose face was wrapped in a scarf and covered by a hat. The witness had been working in the garage at the time of the attack and after being spotted by the killer he was marched out of the building at gunpoint and forced to hand over the car keys. The witness said in Court,

"He came into the garage holding a submachine gun and firing in a constant burst. The gunman ran from the left to the right. He went straight into the spray booth. I saw him as soon as he came into view. He was running and shouting something as he started shooting. I could see him. I looked through the bus which had no windows in it. I was confused as to what was going on. Then he started shouting at me, telling me to come out. I put my arms up, pleading with the gunman not to shoot me. He grabbed my neck, put the gun against me and marched me out to where my car was. I begged him not to shoot me. He edged me into the car and stuck the gun in my neck again.

"'Give me your phone,' he was yelling at me. He laid me on the floor and told me to stay there."

The two defendants were found Not Guilty of murder the week before Christmas, 1999. Following the jury's verdict, Mr. Sinnott's mother, Doris, urged detectives to find the real killer. She told the news,

"Someone has killed my son and ruined our lives. And we want them brought to justice!"

I had talked to Tony on many occasions. He never really discussed any business of what he was involved in. The gang warfare in Liverpool really escalated in the 1980s. I believe it was the importation of drugs. It's been over 25 years now since Tony Sinnott's death. It is hard to believe a young man like him could have come to such a violent end. He was of Irish descent. I think he stepped on the wrong people's toes.

This also happened on a different occasion with a friend of mine from Huyton, Tommy Smyth. We were going into a club, The Driff Inn, in the early 1970s. There were about five of us from Huyton: me, Tommy Smyth, Davey Knox, and the Hughes brothers, Billy and Bobby. As we entered the door there was some well-known family on the door. An argument erupted, and things got heated. This was well before the 1990 feuds and its killings. The men on the door were territorial. My friends became aggressive. Eventually, we were all told to fuck off by the head doorman.

Tommy was a well-known bank robber, but no one thought he would get a gun and decide to go back to the Drift Inn club with Davey Knox. I myself left and went home. So did Billy and Bobby. We actually did not know what would happen that night.

Tommy put his equipment on and loaded the sawn-off shotgun, and drove back into Liverpool. Davey Knox would drive the car. The plan was, when the bouncer opened the door Tommy would blast him and then jump into the waiting car. Davey would drive him away.

When they reached the Drift Inn, Tommy got out and put his mask on. He had the shotgun behind his back. As soon as the bouncer opened the door he let the gun go. Bang! And shot the bouncer in the leg, blasting a hole in his thigh.

The other two bouncers ran after him and caught him as he was getting into the car. They dragged him back to the club. Four men took Tommy in the back of the kitchen. They took Stanley knives out and cut Tommy up. They also took a knife and stuck it in his head. The four men put him in a car wrapped up with towels, and dumped him outside the Royal Infirmary hospital in the centre of Liverpool where the surgeons saved his life. Tommy never said a word to the police when they arrived. He would be charged with a gun offense and malicious wounding with intent to kill. He would receive a sentence of seven years. At the Liverpool Crown Court, one of his eyes would be badly damaged due to the knife going through his head. Also, the men on the door would not identify Tommy. They just settled and went their own separate ways. I would later become friends with the men on the door, Tony Molloy and Pat Heart.

This all could have happened in 1987, when two of my fellow friends got a sawn-off shotgun and were about to kill a known gangster, Joey Wright from Scotland Road. The men sat there with the gun but thank God this never happened.

I told them, "Put the guns away, he is a piece of shit, Joey Wright. You'll get life in prison. It's not worth it." They listened to me.

However, Joey Wright's son was killed a few weeks later. Shot in the head. This is gang warfare in Liverpool. It continued into the 20th century.

CHAPTER 33
BORN TO BE A SCOUSER

My father, Patrick Moogan, would take me to the docks in Liverpool when I was six years old, in 1963. He was a merchant seafarer. He worked on the engine rooms of the ships, putting coal in the boilers. He was a fireman. One of the first voyages that he made was in 1936, on the Queen Mary liner. The blood and the sweat he had put in in his workload paid him barely a pittance of his wages to send home to care for the flock of seven children and my mother, Frances. The port of Liverpool was booming as we had just come out of Hitler's blitz after the Fuhrer aft bombed the shit out of Liverpool.

All the major cruise ships docked in Liverpool. It was a sea-port for cargo from around the world. Dad always made sure I got an ice cream on the cruise ships. My father would take me from ship to ship. A year later, in 1964, the Beatles hit the whole world when they conquered America. With "She Loves You" soaring up to number one in the charts, this really put Liverpool on the map. The following year, the Liverpool football team made it to the FIFA World Cup final in London. In 1971, they made it again, and then they made it again.

In 1974 we were on our way to being known as the greatest football team in the world, with the Beatles right alongside them as the greatest band in the world. Their hit song, "All My Loving," echoed out on the terraces of the Anfield Stadium in 1965. More than 25,000 Kopites were singing "I will send all my love to you." The world was now watching our city.

"It's them scousers once again, with their Liverpool accent!"

Liverpool F.C. would then go on to win the European Cup so many times, especially in Rome in 1977. So much talent was coming out of the city with bands, comedians, and actors. However, Liverpool would have turbulent times in the coming years.

From the mid-20th century Liverpool's docks and traditional manufacturing industries went into sharp decline with the advent of containerization, making the city's docks obsolete. However, the docks and all its warehouses would be turned into luxury apartments, making up for this decline. The Liverpool active city strategy and action plan were launched in 2005, bringing together partners from diverse sectors such as education, transport, and civil society to boost levels of physical activity among the city residents. Panelists said Liverpool had everything you could possibly want and hailed the great restaurants, sights, and the friendly people. The lively city was closely followed in the rankings by Edinburgh in Scotland and York in England.

Liverpool was praised for its rich heritage and ease in getting around, a far cry from the 1950s through the 70s, when the whole of the U.K. had called us 'scousers' in our Liverpool slums. I was inspired to write a poem:

The Scousers are coming up the hill, boys.
They all laugh at us
They all mock us
They all say our days are numbered
Born to be a Scouser
Victorious are we
If ye wanna win a cup
Then you better hurry up,
Cus we're the Liverpool F.C
Victorious and glorious
We took the Margret Thatcher
The four of us
And glory be to God that there isn't any more of us
Cus we'd take the fucking lot

The city's economy is worth over £121 billion, seeing a 15% increase in economic growth year to year. This marks our community as a port city accustomed to newcomers and well-known for hospitality and friendliness.

Liverpool is known also for its great atmosphere, and locals are always willing to help visitors get the most out of their stay in the city. If you ever have a question or are in need of something, you will always find a scouser eager to help. Music also plays an important role in Liverpool culture, from traditional folk music to contemporary music. There is something for every type of music in the city. Liverpool's Philharmonic Hall and Cavern Club draw in music fans from all over the world. Also, of course, it's the birthplace of the beloved Beatles and its landmarks such as the Cavern Club and its pubs and the Story Museum. Overall, Liverpool's vibrant music scene and its rich diverse musical history makes it the best city in the U.K, in my opinion.

Liverpool also has some of the most beautiful art gallery houses with many famous paintings by some of the world's greatest painters.

If you are into architecture you can visit some of the amazing sites found in Liverpool such as St.t George's Hall, Liverpool Cathedral, and the Albert Dock. The city is also bursting with vibrant nightlife with great night spots and an amazing selection of bars, pubs, and clubs that litter the city.

Liverpool's stunning waterfront has some of the most beautiful buildings like the Royal Liver Building, and the Cunard Building. Enjoying a Northern Lights Cruise is a great way to explore the city from the water. Liverpool also has a variety of unique attractions such as the International Slavery Museum, The Beatles Story and the interactive garden festival.

At one point, many across Liverpool felt the establishment had rallied against the city once again. After 23 years of waiting, the 2012 Hillsborough Independent Panel review exonerated football fans of all blame at a game and instead found evidence of an extensive cover up by the police to smear the reputation of fans. It found the police had made substantive amendments to strengthen statements that showed criticism of police management, and the response to the unfolding disaster documents that showed senior officers had discussed the animalistic behavior of drunkenness in the marauding fans. The report also blamed the Sheffield-based news agency for being the originators of the false police reports including the Sun newspaper's shameful front page.

White's report was based on the briefings from the South Yorkshire Police officers. The Hillsborough inquest, which took place four years after the panel report, found by majority verdict that the Liverpool soccer fans were unlawfully killed due to gross negligence from police and ambulance services. Those fans were failed by the police before lies were spread about them by a newspaper that remains among the best-selling.

To this day, Liverpool fans chant, mocking the event at Hillsborough from some supporters. As a result, many football fans in the city don't feel much like supporting England after such treatment from those who should be their fellow supporters. In response to a number of historical factors, there is a rebellious outward-looking streak in Liverpool. Many people believe it doesn't feel very English at all.

The 1980s were tough for Liverpool. The city faced wide-scale poverty and unemployment. There was a feeling that it was left to suffer alone while Margaret Thatcher was Prime Minister. After the Toxteth riots of 1981, when I was watching from Los Angeles, Thatcher's chancellor, Geoffrey Howe, urged the prime minister to abandon Liverpool and place the city through managed decline. He wrote to the prime minister telling her not to commit scarce resources to Liverpool:

"We do not want to find ourselves concentrating all the limited cash that may have to be made available into Liverpool and having nothing left for possibly more promising areas, such as the West Midlands or even the North East. It would be even more regrettable if some of the brighter ideas for renewing economic activity were to be shown only on relatively strong ground on the banks of the River Mersey. I cannot help feeling that the opinion of managed decline is one which we should not forget altogether. We must not expand all our limited resources in trying to make water flow uphill."

Though the suggestions were not adopted, Michael Heseltine argued in favor of ambitious regeneration plans, saying that Liverpool felt let down by the government as a result.

Liverpool has faced brutal cuts from the central government in the past, worsening the lives of so many people in the city. As such, there is a sentiment not to care about Liverpool. Why should Liverpool care about England? Even the milk was stopped in the schools for young children by Margaret Thatcher. However, I can still hear the voices echoing out on the terraces at the Liverpool football club, "All my love, I will send to you. " Twenty-five thousand Kopites, then singing, "We will never walk alone." I am proud to have been born a scouser.

CHAPTER 34
THE INCREDIBLE LIFE OF BRINKS DEPOT ROBBER RONNIE GIBBONS
1993

I first met Ronnie Gibbons in a playground in our local area, Norris Green, Liverpool in 1966. We played football together at St. Matthew's junior high school. He was a nice kid and we got to be friends straight away. He joined our little gang on the streets in Norris Green. W would sit together on the corner of the street. He would be dreaming of wanting to become a professional fighter. We were Franny Jones, John Kelly, David Brooks, and me. Ronnie would sit in the street, sharing his dream of becoming a professional fighter one day. However, he was no different than any other kid. He was a little villain. Our small gang would roam the notorious Norris Green estates and go shoplifting in all the stores, stealing anything we could get our hands on. Ronnie was really game as a young child.

In 1966 he was a year older than me. Any kids in the local area, Ronnie would take them on, and box the hell out of them. He already had a reputation at just ten years old. He joined St. Teresa's boxing club at that age and had a fight once a month. We would scream at him in support. He would always get the decision and win the fight. Then it would spill into the streets for a street fight.

When I came home from approved schools, I would always go to Ronnie's home. He actually showed a close resemblance to me with his black hair and light blue eyes. As we got older Ronnie Gibbons followed his career as a boxer.

When I would run away from the care Homes, the little gang would always meet in Norris Green and we'd go shoplifting in all of the shops, snatching anything we could get our hands on once again, that's all we fucking knew. We would travel to the local factories and steal all the cargo on a Sunday morning, for the likes of cases of jam, biscuits, and Coca Cola. It was always some little caper such as the bread factory, and the list goes on. The likes of the Coca Cola lorries were our favorite, that's when they all loaded up for delivery on Monday morning, and if it wasn't that, it was always something else, often the bread lorries.

I would go to St. Teresa's gym as often as I could to train with Ronnie. However, few kids there could keep up with him. He was so tough and was already starting to establish a reputation for himself. Most of the tough guys in the area feared him.

As we got older, when I was free, we would always get together. Our main thrill was going into the city entre to go shoplifting for clothes. One day there were four guys in the main shopping centre in the city, St. John's Precinct. They had decided to stare Ronnie down. All of a sudden, Ronnie threw a punch on one of the kids' jaws. The kid folded over like a sack of potatoes. The other three sat stunned, staring in amazement. Ronnie shouted back to me,

"Let's go, Terry!"

I knew right then he was special. He would go on to fight for the England International team as an amateur. We were now in our late teens. In the city, we would make our way into local pubs where most men feared Ronnie.

When I got out of prison in 1974 I went to see him. We were now 18 years old. He had developed into a strong kid, big and powerful in stature and aura. He never drank or smoked. He told me his amateur days were over. He was thinking of going to New York to be a professional boxer. It had been his dream.

The next time I would see him would be in a remand centre outside Liverpool, the Risley Remand Centre. He had been arrested in the city entre for carrying a gun in a briefcase. We walked around the exercise yard together. He told me the police had framed him, and he didn't know anything about the gun. Then he was found Not Guilty at the court in Liverpool. He went to America as soon as he was released. A few weeks later he traveled to New York City where he had got the famous boxing trainer, Gil Clancy, to train him. Gil believed in what he saw. Ronnie showed his world-class boxing skills. I would catch up to Ronnie in 1975 when I was a waiter and butler on the Queen Elizabeth II ship.

The Queen Elizabeth docked in New York in November, 1975. My first thoughts as we came into the port were that I had to see Ronnie. I took a taxi to Manhattan, to Gil Clancy's boxing gym. Gil had trained some of the greatest fighters in the world, such as Ken Buchanan, and perhaps most known of all, Muhammad Ali.

The taxi driver dropped me off outside, and I ran up the stairs. There was Gil Clancy, sitting right in front of me. He looked at me.

"Can I help you?" he asked.

"I'm looking for Ronnie Gibbons."

"Oh, he'll be right in."

I soon got to chatting with Gil and told him Ronnie was my old friend. As I sat waiting for Ronnie, Gil asked me a question.

"You from Liverpool, Terry?"

"Yes sir. Great gym you have here."

I noticed a sign hanging from the wall. "Don't be afraid to throw garbage in the waste bin," it read.

I could see it was an old building, guys banging heavy bags and shouting One! Two! One! Two! I noticed the old T-shirts strewn across the radiators. The place stunk of sweat, guys who thought they could move like Muhammad Ali, but really, I thought that it took a lot just to walk in there, even if you weren't a boxer.

All of a sudden in came Ronnie, one of the only white guys on the floor. When he saw me, he jumped for joy.

"Terry! What are you doing here?"

"I'm on the Queen Elizabeth II!"

He held me tight then faced over toward Gil Clancy.

"This here is my best friend!" he said.

Gil just laughed. "Can he box?"

"Oh yes, he can," Ronnie answered for me. "I'm just going to get ready, Terry. I'll be training for about three hours, OK?"

"OK, mate."

Ronnie exited the locker room and entered the gym. He looked like a real man now with his chiseled face. His body was muscular with broad shoulders, and a thick neck. There wasn't an ounce of loose fat on him. He tied his bandages around his fists and began to shadowbox in the mirror. Whup! Whup! With a grunting sound he threw lightning-fast punches. He leaned over to me at one point.

"I'm going to spar now, Terry."

There, waiting for him, were three sparring partners. They thought they could move like Muhammad Ali. But Ronnie had a little surprise for them in the sparring. He whispered again to me under his breath.

"Watch this. I'm going to knock the fuck out of them, Terry."

I just smiled.

They got the shock of their lives. God help their bodies the next day, they probably ended up with black eyes and bruised bodies with his ferocious punching power. When the sparring was over Ronnie just smiled at me once again. He went back to shadow boxing, and then onto the mat for some sit ups. As the sparring partners walked past, Ronnie gave them a tough look. I noticed next to Gil Clancy's office that there was a bulletin board carrying an obituary of Rocky Marciano, and a story about Jack Johnson.

The buzzer sounded again, fists began digging into heavy bags with the boppity-boppity sound of the fists racing against speed bags. There was more Spanish spoken in the gym, I notice, must be from Spanish Harlem. All of a sudden Ronnie was shouting back to me.

"Terry, this is Rodrigo Valdes, the champion of the world."

"Nice to meet you." I had been watching him train. He was all fire.

"OK Terry, let's go, mate."

We shuffled down the stairs on 26th street towards 42nd street.

"I'll be champion of the world soon, Terry, give me a few years."

"I'm with you, lad, all the way,"

It was a long walk on a freezing November night in New York, cold and bitter. We reached 42nd street and went into a diner. We had a salad, Ronnie had his water, while I sipped my beer. We talked about old times, and kept in touch for many years after. Then all of a sudden, Ronnie was in the middle of the Daily Mail newspaper. They had done a full page spread on him in New York, it read, "Mom, I will be Champion of the World."

Eventually, I would lose touch with Ronnie when I got sacked off the Queen Elizabeth II due to the Irish Republican Army, who were going to blow the fucking hell out of the ship with 400 lbs. of dynamite, a plan that had later been exposed. They had done background checks on everybody, and that was the end of my time there. Back in Liverpool, I stayed in touch with Ronnie's brother, Frank.

Ronnie had a fight lined up in Canada against a tough opponent, Francis Margot. Ronnie got knocked out in the first round. This put him back for that title shot. Things didn't go the way Ronnie had planned. He started to get into the club scene in New York. Frank would give me updates on his career. He once informed me that Ronnie had gone missing. Years went by before any news on Ronnie surfaced. Boxer gone missing. How could it be?

The news began to leak out slowly as word of mouth revealed that he had been involved in some bank job. My own feelings told me that it had to be Ronnie. Then the stories began to unfold. I would see Frank again. He told me Ronnie had been missing for years, and that their mother had contacted the F.B.I. in New York. They started the hunt for Ronnie Gibbons. This is what unfolded:

"The incredible life of Brinks Depot Robbery Suspect, Ronnie Gibbons from Liverpool. The Liverpool boxer who was killed for his part in one of America's biggest armed robberies can be revealed. Ronnie Gibbons' family spoke exclusively to *The Liverpool 71* to remember the record-breaking Madison Square Garden figure, who was finally confirmed dead after 17 years. His body was repatriated to Liverpool after a painstaking F.B.I. investigation. A fascinating insight into how the 42-year-old man became embroiled in the infamous Brinks Depot heist in Rochester New York."

Two years after the 1993 raid Ronnie decided to confront the gang over his share of the $7 million loot after driving to New York. He disappeared after last being seen in a car park, leading to his almost certain death. In 1999, the body was found washed up in Lake Ontario, which remained unidentified for twelve years. After exhaustive U.S. police work it was indicated before Christmas that those remains belonged to Liverpool man Ronnie Gibbons. When DNA swabs were taken by his family in Liverpool, they matched his own.

Frank and Rita, his siblings, paid tribute to a man who counted Muhammad Ali and Jake La Motta as his friends and who once dated Karina Hoffman, daughter of the movie star Dustin Hoffman. Ronnie was a gentleman, but tough, and that was the paradox. It was a relief for Frank, Rita, and most of all, Ronnie's mother. He now lies at rest in the Anfield cemetery in Liverpool where he belongs.

What a life at 19 years old! A talented young boxer from St. Teresa's club in Norris Green, he devoted his teenage years to the sport. He didn't smoke or drink. Once across the Atlantic, he joined Gil Clancy at Gleason's gym in Brooklyn. The Hall of Fame trainer soon became his handler. He made it to Madison Square Garden, his second home, under the stewardship of World Champion fighter Emile Griffiths. His record reveals 23 wins out of 25 fights with only a clutch of losses towards the end as Ronnie tried to prolong his career.

After his career ended he opened a clothes store on 59th Street with his mom and Rita, trading in high-end fashions. Next, he turned to illegal casinos in Manhattan, which were frequently busted by the police although quickly reopened. Ronnie made a lot of money but that was never really his focus. The armed raid was the fifth largest in American history with $7 million stolen and $5 million never being recovered.

Ronnie was a great friend to me, and a giant. He was a modern-day Robin Hood, always looking out for someone who needed help. His funeral took place in Liverpool in May, 2013. Over 100 people showed up to respect him. Ronnie was a slender, handsome man. I am glad to be able to say that I was his friend as a child. And I'm alive today to write this chapter on my little mate who took on the world. God bless, Ronnie. We love you.

CHAPTER 35
TIGER WOODS THE GREATEST GOLFER IN THE WORLD

I had moved to Orange County in May, 1987 to be in the employment of Mr. and Mrs. Giles as the head manager and butler on
their five-acre estate. On our days off, me and Annette would
often drive to Newport Beach in California. It was for the mega
rich people where the likes of John Wayne made his home there,
and Shirley Temple. There was Fashion Island, with all its luxury
name-brand shops. Every other car is a Mercedes or a Rolls
Royce. It is home to the millionaires who are housed behind their
gates, the likes of Big Canyon, Lido Isle, Balboa Island, and the
small community of Corona Del Mar.

Then there was the beautiful Laguna Beach. We were spoiled
for choices about where to go. We would watch the sunset at
Laguna Beach on our days off, gazing at Catalina Island in the
distance. We would often sit at Inspiration Point in Corona Del
Mar and watch that magnificent sky with its deep red and purple
colors. You could not ask for a better way to end the evening by
popping into a beautiful English pub, the Five Crowns, a five-star
restaurant. Me and Annette would sit at the bar and sip a glass
of bass beer. I would scan the menu. It gave me great ideas to add
to my own menu. To surprise Mr. and Mrs. Giles for one of their
future meals I noticed a veal piccata.

"I've never attempted that before," I old Annette.

"Try it then, Terry."

We sat in the restaurant located at the back of the garden. The
whole place reminded me of jolly old England. It had an aesthetic
setting of maroon leather chairs with black mahogany tables. The

table settings were beautiful; first class I'd go as far as to say. The waitresses were all dressed in old English costumes, impeccable indeed.

We ordered a Caesar salad and two veal piccata. It was presented to us well and made a delicious meal. I put this on my collection of the top meals I would cook for Giles and their guests, the likes of Oprah Winfrey and Bill Millard, the fifth richest man in the world. What more would you want to end a beautiful evening?

The times when Annette and I had our whole weekends off we would enjoy the natural scenery from Balboa Island, Newport Beach, and Laguna's Main Beach all the way down to South Laguna, and Dana Point. Newport harbor is a lovely spot along the coast of Orange County, about 40 miles southeast of Hollywood. Laguna Beach and Newport Beach are in a sheltered bay filled with white sailboats and yachts, soaring pelicans, and lined with the resort homes of the rich and famous. It was also the vacation home for many stars like Tyrone Power, Humphrey Bogart and Greta Garbo, and even the super-famous like Frank Sinatra and Ronald and Nancy Reagan. Recent generations of new stars also reside in Orange County, including Michelle Pfeiffer, Bo Derrick, and Kelly McGillis, along with Jean Claude Van Dame.

After our daughter, Kelly, was born in 1989, me and Annette were fortunate enough to raise her in Orange County. Annette and I would take Kelly everywhere we went. On Christmas holidays we would dine in the Ritz Carlton in South Laguna. As she became older, we introduced her to the finest education found among private and charter schools. One of the schools she attended was OCSA, an art school. Kelly made her appearance in a couple of short films for U.S.C. in Los Angeles. Eventually, she would go into modeling in New York, where she resided for five years before returning to Orange County. Back home, she attended a fashion school in Los Angeles. When she was 18 years of age I came home one day and told her I had a surprise for her, a black Labrador, his name was Boba.

I was in Corona Del Mar one morning and decided I would stop for breakfast. I had been in the restaurant once before. It was situated in the centre of Corona Del Mar. It read: Coco's, The Best Breakfast in Town. I walked in for a morning meal as the older waiter shouted out with her New York accent. Oh no, I thought to myself, she isn't going to serve me, is she? Next thing she was right in my face.

"Coffee, dear?"

"OK, thank you."

All of the sudden, a man walked in the door to my right and took a seat facing me. I thought, how could he sit there? Wouldn't you think the man would want some privacy? He seemed to grab the menu fast and put his head down. The waitress came back, same thing.

"Coffee, sir?"

He nodded kindly. As we sipped our coffee, our eyes met. I recognized him only then, Tiger Woods.

"Good morning, Mr. Woods."

"Good morning."

Out of nowhere, he asked me, "Are you a scouser?"

I couldn't help but laugh. My only response was, "You're a Chelsea supporter, aren't you? You were at the game when Liverpool played Chelsea?"

I had read about this game, and Tiger Woods was there in London. The waitress interrupted.

"Can I take your order?"

"Could you give us five minutes please?"

"OK," she snapped back, disappearing into the kitchen again. I carried on with Tiger.

"I'll tell you what, Tiger, my name is Terry. I'm not going to sit here and eat my breakfast in front of you. So do you want to join me?"

All of the other patrons in the restaurant were silent, probably listening in to our conversation. But I didn't give a shit.

"OK, Terry." He came over and shook my hand.

The waitress was back now, confused. We both sat together, ordered our breakfast of egg whites and fruit with wheat toast. I had read in the news that his father was not well. Shall I ask or not? I decided to ask him.

"How's your father?"

"Not bad, Terry. Thank you for asking."

I left it at that. We spoke mainly of football that we called soccer in England, and I explained the game to him. There were a couple of eyes on us. We just carried on laughing. I knew Tiger was a lot younger than me, and I knew he was born in Cypress, California. His achievements on the course, 106 wins worldwide, and 15n majors, were amazing. I know his parents, Earl and Kultida Woods, were strict with their son. Tiger Woods's childhood was structured around the game of golf. I knew at the time he was the youngest Masters champion. He was also the winner of the U.S. Junior Amateur championship. It happened in 1991, and he was only 15 years old.

We carried on with our conversation. We talked about the golf course at Hoylake, not far from Liverpool. He started to explain the course to me, and just how tough it was. Then I joked with him, "You should have gone to Anfield to watch Liverpool." He just gave me a smile.

I asked, "You played at St. Andrew's, right?"

"Yes, in 2000. I won the British Open."

It was one of the hardest courses judging by how he explained it: "When the wind blows, it's a tough crack, Terry."

The waitress was back. She looked astonished; you would have thought we'd known each other for thirty years.

"More coffee?" she snapped with her New York accent.

"Yes, go ahead."

This was great, I thought, sitting in a little coffee shop in Corona Del Mar.

Too soon he informed me he had to leave.

"You live around here?" I asked politely.

"No, my mom does. Do you come here often?"

"Yes," I said.

"OK then, in that case I'll be here Tuesday, same time. It was nice meeting you, Terry."

He shook my hand and left. You could hear the whispers from people around us. There were skeptical murmurs of, was that Tiger Woods? I just smiled. I went home and called Kelly. I told her to come and have breakfast with Tiger Woods on Tuesday. She was laughing. "OK, Dad."

Me and Kelly would be waiting for Tiger Woods the following Tuesday. And there he was.

"Tiger, this is Kelly, my daughter."

Kelly shook his hand and smiled.

We all had the same breakfast. He was asking Kelly questions about her life. Kelly told him she had a dog, Boba. He explained he had one, also.

"What's his name?"

"The Pazmanian Devil."

Kelly was laughing.

"I will bring him Sunday," said Tiger.

I had told Kelly his father was not well. She understood the situation.

"OK, Terry, Kelly, I'll be seeing you Sunday then. Ten O'clock on the patio, OK?"

"OK, see you mate."

Tiger seemed to be clever, but deep down, I think he was shy. I also think he didn't have a normal childhood, and he was sheltered.

We arrived the following Sunday, Kelly brought Boba, and Tiger brought the Paz Devil. It was like a Collie dog. We had breakfast together while the dogs entertained themselves on the patio. After our breakfast Tiger asked me and Kelly if we wanted to go down to the beach at Corona del Mar so the dogs could run around on the sand. We walked down to the shore, where Kelly kept an eye on both dogs.

I had so many things I wanted to say, but I held my tongue.

Tiger was talking about the foundation to support underprivileged children. I told him mine wasn't so good. I only told him a small piece. I knew that Tiger had a good heart.

"I'm sorry to hear that, Terry."

As we walked along the beach I noted how glorious of a morning it was. Here I am with one of the greatest golfers in the world, a wealthy man, if not a billionaire. Tiger Woods's life was full of ups and downs, due to the laws of scandal and personal tragedy and back to golf, with one of the most legendary comebacks in sport. Woods is a figure who has seen and lived through it all, just like me. I had seen it all working for the rich, and its famous stars in Beverly Hills. We spoke a little bit about the stars; however, it wasn't really important.

We carried on for many months seeing each other at Coco's in Corona Del Mar and enjoyed ourselves and the company of the day. Eventually, Tiger's father, Earl, would pass away in 2006. It must have had a terrible effect on his life, the man that got him where he is today. Tiger would move back to Florida. I kept a close eye on the news of his life. I heard a knee operation sidelined him for two months. The injury to the knee would plague his career. His personal problems followed tabloid rumors of an extramarital affair, and news of a car collision with a tree and fire hydrant yards from his home. He eventually took a break from the game for a few months.

Tiger released a statement admitting his transgressions, after which numerous sponsors cut ties with him. He had an infamous press conference at the PGA tour headquarters in Florida. He admitted to being unfaithful.

"I had affairs, I cheated," he told the world media, his mother Kultida sitting in the front row.

The comeback in 2019 was against the odds. His old shots were finding their mark. The PGA Championship, the scenes of a stampeding man following Woods as he strode to victory in the season-ending tour Championship, were the stuff of a Hollywood blockbuster. Tiger would have another crash in Rancho Palos

Verdes near Los Angeles. He was driving when he crossed a median and went across two lanes of road before hitting a curb, hitting a tree, and the car landing on its side off the road.

His injuries were great. He underwent surgery on his injured legs and recovered fast for the most part. However, he also did go through five back surgeries. I myself went through three back surgeries, as well as a neck surgery due to a car accident around the same time through a driving error by movie star Tom Hanks's son, Chester Hanks, who was a known habitual drug user.

Regardless of the man Tiger became after we lost touch, I can see it was a pleasure to have met him, and to have shared some beautiful time together. One day, I hope to see him again in Corona Del Mar in California. Then I'll tell him my real story and not talk about football.

CHAPTER 36
SHOULD I JOIN THE LIVERPOOL MAFIA?

I had been in Liverpool a couple of times to visit old friends, individuals who were connected to the underworld of Liverpool's mafia. It gained its strength by brokering a strategic alliance with young black gangs following the 1981 Toxteth riots and became the richest crime group in the United Kingdom. The Liverpool mafia has had several powerful groups over the years, some of which have worked together or fought over control of the cartel at different times. Some of the most notable figures were Curtin Jones, John Hays, the Fitzgeralds, and the Huyton Firms, as well as my late friend, Colin Smith. However, it's those who have gone under the radar who are the most dangerous, the real ones that fit into the group mentioned. I would say that there are many men who dare not get near them.

I would fly to Liverpool every year and was always surprised at the welcome I would receive, not to mention the respect I got. I would be an asset to the firms and their organizations. The history of my life spoke volumes for itself. The downfall of most men in the mafia is revenge in Liverpool. Most of them are veterans. One man I know, Hayes, is still serving 35 years. He made a hell of a lot of money from importation. Young kids in the city were moving into hugely profitable importation. But if these kids make one wrong move, it's the end of their life.

It all went wrong one day when two kids were ambushed and gunned down: one bled to death from his wounds, the other would survive. The veterans, Hayes, and his partner an Irish guard, one of the Queen's guards, was a sharpshooter in the Secret Service, an S.A.S- trained hitman that had mistakenly killed an innocent teenager instead of the real target. He was sentenced at

TERRY MOOGAN

Liverpool's Crown Court after being convicted. Hayes was hired for this contract at the time. One of the kids killed was only 18 years old and because of a feud, both men will have to serve a total of 30 years before being eligible for parole.

I knew Hayes' father well. He told me in Las Vegas that his son was making a fortune. This put a bad taste in my mouth. Killing a kid. There weren't any armed robberies anymore. It was all imported dope these days. Many of my friends were making millions. The work was easy; it was the end of an era for the bank robbers now.

A friend, David, asked me to meet him in the city centre, at a coffee shop on Dale Street. He took four phones out of his coat and placed them on the table before me. He turned the phones on. He made his contacts in Europe. I could hear the voice on the other end of the line.

"Terry is here with me. Say hello to him."

I shouted hello to the person on the other end of the line. I knew he was a member of the Huyton mafia.

I tried to ignore the rest of the conversation, but somehow he really trusted me, as did the other man on the end of the line. When David got off the phone he confirmed who it was. It was Ringo. They had just made £250,000 between the three of them.

" We do that twelve times a year, Terry. We would not let anyone near us; however, we go back to our childhood. We can do you a favor if you want and be our partner?"

I thought to myself, that's three million a year. The temptation really got me going now.

All of the sudden, another man walked in and sat next to my friend. He was heavy set, young, with fair hair and wearing a black tracksuit. He placed two phones on the table.

"Hello, Terry. I'm Justin, I've heard all about you."

I just smiled and listened to what he had to say. He made a comment.

"Have ye done all your calls, mate?"

"Yes, all good." They just smiled at one another.

We sat for another 30 minutes, just talking, before my friend David asked,

"Why don't you take Terry up to your place?"

"OK, that's fine." Justin replied.

As we left the coffee shop I said goodbye to my friend, David, "see you later," and he returned the sentiment.

"Up here, Terry. I'm parked," he said with his thick scouse accent. We both walked through the city centre into a car park in Old Hall Street. He unlocked his car, a black Range Rover. "

"Jump in, Terry."

We drove out of the city.

"You will be OK, Terry, we're safe. I live just outside Liverpool, on the Southport Road."

We headed through the city, up the dock road into Maghull, then on to the bypass to Southport. Just before we got there Justin pulled up to a big mansion. We rolled through the gate. I was just observing.

"My wife's home Terry, so we'll have a cup of tea and a few biscuits,"

The home was absolutely beautiful, with lush green gardens and a swimming pool in the rear of the back garden. As we entered the front door his wife greeted both of us.

"This is my wife, Susan, Terry."

"Hello, dear, how are you?" I asked politely.

"Oh! You're the man from America they've all been talking about." I just smiled.

Susan made us a cup of tea and served a plate of chocolate biscuits.

"Come upstairs, Terry."

We entered the back bedroom. There was a large table in the corner.

"I'm just going to count some money Terry." he said, and as he did so he pulled back the carpet in the corner of the bedroom. Lifting one of the floorboards up, he pulled out a large plastic bag.

"I've got to count this Terry. Gotta take £300,000 to Spain on a yacht. You can come with me."

My eyes darted right up to meet him.

"We'll see, if I have the time," I said.

The trust that they had in me was amazing. Then all of a sudden he took a gun from his pocket and placed it on the table, smiling as he did so. I thought, there's seven years in prison right there, just for carrying the fucking gun.

Organized criminal gangs from Liverpool have risen to the summit of the U.K.'s underworld and dominate the firearms and drugs trade outside London. That was the intelligence I had read. A few months before my visit to the U.K. Liverpool gangs were the second biggest users of guns and drugs, ranking high in overall crime. They were seen as some of the most troublesome in the U.K.

I read, "The recent jailing of the Anfield drug gang led to Liverpool Crown Court hearing about county lines, a distribution system harnessed by criminals in their ruthless pursuit of profit."

The Anfield gang was run by none other than my friend Leslie Collins and his family who'd been jailed for more than 80 years. This got my mind thinking. Justin and my friend had me already in with them. I didn't even know it.

"This is for you, Terry, for your expenses." He handed me a parcel of cash in a plastic bag.

"Just leave it there, mate, I'll take it when I leave."

"I just wanted to thank you, Terry, for doing my family a favor." I was sort of surprised. "It's for taking care of Jim when you took him to see that doctor in the United States."

"Oh, is he your family member?"

"Yes, he's my younger cousin."

A year prior my friend's nephew wanted a physical. His younger brother had died at only 14 years old due to a hole in the heart. Jim was panicking that he would go out the same way as his younger brother and die. I had flown back a year before and taken him back to America for a physical and got him and E.K.G. on his heart. We had paid the doctor in California, the results were positive, and Jim was fine after that.

Eventually, we left the house. Justin brought the bag into the Range Rover.

"Just drop me into the city, Justin, we'll be in touch, OK?"

We drove to the city centre.

"All will be well, Terry, when we go to Spain. I have a nice apartment there, mate."

"OK. I'll let you know," was my only reply. He dropped me off at Lime Street Station in the city.

"See ya later, mate."

"OK, Terry, take your bag."

I took hold of the bag, and placed it inside my coat, holding it close to my arm.

I got a taxi to Huyton, on the outskirts of Liverpool, where I was staying with my friend, Rene.

"Hello, Terry," she greeted me at the door. "All OK?"

"Yes, Rene." I went upstairs and dumped the bag onto the bed. I pulled the bundles of ten pound notes out and counted them. Right there in front of me was a total of £15,000. However, my mind was not clear on what to do. I yelled down to Rene:

"Let's go out for a meal!"

"OK, Terry! That Chinese place in Prescot sound good?"

"Yes. Call Dawn as well, tell her to meet us down there."

Dawn was Rene's daughter and an old friend of mine and also Annette's, from childhood. She arrived at the Chinese restaurant, and we had a bottle of wine with our nice meal. Dawn followed us back to her mother's home and the two of us sat in the living room while Rene went up to bed.

"What have you been doing Terry?"

"Oh, I was with some of the old school mates."

She gave me a stern look. "Be careful with that lot Terry. If you get caught, you'll be going away for a long time. You won't be seeing Kelly or Annette, and your life will be destroyed, not to mention theirs." She paused for a moment. "This city is getting destroyed," she said once again. "The sentences the judges are giving now are unbelievable. Terry, think about your family, really.

You have a great life in the U.S. Don't spoil yourself, lad, you're too good for that."

The top men now were taking on the world. One man, Christopher Ward, taught the Liverpool mafia to think global and take on every nation. Christopher had spent most of his adult life behind bars, even dealing with Columbia's cartels made famous by the Netflix drama, "Narcos."

This was simple. I would go and see my old friend Tony Malloy, from the south of Liverpool. He had a club called Club Thirty-Three. The following day, Rene made me some breakfast. I sat with her as the rain was coming down. Rene was getting older now. She had a total of seven children, whom I knew well. She was a beautiful looking woman who had lost her husband some time before to cancer.

"Phone Dawn, Rene."

"OK, Terry."

"Tell her to come over."

Dawn arrived twenty-five minutes later.

"Can you take me to the city centre, Dawn?"

"Sure, Terry."

We drove to the city entre, her voice ringing in my head with the words "be careful." I will, Dawn, I thought to myself. Just going to see a friend.

We arrived in the city centre and I stepped out of the car, before turning back around to face Dawn in the open window of the passenger's seat. She leaned over.

"I wouldn't like to see you get into trouble, Terry. It would kill Annette, and you have Kelly now, remember that."

I smiled back and said, "I'm fine. Thank you, once again. Catch you tonight then. Goodbye."

"Goodbye, Terry," she said, and drove off.

I walked down North John Street, to Club Thirty-Three. I walked in. There was a guy sitting at the bar. I knew him straight away. He was from Scotland Road.

"Hello, John, how are you?"

"Good, Terry. Been a while."

John Cummings was a real tough man from Scotland Road.

"Is Tony here, John?"

"He should be here any minute."

We carried on chatting for a few minutes, then Tony arrived.

"Alright, Tony?"

"Oh my God. Terry!"

Tony had come from the south end of Liverpool, the Dingle. I knew him from the club scene in the late 1970s and also from being on the Queen Elizabeth II when he was doing the world cruise as a waiter. He had a feared reputation, along with that of his family. He knew everything about importation and the men behind it, even though he himself was not involved. We sat and talked for a while. Then I asked him a question.

"Would you have a go at this, Tony?"

"No way Terry. You can't trust anyone. We are old school; no one likes us. You get caught, Terry, you're going down for 25 years at least, mate."

I spent a few hours with Tony and his brother Jimmy. All of a sudden, I realized I was a free man. Then the penny dropped in my head. I said my goodbyes. I walked through the city centre, down Dale Street and over to Sir Thomas Street. I stumbled across the Magistrates courts and looked up. The memories came flooding back to me from when I was a kid. That's where they would sentence me to government Homes. I thought about my mother and father. It must have broken their hearts. Now they are no longer here. I remember my mother would stand on the corner, waiting for the police van to leave the court so she could wave at me.

The rain started to pelt down. I stood at Dale Street in the city centre of Liverpool, waiting for a taxi back to Rene's home. I looked up at the sky and its dark, brooding clouds. It took me back to the feeling of the prisons I was in when I was young, when I would look out the window at night, listening to the rain.

All of a sudden a black cab was coming down the street. I waved him down. He stopped at the curbside to pick me up. My clothes were ringing wet, and the rain had drenched my whole body. I hopped in quickly.

"Where ya going,' mate?"

"Huyton, Knowsley Lane."

I sat back against the seat to rest. The fabric of the car is already warming my body compared to the cold outside. He asked me how my day was.

"Not bad, mate."

This time I was not going to see any gangsters in Huyton, only my friend Rene and Dawn on a miserable night. Upon arriving at Rene's, I could see she had been having a couple of drinks. I joined her. We spoke for a few minutes. All of a sudden, an idea came to mind.

"Would you ever dream of going to Hawaii, Rene?"

"I'd love to," she replied without hesitation.

"Would you like to come with me, Annette, and Kelly?"

"OK."

"Get ye bags packed then. I'm leaving soon to go back home to California."

Tucker Comerford was now dead. Colin Smith was gunned down. Tony Sinnott was struck by a machine gun and left to bleed to death. Joey Wright was dead. The Friday Night Gunmen were all dead. Billy and Bobby Hughes were dead. Austy McCormack, Tommy Gilday, all dead. The list went on. There was a threatening, ferocious war between Britain's original drug syndicate and the so-called Liverpool mafia. Thank God I made the right decision that night.

A few days later I was carrying Rene's suitcase through London and boarding a 747 Virgin Atlantic flight to California. We sat on the plane together, sipping our glasses of champagne.

"Cheers, Rene."

I woke up in the morning in sunny California. I'm a millionaire. I go to bed at night, no prison guard in sight, I'm a millionaire. I walk along Laguna Beach in California; I'm a free man and I'm a millionaire. No prison guards to lock me up. I'm a millionaire.

CHAPTER 37
HAWAIIAN ISLANDS WITH RENE
1993

Captain James Cook visited the islands on January 18, 1778, and named them the Sandwich Islands in honor of the fourth Earl of Sandwich, who was the First Lord of the Admiralty and one of his sponsors. This name was in use until the 1840s when the local name Hawaii gradually began to take precedence.

There are six major islands to visit in Hawaii: Kauai, Oahu, Malakai, Lanai, Maui, and Hawaii. Each has its own distinct personality, adventures, activities and sights. There is also another island called the Forbidden Island also known as Niihau, with fewer than 200 residents. It is the least inhabited of the Hawaiian Islands and was once owned by royalty.

I first visited Oahu in January, 1984 on my way back from Australia. Me and Annette would spend two weeks at the Kamala Hilton at the request of Mr. Weinberg, who owned the hotel. I had worked at his home in West Hollywood for a short period of time. He was also a land developer. We had a beachfront room overlooking the ocean on the famous Waikiki beach.

I remember the morning getting up with Annette and walking down the beach, with its crisp, soft, golden sand and a green mountainside reflected in the beautiful blue ocean. It was a wonderful feeling, sitting on the hotel's deck overlooking the ocean.

Years later in the 90s, I would return to visit Maui and Kauai. Kelly was two years of age at the time. The hotel, situated on Kaanapali beach, was the Royal Lahaina Hotel. We had a beautiful ocean view. We would wake early in the morning and walk along Kaanapali beach where the sand was like walking on salt, and the deep, blue ocean was incredible. Now this was life! I couldn't imagine anything else. A far cry from the abusive Homes and Britain's institutions. I would look at Kelly and think to myself, this is the peace and quiet this child needs and let her not forget the beauty of Hawaii and its many islands so that she may continue to visit them for the rest of her life.

Me and Annette would plant the seeds for her for the future, to visit the Hawaiian Islands. We would sit at night on the balcony and watch the shooting stars dash across the dark blue sky. The sunsets would be an unusual dark red, yellow and orange. It was quite the sight.

The sound of the early morning, of the birds singing, was enough to put you in a deep relaxing trance and go back to sleep, something I had never experienced before. The freedom of the island and its people was an amazing experience as well. Kelly would dance at night with all the Hawaiian dancers that put the shows on at the hotels. They embraced her like one of their own. Once a year we would visit either Kauai or Maui to embrace its beauty, away from the hectic life in California with all its traffic.

Kauai was called the garden island. It produced pineapples that would be shipped across the world. After the hurricane, Iniki, hit in 1992 the damage amounted to about $1.8 billion. This was the most destructive hurricane on record anywhere in the United States. Seven people died and more than a 100 had been injured because of Iniki. The following year, in 1993, we decided to visit Kauai. The price was $100 each night for a massive home, only one mile from Poipu Beach, one of the best beaches in the world that catered to film stars. But now the hotels were all empty and the destruction was still not fixed. All the palm trees were flattened. We were spending most of our days on the beach just relaxing with Kelly. We would drive around the island, sightseeing the destruction. It was one hell of a sight.

The Coco Palms was a famous hotel on Kauai for Elvis Presley's film, *Blue Hawaii*. But it had already lost its luster by the time the hurricane hit with winds that reached up to 145 miles per hour.

The hotel was closed and abandoned and looked worse with each passing year. It became an eyesore. The rooms had been gutted, leaving an empty shell of a once-flourishing establishment rather than the owners deciding to tear the place down. The hotel was passed from one investor to the next, each fueled by the nostalgia of what Coco Palms once was.

All of them saw dollar signs but in each case their plans for development failed, and the unsightly remains of the Coco Palms are still there. There will never be a hotel like it because times have changed. However, we have great memories. But most of all, we have Kelly Moogan. Aloha! A far cry from my own experiences as a child in the hell hole of Britain's institutions.

As we touched down in Kahului Airport in Maui, Rene, Annette, me, and Kelly were so excited. We were welcomed with a warm Hawaiian trade wind breeze on our faces, with the majestic green mountains in the background. I knew this was Rene's dream. I planned to make it beautiful for her.

As we entered the airport her eyes were all over the place. I was just observing her. I walked over to a beautiful Hawaiian lady who was selling flowers. She had a beautiful Hawaiian smile on her face, and her long black hair and dark tan skin were glowing in the sun, a pink Hawaiian flower tucked behind her ear. She made leis, a garland necklace made of flowers knotted together and given in Hawaii as a token of welcome or farewell. I placed the garland necklaces of flowers around our necks. Leis are most commonly made of carnations, of Kika blossoms, ginger blossoms, or even jasmine blossoms. About 18 inches long, they are bestowed with a kiss, a sign of hospitality.

The warm breeze and the trade winds were blowing, and we couldn't help but look up at the beautiful deep blue skies every now and again. The temperature was perfect. We headed to get a car from the hire company. Rene was asking Annette a lot of questions. Then she would finish, "Isn't it beautiful?"

For Kelly, it was normal. I had hired a stunning red Mustang convertible. We all piled in, listening to the beautiful melodies of Hawaiian music, making our way along the highway heading towards Kaanapali. I had booked a penthouse room at the top of the Royal Lahaina Hotel with two bedrooms. Rene would also get her own master suite. As we were heading north along the Kahekili highway I could just hear Rene saying how beautiful the place was going to be as we drove towards Kapalua. It offers a unique experience of discovering another little-known facet of the Hawaiian Islands. It offers spectacular scenery, paradisiacal beaches, and endless green beauty as far as the eye can see that comes to rest in the blue ocean.

We arrived at the Royal Lahaina late that afternoon. The porter unloaded the bags and parked the Mustang. I told Annette to go to the bar and sit for half an hour and get a drink with Rene while I checked in.

"Aloha, Mr. Moogan," the kind looking woman behind the reception desk said to me, a smile beaming on her face with a beautiful flower tucked inside her hair "Here are the keys to your room, Mr. Moogan Your bags will be delivered shortly, mahalo."

"Thank you." I said, nodding.

We all exited from the elevator to the penthouse room. Rene's jaw dropped. There were three balconies overlooking the magnificent blue ocean, and one looking over the magnificent Hawaiian mountains. There were two master suites, Hawaiian furniture much of it made from koa wood, a symbol of Hawaiian heritage and its natural beauty. There was a Jacuzzi for Rene. The room was exquisitely designed, with mirrors on the walls and an overall light-yellow theme with its beautiful furniture. Rene opened the door to the balcony, her voice booming.

"It's out of this world!"

You could see the full-length swimming pool below. I told her this was my beachfront escape, as I cracked open a bottle of Moet et Chandon to celebrate life to her and Annette and most of all to Kelly Moogan, the apple of our eye.

"Cheers, Rene. God bless you, and you Annette, and you too, Kelly."

My eyes moved out towards the ocean. I thought, I am free.

The Royal Lahaina Hotel sits on 27 acres of sun-kissed tropical gardens and offers an island-inspired ambiance on a regal beach, a timeless yet unstuffy setting. It was built in 1962, in one of Maui's first resorts. Today, the powder-white sand and transparent water makes Kaanapali beach one of the world's most picturesque. The hotel is set on one of the world's best beaches. This classic oceanfront paradise has been the best place I have experienced in my life, and I just knew Rene would enjoy this beautiful hotel.

Rene was now 74 years old. She had worked all her life in Liverpool. Annette had met Rene and a local office, where Annette was an apprentice operator. Rene was the first one to assist Annette, and they formed a friendship that would last over 50 years.

I urged Rene to go in the beautiful blue ocean one afternoon. I guided her in slowly, with Kelly at her side. I could feel the sincere peace she was having in that moment, surrounded by the beautiful waters in Maui. She had deserved every minute of it. Rene had worked hard all her life and raised seven children. Her husband, Billy, had passed away. Rene was in the golden years of her life. This was my treat to make sure Rene would never forget this beautiful experience. It was also a special experience for Kelly as she had lost her grandmother when she was only two. It was bringing Annette so much joy, as well.

In the evening, Kelly would fill the Jacuzzi up and add bubble bath salts. Rene and Kelly would get in together. I would serve Rene a bottle of Moët et Chandon. Kelly would splash the bubble bath water all over the high mirrors. It was quite a scene, looking out at that big blue ocean with Molokai in the background. Our days would be spent around the pool and walking along the beautiful golden sands of Maui.

One day I decided to take Rene to Hana on the other side of Maui. It was quite an experience. Rene wanted to meet some local Hawaiian people. She seemed to be aware of the people and their beauty and compassion. Rene talked to the Hawaiian people about their heritage and Maui being their birthplace of the revered Hawaiian Demigod. Rene was overwhelmed with their culture and kindness, and their love for people around the world.

The scenic road to Hana that connects Kahului to Hana, east Maui, is a 64-four-mile drive. It features narrow winding roads and 50 bridges, taking you past gorgeous beaches on the rugged coastline, lush forests, beautiful waterfalls, pools, and hiking trails.

When we eventually got to Hana, we engaged with the local Hawaiian people. Rene would buy pineapples off them, and we would sit at the local park watching the ocean. Walking along the black sandy beach, Rene thought she was in heaven.

On the way home, after a beautiful day spent in Hana I had an idea. I would take Rene to Mama's world-famous Fish House overlooking the ocean. It sat overlooking the ocean. The decor was of French Polynesian wood that surrounded the entire place. I suggested to Rene that she have the Mahi, with some explaining as to what it was, Hawaiian fish.

"OK, I'll try it," she said.

She was always down to try something new, was adventurous Rene.

It was the best fresh fish she had ever tasted, caught straight from the ocean that same day. As we drove back to Kaanapali that night to the Royal Lahaina, it was so peaceful watching the sun with a beautiful color of red, descend over Molokai.

Rene said, "This was one of the best holidays of my life so far. Thank you, Terry."

Me, Kelly and Annette just smiled.

The following day, Rene and Kelly would swim in the beautiful sparkling sea. Occasionally, a turtle would pop its head up out of the ocean. Rene would be so excited. You could see when she was relaxing at the pool that she was at peace. Our time was so short on Maui.

The morning we were leaving to fly back to Los Angeles we all decided to take one more photo at the lookout. We all got out of the car on the way to the airport. We stood on the cliff overlooking the windsurfers near Paia and took our last pictures of that spectacular emerald ocean. We all took in the deep breath of the olfactory delight that is Maui and promised we would return, sealing it with a kiss.

A couple of years later me, Kelly and Annette would return. As for Rene, life sometimes gets to us. After returning to the U.K., Rene went into a care home. She passed away, her dream of returning to the beautiful islands going right along with her. The Hawaiian Islands, mahalo, goodbye. Rest in peace, Rene, love, Terry, Annette and Kelly.

CHAPTER 38
THE FULL STORY OF QUEEN ELIZABETH II'S BOMB SCARE

As I was disembarking the greatest ship in the world, the Queen Elizabeth II, in Southampton on a beautiful summer morning in July 1977, I was carrying my suitcase. The Purser's officer had put me on leave for 21 days. This was unexpected, to say the least. All of a sudden, I was walking down the corridor and as I got to the gangplank two men approached me. They were both tall and wearing dark suits.

"Mr. Moogan, would you please sit down here?"

Two more men showed up There were four of them now.

"What's the problem?" I asked.

"Hold on here," one of the men ordered. I noticed he was wearing a dark, grey suit, the same as the other man. I could tell straight away that they were policemen, as bitter experience had taught me. The thoughts in my head began racing. Oh no, I thought, the jewelers! They might get me for it. Stay calm, my mind said.

"We are from the Ministry of Defense, Terry. We are taking you to the Cunard Building in Southampton for some questions. You are a suspect. We have had you under surveillance."

I said nothing. Within a minute another two men were coming around the corner to join them. I thought to myself, there were four of them! Now there are six. This must be serious.

"We are from London's Special Branch Police Department."

My mind was really going now.

"What's the problem?" I asked.

But there wasn't a reply from any of them. As past experience had taught me, be fucking quiet, Terry.

They guided me down the gangplank and we walked along the quay, one of them holding tightly to the handle of my suitcase.

"I'll take that, Terry. Here, get in."

I gave the suitcase to him freely as a black Ford Grenada four-door car pulled up in front of me. They opened the boot.

"I'll put your suitcase in here."

They threw it in like a piece of shit.

Within half a mile we were at the Cunard Building. There wasn't a murmur from any of them in the car the whole ride over. It was the same building where they had accepted my fraudulent documents of references to get on the ship through a man named John Callo, who had done my brother, Alan, a favor after I'd just come out of a two-year prison sentence. John, whom I'd met, had told me not to worry, he had checked my references.

"I've pushed you through to join the Merchant Navy," he'd said so long ago. This was how I'd made it onto the Queen Elizabeth ship in the first place.

They led me into an office. The room was far more opulent than any police station that I had been interviewed in the past.

"Sit down there on that chair," one of them said. "Now, do you know why you are here, Terry?"

"No," I said.

A large, 6 ft. man, said in a deep voice,

"You drink with Irishmen Terry?"

"Yes," I said.

"Do you know Brendan Hughes, Terry?"

"Yes, I do."

"Do you know Peter Walsh?"

"Yes, I do."

"How about Billy Boyle?"

"Yes."

"And Brian McCafferty."

"Yes, I do."

"Terry," another man interrupted, "let me tell you why you are here. We believe that you are part of the I.R.A., the Irish Republican Army, and a co-conspirator."

"Come on, don't be stupid."

"Were you smuggled onto this ship Terry?" one of the men was asking me now, the cop who had introduced himself from London's Special Branch.

"Do you know John Callo?" said another.

"Yes, I do." Oh no, I thought, they know about my references.

"We have been watching you for a long time, Terry. You know, the men you drink with smuggle guns from New York to Southampton."

"No, I didn't." Fuck. Here we go. Am I going to be classified now as an I.R.A. man?

"Well, Terry, all the men's names we have mentioned have been arrested. You will be next, Terry, if you don't come clean, that is."

He said this to me with that deep, horrible voice once again. He could scare the shit out of any man, but not me; however. I was well used to it from my days in investigations in the past.

"What's that got to do with me?"

The six-foot-tall man was speaking once again, his deep stern voice seemed to rattle bones when he said,

"You're a member of the I.R.A. Terry."

I stared back at the four of them, making eye contact.

"I might know John Callowell, but I sure don't know these men well. I drink with them, that's it. Have you ever seen me in a pub with them besides on the ship?"

"That's not the point," one of them was piping in. "You're involved, Terry."

I was starting to get a bit aggressive now. The interrogation room felt like a suffocating box with every tick off the clock.

"Am I? Fuck."

"We will be holding you in Winchester Prison, Terry, on the Terrorism Act."

Another one of the men stood up.

"Tell us your part, Terry."

"I don't have a part."

Seven grueling hours passed as we kept up this banter, yet to no avail in that they could not entrap me. They kept the pressure on. However, I had nothing to worry about.

"Have you ever brought any weapons in from New York on the ship Terry?"

"Of course not," I said.

The man with the deep voice was shouting angrily now: "You drink in a bar called McCardle's in New York?"

Fuck. My mind was racing, my head spinning, they'd been on to me for a while now.

"Yes, I have been drinking there. I'm not denying being there."

"Well, Terry, that's where the guns were smuggled from you and the Irish Republican Army. The plan was to smuggle them onto the Queen Elizabeth! We watched you!" the clone barked, sweat rolling down his forehead.

Another one of the government clones stood up. Yes, I thought, you've got fuck all on me. You just lied, you lying bastard. You've never seen me do shit. I knew my alibi was concrete,

"Yes, and the grenades, Terry." I once again denied any involvement.

"You smuggle them onto the ship for this operation, Terry."

After much more time checking, I eventually said I had smuggled myself on the ship for a better life, to work, in hopes for a brighter future. I had to get them off this I.R.A. shit.

"Terry, you know John Callo died last year?"

"Yes, I do. He was a good man; he tried to help me because my brother, Alan, worked with him."

Just then one of them was opening a file.

"We have those references, Terry."

"Good," I said. "Don't ask me any more questions about the I.R.A. OK? I'm not answering anymore."

Three of them left the room. One brought a sandwich in and a cup of tea. I left the sandwich and drank the tea. They went back in time to my childhood.

"You sure went through it, Terry."

"Yes, I did."

They were starting to soften up now.

"You know there's over 200 soldiers, police and customs' officials hunting your friends, Terry."

"No, I don't."

"Yes, they have smuggled explosives, guns, and gelignite onto the Queen Elizabeth, Terry. They are going from cabin to cabin as we speak, looking for this shipment."

I just shook my head.

"Has anybody ever mentioned to you, Terry, the I.R.A.? On the ship?"

"No," I said.

"Did you know these men were part of the I.R.A, Terry?"

Just then, one of them brought my suitcase into the room. They had torn it apart looking for evidence.

"You like cigars, Terry?"

"Yes, I do."

"Why do you have five boxes Terry? You're only allowed one box."

"They're not bombs," I replied.

They had bigger fish to fry here. They weren't interested in cigars. Then all of a sudden a new man walked in.

"Hello, Terry. I'm Billy Malone from the Ministry Department. We have everything checked, you'll be free to go in a few hours. However, your days on the Queen Elizabeth are over. Your seaman's documents will be cancelled in the Merchant Navy. We have some documents for you to sign." He exited the room after this.

I was actually relieved. I thought my life was on the line there for a minute. Now they were being kind to me, asking friendly questions as if the past several hours had never happened.

"You're a butler, Terry?"

"Yes, I am. I worked hard to get here; it took me years."

"Yes, you're popular on the ship, everyone seems to know you."

Billy was talking again. "You're free to go, Terry. Just sign here. Here is your suitcase. And Terry, don't smoke too many of those cigars at once." He gave a little chuckle. "Or were you just planning on selling them?" I just smiled.

I walked out of the Cunard Building and got myself to a bed and breakfast. That was the end of my beautiful life aboard the greatest ship in the world, the Queen Elizabeth II.

Brendan Hughes, a top I.R.A. man, said he used the Queen Elizabeth to smuggle weapons into Britain from New York throughout the 1970s. Brendan Hughes went to Southampton, put together a wee squad, all Belfast men, and practically ruled the Southampton docks in the 1970s.

"He would drive into the docks, all rearranged through contact, and eventually get on to Queen Elizabeth to take the weapons off, " the Sunday Times newspaper quoted.

The shipment would have been five or six, eight or ten weapons at the most and maybe a couple of hand grenades. The seamen would go ashore in New York, carry the stuff on board, in their lockers, or on the boat somewhere, and then have it ready to conceal in the panels of cars. Once the weapons were brought ashore, they would then be transported to Northern Ireland, normally through the Scottish part of Stranraer.

The British authorities became suspicious that the Queen Elizabeth II might be used to smuggle weapons when they discovered explosives in an apartment in Southampton in 1977. Six Irish people, crew members on the Queen Elizabeth, were arrested, me among them. A total of 874 sticks of gelignite were found in the apartment. The Queen Elizabeth, which was the flagship of the Cunard Cruise Line for 35 years, made two transatlantic trips per month. But Cunard has always stated that it was not aware of any arms smuggling on the ship. The 200 soldiers, police and customs officials hunted the men and their explosives on the ship, cabin by cabin.

On their last night of searching, they discovered 400 lbs. of gelignite. The full total of 44 men and one woman, along with myself and crew members, had been seized by the police under emergency regulations designed to quell terrorism. Detectives and Army explosive experts believed that Irish Republican Army sympathizers in the United States may have been using the 67,000-ton liner to transport gelignite and detonators to terrorists in Britain.

The 400 lbs. of gelignite were enough for 80 bombs of the kind recently used in London, which had been found in the apartment overlooking the Southampton Docks. The police were working on the theory that bomb kits, including explosive battery wires and detonator caps were being smuggled onto the ship in American docks. The kits were then reportedly removed by crew members and hidden in the lockers and behind paneling during the voyage to England. The kits themselves were slipped out of the ship in clothing, duffel bags and valises. They were then handed to contact men for storage in buildings such as Albion Towers in Southampton House, where the bomb cache was found.

As for Peter Walsh, Billy Boyle, and Brian McCafferty, they all went on trial and were found Guilty. They each received a sentence of 20 years. Brendan Hughes was never caught and later passed away. However, he left transcripts of the events. His voice spoke from the grave.

For me, it was quite an experience. I could have been dragged into the whole conspiracy, found myself locked away just like all the other boys. Thank God I was not terrified and did not show how anxious I was.

CHAPTER 39
GRIEF IS THE PRICE WE PAY FOR CRIMES

I don't think much has changed today in this world as it was in the late 1960s through to the 1980s. The punishment for committing a crime can vary depending on the severity of the crime, the defendant's criminal history, previous jail time and other factors. Some common punishments for crime include fines, probation, incarceration, and in the most serious of cases, death. This single most important root of crimes is self-hatred, nurtured in early years by parents so plagued by self-hatred themselves that they express hostility.

Crime is primarily the outcome of multiple adverse social, economic, cultural and family conditions. Some individuals commit crimes out of necessity. Others are driven by anger, rejection of authority, a manipulative personality, or psychopathic punishment. Those who have not cherished themselves, like myself and those dearest to me, know nothing of what it means to cherish another. Grief is the price we pay for crimes.

However, on the other end of the spectrum, what grief do we pay for our crimes? Let's take a look at my dear friend Franny Jones. He lacked everything in life. Eventually, when he was ten, he was taken into the British care system, and spent his youthful years locked up in what was infamous for its child killer, Mary Bell. Franny was only ten years old, locked away in Red Banks Secure Unit Institution, outside Liverpool. I would eventually also find myself locked up with Franny three years later at St. Aidan's Approved School.

Our anger unfolded because of those institutions. It had a terrible effect on the brain regarding the so-called teachers that were caring for us. One day, we would attack them, and put them into submission, then escape. That was our plan. These so-called teachers were ignorant to the core.

It is now 50 years later that I am writing about Franny Jones, my cherished dear friend. I am now looking over the beautiful California coast, Laguna Beach, to this day, thinking about him as I write this chapter. I had not seen Franny for many years. But I could never forget him. I was on my holiday from the Queen Elizabeth II cruise liner. There was a knock on the door where we lived, one early evening where we grew up as lads together on the corner of the street when we moved out of the city.

"Hello, Terry," John said.

"Hello, mate, come in. Do ye want a cup of tea, John?"

"Yeah, go ahead."

He had a worried expression on his face and looked nervous.

Then he started to tell me, "Franny is in the hospital, Terry. There's something wrong with him. He's been asking for you. Will you come and see him, Terry? He's in Walton hospital."

"OK, John, I'll go tomorrow."

"OK, Terry."

We sat and talked. John told me Franny had been let out of prison. He was serving two years for some stupid crime.

I entered Walton Hospital in Liverpool, found the ward, and knocked on the nurse's station door. I looked across the ward nervously.

"I'm here to see Franny Jones, Miss."

"What's your name?" She looked up from her clipboard. "Oh, are you Terry?"

"Yes, Terry Moogan."

She wrote it down on the visitors list. I could smell the stench of the cleaning materials, and the wooden floors. Rows of beds lined the ward. It looked the same with green blankets on the top of the beds with cream white sheets. I was looking around the ward wondering where he was with anticipation. I was in for a shock.as the nurse walked towards the bed in the corner of the ward.

"He's been waiting for you, talking about you all day."

I just smiled. There he was, my old friend. It looked like life had taken its toll on him. He was just lying there, staring, with his round spectacles on, half asleep. The nurse touched him on the shoulder.

"Francis, your friend is here."

He seemed to come out of a trance. He stared at me. I hadn't seen him for several years. He looked so different. His face was swollen, and his body was bulked up. He pushed his spectacles closer to his eyes and stared at me and said with a shallow voice,

"Hello, Terry how are you, mate?" The words came out of his mouth slowly. "Terry, how are you?" he said once again. "Did you bring me any cigarettes?"

I just started laughing, that was Franny, cheeky as fuck. He got excited and sat up, pushing himself up with the little strength he had, using the bed rail to hold on to.

"Go and get me twenty cigarettes, Terry."

"OK, I'll go down to the shop for you." Then he was asking, "Get me forty Terry."

The inflection in his voice got louder. I slowly got up, letting the nurse know I'd be back in f15 minutes. I returned with forty cigarettes from the local shop.

"Here ye go, mate."

"Lovely, Terry. I like the Embassy, they're really good."

I watched as he opened the packet. I noticed his fingers fiddling with the paper, then I observed his whole body. It was totally swollen. His hands were shaking as he tried to open the packet of cigarettes. He pulled the sheet back that was covering his legs.

"See that, Terry?"

"Yes, Franny."

"They're the markings where they will take my leg off tomorrow."

My heart sank. He began to tell me that he had cancer. I touched him on the shoulder.

"You will be OK, mate."

I felt haunted. He just stared at me with his glasses slipping on his nose. He looked shattered.

Franny was quick to remind me of all the little capers we did when we were children.

"Remember that one, Terry? When we robbed all the money from the Woolworth shop?" he would say as he explained when we robbed them in 1966, getting away with £45. He puffed again from his third cigarette and took a massive inhale of smoke. I noticed his eyes were sunk in his head.

"Get some rest mate," I told him. "I'll see you tomorrow."

He said goodbye in his shallow shell of a voice, his eyelids shutting slowly. Then, all of a sudden an orderly came down between the two beds to pick up the soup bowl up from the tray at the side of the bed. The bowl was still full with only a few spoonful's taken out. I looked over at the needle in his hand and the tube that was attached to it leading to a bag above his head. I guessed it was morphine to kill his pain.

"OK, Franny, see you tomorrow."

I walked out of the hospital in tears and sat for a little while to get my thoughts together. I felt terrified for him. Franny was a product of Britain's institutions. I would say he was institutionalized.

A few days later I went to visit him again, the same routine, but this time, there were no cigarettes. He was lying there, motionless as I touched him.

"You OK, mate?" There was no answer this time.

He just stared at me and blinked his eyes. I left the hospital once again heartbroken and had to leave to go back now to Southampton, to the Queen Elizabeth II. I walked away from his bedside knowing I would not see him again. My little childhood friend was dying and one of his legs had been removed.

A couple of months later I was home again. I went to the house where Franny's mother lived. I knocked on the door. His mother opened the door, she was older now, and not the same woman I knew, with long gray hair and her small, thin frame. Life had taken its toll on her.

"Hello Terry, come in."

"How is Franny?"

"He passed away, Terry." I couldn't say a word. "He went into a coma; Franny's brother John would talk to him every day to try and bring him out of that coma. It was always a fruitless attempt."

He was only a young man, 22 years of age. He had spent most of his life in institutions, along with part of his adult life. It was grief alright. The love that he never received, only the hatred from Britain's institutions.

Me and Franny also had another dear friend in our gang from back in 1965, David Brooks. David lived on the same street as me when we were children. We met hanging out on the corner of Finborough Road, Walton, Liverpool. He was one year older than me, and we clicked automatically. He had blond hair with blue eyes, a beautiful-looking kid. His mother would come to the corner, marching and shouting, "David! David, come home!"

David would look at her, tell her to fuck off, and walk away.

"Come on, Terry," he'd say.

We would run up the street to Norris Green, The Broadway. We would go on a shoplifting campaign and hide out on the railway lines, eating our stolen chocolate and milk. David never got caught and was not sent to a government Home. However, one morning he was with another boy, Brian Steel, and decided not to go to school. They climbed into a loft at a local community centre. A couple of lads from a special school came and lit some fish boxes, and they got trapped. By the time David and Brian were rescued Brian had 90% burns on his body and David had 25% on his. It would take years for them to recover, along with many surgeries, especially for Brian. Before he could ever get a chance to fully come back to life, he would pass away the same year.

I would still sit with David when I was 19 and have a drink with him. His hands were burnt to a cinder, and he could not move his fingers, let alone hold a pint of beer. His fingers were all bent out of shape from the operations he'd had. As if life wasn't already tough, this was another blow to his mental capacity. It would affect his whole life. He had moved out of the area to the suburbs of Kirby, a well-known tough place where it bred real criminals.

David turned to crime once again and became a major shop-lifter on a professional level, providing for his children and wife. He would spend many months in prison for his crimes on several misdemeanors. Sometimes he would binge-drink when I was in his company. Even with his disability he always managed to laugh.

Later on in his life, however, he became quite the recluse. There were many reasons why he may have chosen this, not to connect with others, anxiety, shame, fear, vulnerability, and potential rejection. This can be a reflection of an underlying mental condition. This was the opposite of his youth. However, you could see it in him as a child.

I got a call in November, 2023 from his daughter, Katie. She informed me David had passed away and asked me if I could make a video for his service, which of course, I did and sent it to Katie. I spoke about our childhood and told Katie what kind of a boy he was. She confided in me that he had not been out for years. I understood his condition. Apathy, a phobia, schizoid personality, various anxiety disorders. We will never know; this could have been the toll it took on him that he developed throughout his adulthood due to his accident when he had been burned.

The hardest thing that Katie, his daughter, had faced, was love, the hardest stage of grief, his acceptance. It often occurs later in the grieving process and is considered the hardest stage of grief, simply because it requires fully accepting a loved one. David is gone, though he will be remembered for the rest of my life. My dear childhood friend, David Brooks. Amen.

The third last friend, Edward Langley, was from Scotland Road. We had been in Homes together since 1969. He had been punished for his petty crimes. He had been in detention in Borstal Prison. However, his strength carried him through. I'd never seen the weight on a man's soul so much as Eddie's. He had become successful as he got older and was well respected in the city. He had flown out to see me in 1994, when Brazil played Italia in the World Cup final in Pasadena, Los Angeles.

We spoke about old times and his life. I had also seen him in Liverpool in the early 2000s and visited his home in the city centre. We had some great laughs sitting there on the Mersey, Liverpool, having a pint of beer. He was a man that could not be broken. A few years later, I called his brother, Jim. I heard Edward was in trouble and had been sentenced to three years in prison. The Serious Organized Crime Agency had begun to investigate him further for some unsolved crimes, paying him a visit in prison. They threatened him that he would be charged with laundering millions of English pounds and also take all of his assets away from him.

Mr. Justice Smith, after several months of considering the case, granted SOCA's application. He said he had no doubt the stake of money used in finance in extensive gambling activity in 1998 was the product of criminal activity. All of Edward's assets were seized, £1 million. Also, there were new charges coming in the near future for Edward, all of which would carry an extensive sentence, he had been told. It was all too much for him, my dear friend Edward. We suspected that trigeminal neuralgia as well as douloureux had set in his brain which affects the trigeminal nerve which delivers sensations to the face and surface of the eyes. It is called the suicide disease He went back to his cell and killed himself in 2008 while serving his three-year sentence for money laundering. Franny Jones, David Brooks, and Edward Langley did not die of grief for love. They died for the grief; they paid for their crimes. Amen.

CHAPTER 40
THE BRAWL IN BEVERLY HILLS: FRANK SINATRA AND DEAN MARTIN

My former boss, Frederick Weismann, after the brawl in the Beverly Hills Polo Lounge at the Beverly Hills hotel, was the most prominent millionaire who died.

Frank Sinatra and Dean Martin had gotten into a barroom brawl in Beverly Hills that nearly left Frederick Weismann dead. The details to this day, decades later, still remain murky. This was one of the most outrageous incidents to occur in the star-studded city.

These two guys were at the top of the entertainment food chain. They couldn't have been more popular; they couldn't have been well-paid and more iconic when the incident happened. For something like this, a monkey wrench so powerful to get thrown into their lives, something as simple as a couple of cross words and racial epithets thrown around in a bar, led to fisticuffs that ultimately threatened their careers, and took a really dark turn, said the news. It's a little-explored facet of both men's careers. It hinged on one night in both of their lives that should have been a celebration of Dean's 49th birthday.

On the night of June 8, 1966 Sinatra and Martin were at the Polo Lounge alongside Sinatra's bodyguard, Pal. Jill Rizzo, actor Richard Conte, as well as plenty of ladies, were sitting next to them at a booth as well as Frederick Weismann, my former boss and president of Hunt's Food. He was accompanied by businessman Franklin H. Fox. The men were barely sitting for ten minutes when Weismann grew increasingly annoyed by the rowdy laughter of the celebrity guests. That's when Weismann got up and said something few people dared to do, asking Frank Sinatra and his pals to quiet down.

Sinatra claimed that Weismann told him, "You talk too fucking loud, and you have a bunch of loudmouth friends" before using a certain "f" word and a certain "c" word that Italian-Americans typically object to. Some claimed that Weismann also scolded Sinatra for using foul language in front of ladies. Sinatra allegedly responded with an antisemitism remark.

"Fuck off, you little Jew," Weismann told me Sinatra said.

Then all of the sudden Weismann decked him in his right eye before slipping and falling, breaking the base of a cocktail table as he crashed to the floor. Sinatra made claims to biographer Kitty Kelly that the singer stalked out of the room when things came to blows. According to reports the hotel security guard tried to keep the two men apart as Martin pleaded, "Let's get outta here, Frank."

That's when Sinatra grabbed one of the booth's side telephones and hurled it at Weismann, knocking him out cold. It is also possible that after lunging at each other, Weismann slipped and fell. What's known for certain is that Weismann had landed on the floor flat on his back amid an upturned ashtray, a tablecloth and a clutter of broken crystal. It sounded as if he was snoring, and he wasn't getting up. What we know for sure was that Weismann objected to some of the language that was being used by Frank Sinatra and Dean Martin. It turned into a typical barroom confrontation, explained by the security guard.

What we don't know exactly is who swung first, who did what to whom, and in what order. But it ended up with somebody clubbing Frederick Weismann over the head with one of the famous pink telephones that sat booth-side at all the banquets in the Polo Lounge. He ended up unconscious on the floor.

He was revived within the day, and then he was comatose again. He was in the hospital and underwent surgery and it could have been particularly bad. He could have died, he later told me. That's when Frank Sinatra and Dean Martin separately left Los

Angeles to wait for the news while police investigated. That's where we get all of these conflicting stories, Weismann explained, where nobody knows or saw exactly what happened. Nobody gave the same story.

According to Mr. Weismann, he told me he endured a nearly three-hour operation to alleviate a skull fracture. Doctors couldn't guarantee that he would survive. Sinatra fled to Los Angeles where he was sweating it out with his much younger girlfriend, actress Mia Farrow. Martin went to Lake Tahoe to play golf. He had nothing to say when the police questioned him.

Frank was 50 years old at the time. He was grappling with a little bit of how large he was, how iconic he had become, and how he was involved with somebody half his age. So, there was a lot of stress on him even though he was on top of the world. And I think this occasionally expressed itself in outbursts. He was an emotional guy. Was he mobbed up? I think there's a lot of debate to be put on that. Was he a violent character? I don't know if that's true either, but there were certainly incidents that suggest that if he lost his temper, things would go poorly.

Jilly Rizzo was Frank Sinatra's best and most loyal friend, more so than any of the more famous figures in the rat pack. Jilly was at his side pretty much until the end of Jilly's days. They had a special bond; they were like brothers.

Jilly had come from the New York nightclub world. He had his own restaurant. He was built like a tractor-trailer. He kind of appointed himself as Frank's bodyguard, and so if trouble started it is way easy to imagine that Jilly was the one to step in and handle it. There were subsequent incidents in the years ahead in which Jilly did the exact same thing. Was it because he was a violent man? Everybody who knew him in Hollywood seemed to absolutely adore him and be charmed by him. However, if he thought his best friend was in trouble, or being threatened, out came the fists although Rizzo repeatedly denied ever being Sinatra's bodyguard in any official capacity.

"Sinatra doesn't need no protection," Rizzo was quoted as

saying. "He's man enough to stand up and defend himself in his own way like any man should."

Sinatra insisted to a detective that he didn't initiate the fight. However, Weismann told me differently.

"The guy was cursing at me."

Sinatra complained he was using four letter words. He told this to investigators, as quoted by the police:

"I don't think you ought to be sitting there with your glasses on making that kind of conversation. Then the guy got up and lunged at me. I defended myself, naturally."

Sinatra contended that after Weismann slugged him, someone tried to separate them. That's when Weismann fell without anyone laying a finger on him, it was claimed.

"I, at no time, saw no one hit him, and I certainly did not," said Sinatra.

He noted that on his way out, he saw a man hit the floor.

Weismann eventually gained consciousness but was still suffering from confusion and memory loss. Police who listed Sinatra as their prime suspect were eager to interview Weismann, who told them that he could remember everything leading up to the altercation, but nothing else. The whole incident was a blank to him, his condition described by doctors as retrograde amnesia.

According to the news, Weismann's family had been incensed and wanted to press charges against Sinatra. However, they thought better of it. A family member of Weismann's told the police they were receiving anonymous telephone threats from ominous-sounding figures. Hollywood attorney Grant Cooper announced that Weismann wanted to forget the incident and move on. The detectives, unable to do more, closed the case.

According to Frank's publicist, money was exchanged. Frank was supposed to be there with a group celebrating that night and made a habit not to be involved. So, if anything did go badly, he was in a good position to clean things up. He said the patrons, the bartenders, waiters, and all the staff at the Polo Lounge all received some kind of compensation to keep their stories vague.

Weismann was plagued by amnesia for months but did go on to live a long and prosperous life, dying in 1974 at age 82.

An elated Sinatra, who realized that the whole ordeal wouldn't derail his career, swiftly purchased an $85,000, 9-carat engagement ring. Sinatra and Farrow married in 1966.

According to the media, Dean Martin got the thankless task of informing the Sinatra children so much closer in age to Mia than their father was, of the nuptials just as the ceremony was taking place.

What really happened at the Polo Lounge remains shrouded in mystery? There are rumors that Frederick Weismann and his family may have received a payout because they never chose to press charges. Or so the speculation goes. But it does sound like it was papered over with green paper!

I had the pleasure of being Mr. Weismann's butler, houseman, and chauffeur in 1983. Frederick Weismann was one of a kind, the son of Russian Jews who came to the U.S.A. to make a better life. He excelled in business as a young man and rose to the position of Chairman of Hunt's Foods by the time he was 31 years old. He also formed a business alliance with a select group of Japanese businessmen which led to the formation of the Mid-Atlantic Toyota. It became the largest distributer of Toyota vehicles in the United States.

He also collected over one billion worth of various artworks in a private collection at his $40 million home set in Holmby Hills, California including those of Francis Bacon, Andy Warhol, David Hockney, and perhaps most famous of all, Pablo Picasso.

He discussed the Polo Lounge incident with me one day when his neck became too stiff to drive his Bentley. However, he kept it short, using the word 'motherfucker' at the end of every sentence of the conversation.

"Yes, Mr. Weismann, I understand," I said, "and I'm impressed you've got balls. I can't believe you turned old blue eyes into swollen black eyes."

We both laughed so hard.

CHAPTER 41
THE END GAME
1980

The Scotland Road bank job. On a Monday evening in October, 1980 four men sat in a damp tenement council flat on the outskirts of Scotland Road in Liverpool's most notorious area. As smoke filled the air one man flicked the ash from his cigarette onto the floor. He looked like he hadn't slept for a week. He was unshaven, his eyes were glassy, and his face was pale. You would never know with this guy which mood he would be in. His name was Joey Wright, an old friend from Huyton from 1974 but originally from Soho Street in the city centre where well-known professional criminals lived.

The other two men were also from Huyton on the outskirts of Liverpool. They had the reputation of being ruthless bank robbers. I had known these three men for many years and could not fault them. Then there was myself in the group. I would lead the main criminal operation and planning.

The plan was to hijack a Securicor van carrying well over £100,000. That would be equivalent to millions today. Joey Wright was a tough guy and most men feared him. He was 5ft. 8in." with a stocky build, black hair, deep blue eyes, and a long scar on his face. He was also a bully and known for his crazy mood swings. His nickname was Crazy Joey. He had just served a three-year sentence for robbery and had only been out of jail for six months, and here he was at it again. Billy and Bobby Hughes were ruthless and had been at the game for years, with Billy having served seven years for robbery.

The three men were on Liverpool's most wanted criminals

list as I was myself. The two brothers, with their blond cropped hair and green eyes, had a Steve McQueen movie star look about them. I first met them at a pub in Huyton. At first they were suspicious of me until I mentioned I had been in prison with their brother John in 1974. That cleared the air straight away, and we became friends.

"You know; my aunt works in the bank, Terry?" Joey said.

"I didn't know that. Did she give you all the information about how much they bring into the bank, Joey?"

"Yes. It's all sorted out, Terry."

Billy and Bobby just stared, Bobby, muttering, "It's on then, lad."

"You got the gun, Joey?" Billy asked.

I took a look at Billy and Joey, letting them know without words that there was no way we could use guns. That would depend once again on Joey's mood that day.

"Did you speak to your auntie at all, Joey?" I asked.

"Yes. She told me it's about £100k."

I knew right then he was not bullshitting.

He took a long drag from his Embassy cigarette and blew it out slowly.

"She is safe, Terry, we can give her a couple of quid, is that OK?"

"Sure," I replied. "OK. We'll all meet on Monday at twelve, at the Throstles Nest pub next to the bank on Scotland Road."

"OK." Bobby said. "Let's get off, then."

"See ya next Monday," I said.

I slowly walked down Walton Road towards Kirkdale with Joey. We stopped at a pub, the Halfway House, and went into the bar.

"It's going to be a piece of cake, Terry." said Joey.

I ordered two glasses of lager.

"Listen to me, Joey, no fucking guns, okay?"

Joey snapped at the bartender, "Two whiskeys with ice, mate."

The bartender gave him a weird look. "Here, drink that, lad."

Joey threw the whiskey right down his throat before it touched his tongue.

"OK, Terry, we will be sound."

"I know Billy and Bobby love guns, lad, but we don't fucking need them."

"Terry, this will make our lives better. We can all buy a lovely house in Spain, one each!"

"OK," I said. "Let's finish this and get the hell out of here."

"I'll see you next Monday at Throstles, Terry."

"OK, Joey lad, I'll see you there."

I thought about the whole situation. It would be a large amount of money if Joey's auntie was correct. As I drove home, my head was going twenty-to-the-dozen. I kept my eyes on my rear view mirror every 30 seconds to see if there was any surveillance keeping tabs on me as I had been found Not Guilty in the Liverpool Crown Court a year before on a robbery with force on a Securicor van that netted over £33,000. My observations through the rear-view mirror were all clear, with no evidence of anybody following me.

The Royal Bank sat on Scotland Road in an old building. The people who lived there were tough and impoverished. It was on a decline at the beginning of 1980. The bank paid customers with their government checks and withdrawals from the little amount of life savings they had. Scotland Road had one hell of a reputation for toughness and especially for its drinking on the weekends. There were once over 200 pubs on Scotland Road. Now, there is only one left. The McMullens were the owners of the Throstles Nest. Joey knew them well. They were sound people. If you mentioned the Throstles Nest on Scotland Road, people automatically thought you were tough, especially if you drank there as a local. The Throstle's Nest opened in 1804 and remains open today.

I figured out which route the getaway vehicle would take, switching to the second car and its location, and then on to the safe house. I decided this was to be my plan and reported it back to Joey, Billy, and Bobby. They, of course, accepted it, judging the plan from the history of our past endeavors

We would steal a van, me and Joey, the night before the robbery, drive one mile to Kirkdale, then change cars into a Jaguar. From there we'd make our way to the safe house in Anfield. That was the plan. The safe house that my friend owned was an old building in an area of Anfield

I met Joey, Billy, and Bobby on Monday at twelve o'clock on the dot. Joey blurted out, "You got it all sorted, Terry?"

I bowed my head slowly. "Yeah, mate."

We sipped on a glass of orange juice while Joey had his pint of lager as usual.

Joey piped up, "the Securicor van will be arriving at one o'clock, boys. Let's head outside."

We all walked across the street, stood there and watched the guards from a tenement building on Sylvester Street as they delivered cash in big brown boxes that were transferred by two of the guards into the bank. They didn't seem to flinch as they walked into the bank for the delivery.

Bobby, with three words coming out the side of his mouth, said, "That's ours, fucking hell, Terry!"

I whispered back to him, "That's next Monday, mate. No guns."

The plan would be executed the following Monday to ambush the guards taking the boxes into the bank at one p.m. We were all excited, and all set to go.

A few days later me and Joey headed into the city centre. Our plan was to steal a Ford van with no windows in the sides. We went into a car park on Old Hall Street. After a few hours we found a Ford transit van parked on the third floor.

"Do ye thing," I told Joey.

Within five minutes Joey had placed his screwdriver into the ignition, got in, and cranked the engine up as he drove out of the city. I followed him to Scotland Road in my Cortina. Our plan was to park at an old friend's house, Joe Cavanagh's, so he could keep an eye on the cars till the following Monday. The next day, me and Bobby went to the same car park, this time in a Ford Granada, a fast car. It would be an easy run from the police if we were chased. The Ford Granada was one of the fastest cars on the road. Bobby got in, starting up the ignition with a stolen car key from a local friend.

We were off once again to Joe's house through the city centre. The two cars were parked behind the tenements on Vauxhall Road. Joe kept his eye on them until Monday. Our arrangement was to meet on Sunday evening, me, Billy, Bobby, and Joey at a local pub in the city centre. I walked into the Cavern Pub on Sunday evening. It was the local pub and nightclub where the four lads, John, Paul, George, and Ringo were discovered before they became the Beatles.

We sat in the corner. Billy and Bobby were always dead serious men. Joey and I had no problem with that. Sometimes there was a clash of personalities and I'd say just said two words, "That's enough!"

We would meet at Joe's house, just off Scotland Road. The plan was to block the door at the bank with a ladder and a bucket, as if the window cleaner was cleaning the windows above the bank door. Me, Bobby, and Billy would come from behind and put the men on the floor as soon they removed the boxes from the vault in the Securicor van. There was a bus stop outside the bank, 30ft. away, which was perfect. We took the ladder that Bobby had purchased a couple of days before, out of the van.

We all headed to the bus stop, as if we were waiting for the bus into the city centre, Bobby leaned the ladder up against the wall outside the bank. It was 12.50 p.m., and quite a grey, cold day. The traffic was light going into the city. The streets did not have many people about due to the inclement weather. We were dressed in jeans, big black overcoats, and dark grey caps just like the Peaky Blinders.

Once we'd seen the van coming we put our masks on up over our caps. Bobby was putting the ladder in place, moving it around the bank building as if he was working on cleaning the bank's windows. Unfortunately, we were the only ones at the bus stop shelter. As the van approached we waited anxiously, my heart banging like fuck. The two guards got out and opened the back of the security van. They were dressed in blue uniforms with a massive blue motorbike helmet to protect them just in case of an attack.

I noticed Bobby had moved the ladder, blocking the doorway. As the two guards pulled the big brown boxes out of the secured position at the back of the van and closed the door on the security van, we made our move and pounced on them, Joey putting one of the guards onto the floor and grabbing a box. I grabbed the other one while Billy and Bobby had the other guard pinned down. Within five seconds we were running across Scotland Road into the tenements. Joey jumped into the Ford transit van, and I lay down in the back. The boxes of cash were next to Joey. I shouted to him,

"Go!"

"Where's Billy and Bobby?"

"I don't fucking know!"

Billy and Bobby had their own plan. They must have had a friend pick them up and drive them away. As Joey was driving to the safe house five minutes later, we could hear all the sirens echoing over the city. The police were scrambling everywhere, blocking off roads into the city from Scotland Road

"Stay calm, Joey."

The second car was in position a couple of miles away. Then suddenly Joey blurted out, "There are two police cars behind me, Terry!"

Joey put his foot on the accelerator, swerving around the side of a car and smashing the whole side in, forcing the car off the road.

"Terry, there's about four of them now!"

"Go to the safe house!" I shouted. I knew we were fucked.

One of the police cars came up to the side of the van at a stoplight, its siren screaming. He was shouting at Joey.

"Pull over! Pull over now!"

Joey ignored him, putting his face down speeding off,

We headed up Everton Valley towards Anfield. We were one block away from the safe house. Joey pulled into Anfield Road and shouted, "Bail, Terry, every man for himself with the police on our tail!"

I leaned over and grabbed the box. As Joey pulled up slowly, I jumped out with the box under my arm. There were two cops after me, the chase was on now. I zigzagged through the alleyways of the streets of Anfield, all the way to the safe house. I blew the cops off with my physical fitness, well, I thought I did. As I entered the safe house, my old friend Dave had left the door open for us to his flat. I locked the door after I entered, ran upstairs to the top flat which was already open. I put the box under the bed. All of a sudden, I heard the smash of glass. Oh fuck, I thought. The door flew off its hinges and about eight policemen had me on the ground in seconds. I thought to myself frantically, it's the end game now.

They overpowered me, put the cuffs on, and marched me down the stairs with the cops puffing and panting, out of breath.

"We got you now, you bastard!" one of them shouted with excitement.

They threw me in the police car.

"What's your name?"

I kept quiet.

"What's your fucking name?" they asked me again.

I didn't open my mouth.

I was taken by an escort of five police cars to Walton Lane Police Station for questioning. The Serious Crime Squad came from all over the city to have a look at me in my cell, and then interviewed me for several hours.

"We got you now, Terry. You will be charged," the lead detective, McAtteer, said.

They never had any luck throughout the night. I kept quiet. I had been in my cell for approximately five hours when I heard a voice:

"Terry! Terry!"

I thought I was dreaming.

"Joey, is that you?"

"Yes! Have you been charged with anything, Terry?" Joey asked.

"No." I replied.

"I have."

"For what?" I asked him.

"Robbery with force. They said they found glass on my clothes from the driver who was delivering the money to the bank."

All of a sudden, the door opened.

"Come on out, Moogan," the sergeant snapped as McAtteer and Bailey watched me. I got up slowly from the concrete floor. I was dressed with only a pair of boxer shorts on.

"Stand at the desk."

A big sergeant was staring at me along with about six detectives. Detective Bailey and McAtteer announced, "He will be charged on Section Eight of the Theft Act of1968.'"

This section states that a person is guilty of robbery if they steal property while using force or threatening force against another person immediately before or at the time of the theft. The custodial sentence for robbery is five years to a life of imprisonment. I was silent once again and placed back into the cell.

I thought it was morning again when the cell door banged open.

"Up, Moogan," the sergeant said. "You're going to the Bridewell Main Prison in the city."

I noticed Joey was behind me.

"Put these blankets over your head," the sergeant snapped.

Detectives Bailey and Walker and the rest of the detectives followed, placing the blankets over our heads, and handcuffed us to their arms. I was handcuffed to Bailey, and Joey handcuffed to McAtteer, a precaution in case we tried to escape.

We were put into a massive police vehicle and escorted by four police cars into the city. The following morning, I was lying in my cell when the door opened.

"Put these clothes on," Bailey said.

All of a sudden Joey was put in my cell and five minutes later we were paraded from the underground courts to the main court. There were high security police at every entrance just in case we escaped. The hearing lasted five minutes as the prosecution opposed bail. We were back in the same cell together, waiting in custody to be transferred to a top-security remand centre on the outskirts of Liverpool, Grizzly Risley, our home for the next two weeks. Both of us had been sleep-deprived and were scanning for danger. We entered the shitty cell together on the first floor. Once we were allocated to our cell I was able to talk to Joey. The massive metal door slammed closed as the prison guard turned his key to lock both of us in, I took the top bunk while Joey took the bottom bunk. We were just two bricks now in a cell once again.

"Don't worry, Terry," Joey said.

I just brushed it off. My mind took me back to when I was 14 years old, one of the youngest prisoners in Risley. My mind started to drift off to sleep when Joey said, "Fuck, Terry, I'm sick. I just did three years in prison; I'll probably get ten years now."

Joey wanted out. Now, he seemed to be petrified. The prison was horrible, the stench of the cell stung. Risley was known for prisoners to commit suicide. I wondered if Joey would be next the way he was behaving. After a few days, at 12 o'clock midday, when the cell door opened.

The prison guard shouted "Out, Joey Wright!"

Joey got up and was keen to leave the cell. He returned an hour later.

"Terry," he announced as he stood there sluggishly in front of me staring out the caged window of the cell, "I want to talk."

"What, Joey?"

"The police have been to visit me. Their names are Smith and Bailey. Terry, I've made a deal. We will be out in two weeks. The police won't show up for the bail hearing. By law, the magistrate will release us. It was hilarious. I've paid Smith £5,000 for our freedom."

It was obvious he was conspiring with Detective Smith, I knew then there was something wrong with Joey, but what could I do? He was so convincing I couldn't do anything.

The day soon came that we stood in front of the magistrate. I noticed there were no police detectives and no security around the courtroom. I thought, This is it, we're out! The prosecution was dumbfounded; the magistrate was shouting: "I can't release these two men!" The magistrate seemed petrified: "These are serious charges."

After arguing back and forth the magistrate gave up and released us on bail with no restrictions. I couldn't believe it, then I knew. Joey was with Smith the detective, he was a police informer. We had wondered why men were getting caught for robberies; it was Joey all along giving Smith information, the dirty stool pigeon.

As we walked out of the court to Dale Street in the city centre my wife was there waiting for me. Joey's wife was also there, lots of tension in the air now between both of us.

"I'll see you later, Joey." I had to be nice to him, but I wanted to beat the fucking daylights out of him also.

"OK. Terry."

I turned to my wife as I was stepping into the car. "Go follow him."

"OK," Annette said. "Joey got in Detective Smith's car, Terry," Annette said to me.

"What color was the car?" I asked.

"Green."

That was the Detective Smith who had been following me for years, I told her. Joey was a police informer, but there was nothing I could do. He got me out. But it would come back to haunt him years later.

After my meeting with a solicitor, Rob Broudie, and Paul Rooney, I took the Pan Am midnight express flight in December, 1980, just after John Lennon's death. My trial was set for October, 1981 in my absence.

I kept in touch with Joey, calling him from a local phone box outside a pub, the Cock 'n' Bull, that my brother and I owned in Santa Monica. The operator spoke: "$3.50 for three minutes, sir."

"Hello, Joey, how's it going?"

"They framed us, Terry. They put the glass on our clothes from the security guard's glasses. They got us on the forensics, from when the guard was attacked. His glasses smashed on the ground when Billy and Bobby attacked him."

Billy and Bobby were nowhere to be found after the robbery. They had their own plan and escaped in their own getaway car with friends.

"I want you to listen to me, Joey. Get John and Alan to follow six of the jurors home to see where they live after they leave the court in the evening. Tell John and Alan to sit in the back of the bus next to them when they're on their way home from the court. Tell them this, Joey that they make sure to come in with a Not Guilty verdict, telling them, 'These men, Joey and Terry, are innocent, they have been framed by the police.' Then say this, Joey: 'We know where you live.' It will work with six of them; it will confuse them and scare them, Joey, OK?"

"OK, Terry. What a great idea! Fucking brilliant!" he said.

"Fucking do it, OK?" It was the last thing I said as the phone line went dead. A few days later I got another message to Joey: to be on the phone at eight p.m. tonight.

I stood at Armand Hammer Park in Beverly Hills on a beautiful October day under the California sun. I stood staring up at the Beverly Hills mansions. This was my future now. I had $25 in quarters from a local liquor store.

Later, I stepped out of my convertible Cadillac in Beverly Hills and headed across the park. The park was beautiful. People were walking peacefully in the morning with their dogs, not a care in the world. Children were playing on the swings; I could hear their innocent voices as I picked up the receiver of the phone. I dialed the operator.

"A call to the U.K. please."

"That will be $3.50, sir."

My mind was going fucking crazy. Had Joey done as I'd told him, or did he snitch put down the whole robbery down to me and make a statement against me to save his own life?

"Hi, Joey,"

"We were Not Guilty, Terry!" he shouted down the phone.

My heart lifted. It worked.

"The Liverpool jury, they are the best, Terry. The coppers left the courtroom with red faces of embarrassment. But listen, Terry, the police made an application to the judge for a warrant out for your arrest, and it was granted. So be careful, mate."

In Liverpool's streets I was a marked man now.

"What about Billy and Bobby?"

"They want them too, Terry."

"Don't forget the £20,000 you owe me, Joey."

"I will give you the money. I owe you," he replied. "Honest, mate."

"Take care, Joey."

Joey Wright was nothing but a snake and a reservoir dog, Liverpool's worst police informer. He would be sentenced to 25 years in Scotland a few years later for heroin trafficking. After his release, he would only live another few years. He was tagged as a reservoir dog. My friends spared his life. I told them he's not worth the time.

As for Billy and Bobby, they would hijack a sorting office, with four other men, from the Huyton firm that distributed money to post offices in Worcester in January, 1981. In an ambush by armed police a pitched battle erupted as the police opened fire on one of my old friends. Tommy Smith got shot through the arm. Their luck had run out. They were sentenced to 12 years each when found Guilty.

Years later, Billy and Bobby would pass away. Tommy Smith followed them in 2024. The greatest notorious gang of bank robbers ever to come out of Liverpool had lived infamously. The Serious Crime Squad had the Huyton firm down as the

"Operation Transit Gang." They have gone down in history, the Huyton firm. As for me, I got into my red convertible Cadillac and drove through Beverly Hills, stopping at the Beverly Hills Hotel to sit in the Polo Lounge where Weisman was whacked. I sat and had a beer and reflected on my whole life up until that point.

I was 25 years of age. I had been battered by Britain's institutions and was not out of my head. I hadn't committed suicide like so many others. I didn't sink into insanity like most had. All of them lonely people who worshipped drugs due to their abuse and depression and loneliness, I kept my balance and away from alcohol and drugs. However, I was tormented inside with anxiety and depression. The list goes on. I wasn't far away from mass destruction.

As for the warrant, I stayed away for ten years, just as I was told to by my friends, the solicitors Rob Broudie and Paul Rooney, until the warrant ran out. They were the same solicitors who told me to take the midnight express flight ten years earlier.

We all walked down to the same cafe on Dale Street as in 1990 and had a cup of coffee This time it was a young girl serving us.it was a younger generation now. Rob Broudie pushed a piece of paper across the table. It was from the Department of Prosecutions office. It read: Regarding Mr. Terence Moogan. Urgent. No warrants.

I smiled. I would have loved to have seen the faces of the detectives when the foreman of the jury announced that I was Not Guilty in the courtroom on that October day in 1981.

I was not a broken man. I had returned to California to resume my life and raise my little baby, the Hollywood butler's daughter, Kelly Moogan, who was only one year old at the time, and my wife Annette. That was the end game of Liverpool' notorious bank robbers. It read the next night in *The Liverpool Echo*: Man Escapes to America. Unfortunately, Rob Broudie committed suicide years later.

CHAPTER 42
AN ANGRY SOUL

An angry person may refer to someone who feels angry often or has a difficult time controlling their anger. Anger can be a symptom of deep issues such as past hurts, guilt, or a sense of powerlessness. The causes in my life, I think, started with trauma in the middle of the night. Past hurts. I think at the time that being a small child can damage your trust and safety. This then creates fear and distance.

I always remember when my mother would call me to come in off the street and I would run away. At that time I was seven years old. From there on it would only get worse throughout my little childhood which would cause me to lose that childhood. It did create fear and distance with my mother and eventually my father, which led me to feelings of anxiety and negativity and confusion in my mind. There was no way to communicate, as I would be judged differently as a child.

Every time we have a new experience we inevitably get some-thing new out of it. This isn't because things change but because *we* do. Meaning is stable, but we need to grow to mature. At least, we ought to, and as we do we become attentive to truth in new ways. We have a broader and richer framework that enables us to see more in life. This is true even of children who become angry. The journey in my life and experiences were beyond me, which in my thoughts were normal.

I fought so many battles, but I had passions that brought instinctive emotions to my soul. They are good but dangerous. They are immediate reactions to reality, such as fear, anxiety, desire, pity, grief, and anger. It's this last passion that figures prominently in the final battle of our life. What happens when our anger, however justified in itself, goes unchecked? It becomes rash. Are there any ways to reign in?

Anger invites more anger. An example of this would be my childhood friend, Ronnie Parr, who was abused by the teachers in St. George's Approved School. One particular teacher, Forrester, constantly picked on Ronnie Parr and bullied him and beat him to a pulp. When we look at this anger within ourselves, we become speechless. In his grief and anger Ronnie Parr then went on into the real world and invited more anger. When he got older, he was picked on in a pub on the outskirts of Liverpool, in Widnes, and bullied once again.

Eventually, he returned with a shotgun. When the men were leaving the pub he turned on the villains and murdered both of them. He could not control that anger. It was embedded into him from the abuse he took from Forrester at St. George's. The issue was that he was too angry to think. The rashness of that evil he was reacting to unintentionally came as a result of great harm. Ronnie Parr was sentenced to life in prison. Whose fault was it? Was he born that way, or was it embedded in him by abuse? If unchecked and rash anger leads to great folly, evil and bloodshed, what can check anger?

We don't have to wait long for some of that evil to manifest. When some people come upon a horse being beaten and whipped by soldiers, their anger reaches a fever pitch. When we were young, getting neglected and beaten, we were formed by anger, especially my friend Franny Jones. Everywhere he went, he was angry. Looking back on him today, he would tell everyone to fuck off. Surprisingly to me, he was quite loving. But this anger was inside him.

So how might we apply wisdom in checking our anger today? As we feel the temperature of our souls rising, we stop and remind ourselves and one another first that ungodly anger will only add iniquity to our injury, and second, that the Lord himself has said "Vengeance is mine. I will repay."

That vengeance came to me one day when I went to meet

a friend who had been raped by a man, John McCardle, in St. George's Approved School. He was weak and I was strong. The anger was waging war against our flesh. They often wage wars against your soul, also. We decided to kidnap him and do a lot of harm, probably kill him. However, after a couple of hours, I remembered an old doctor, Carol Way. He said to entrust yourself to God. Look to Him to fight your battles and to vindicate. I passed this on to my friend, and he became calm. So did I. Our souls became calmer and we had a cup of tea in the rose garden. Then all of a sudden, the sun shone. This doesn't make us passive, we thought. We were David against Goliath. We trusted that our lives are bound in the bundle of living in the care of our Lord, that we always live between the paws of the true Asian.

I had the pleasure of working with Mr. Weismann in the capacity as his butler and chauffeur. This man had been black-jacked over the head with a phone and sustained a tumor. One morning, I was outside the home picking some flowers in the rose garden for the centrepiece in the dining room. That evening, there would be six guests. For a formal dinner, you'd think he would be jolly. Then all of a sudden, he was there in front of me shouting,

"Answer the fucking phone, Terry!"

"I'm sorry Mr. Weismann. I didn't hear it."

He shook his head and walked back into the house. The sound of the phone made him angry and must have given him images of the trauma. I noticed the anger. Years later, after I had counseling, I realized that when he was banged on the head with the phone in the Polo Lounge, which caused a tumor in his brain, it caused anger for him, to have that trigger which created the anger for him to scream at me. His soul might be considered angry, perhaps harboring deep-seated resentment, unprocessed negative emotions, or significant unresolved trauma which can manifest as a persistent feeling of anger. It can be linked to a sense of injustice or deep hurtful experiences in life.

The key points are unresolved conflict and negative thought patterns. Spiritual interpretation replaying hurtful events in one's mind can perpetuate anger and make it feel part of the soul. In most interpretations, the conclusion of the angry soul signifies a moment of realization where the individual chooses to let go of their consuming anger, embracing forgiveness and compassion with inner peace, often recognizing the destructive nature of the rage and potential of healing through self-reflection and positive change. Then, essentially, the angry soul moves towards a more tranquil state.

I work most days now. I make the choice to let go, to embrace positive emotions, and most of all, make peace with my soul.

CHAPTER 43
THE LAST MAN STANDING
2025

I didn't know that I would get to this point in my life as there was always a battle in my life. Who would ever give a little imp a chance to write two books? I was made for something bigger, something better, I had belief in myself. Every step I took was purposeful and did not shy away from challenges. I didn't stop for fear. I was confident that I knew I could do anything. It started with belief and consistency. I didn't want to live in the dark. I knew the storm would run out of rain and the sun would shine every day. I would become a stronger man and I would overcome every obstacle. My failures were lessons, not defeats. I knew I would get better each day with action and my future would be bright. I kept my eyes on the horizon and kept pushing, knowing I would get better every day.

I stayed patient; every challenge I faced taught me something new. I will work hard; there are no shortcuts in life. I have pushed through the discomfort once again, no excuses. Life didn't wait for me to be ready. Greatness was in my blood; every decision I made was preparing me for success. I was born to do great things I wanted to walk in my purpose. The court's opinion would never affect me. I was on my own path. I wasn't born to fit in anybody's box. Life is precious, there are no short cuts in life, no excuses. I didn't give up on my potential. I was born for this. Once again, the court's opinion didn't affect me. I kept moving forward.

Life is precious. I believed in my path and the beauty around me, especially my beautiful daughter, Kelly. I have made it this far. Thank God I didn't succumb to the courts, especially after standing in the Magistrate Courthouse in Liverpool in 1967, in front of three magistrates who did not give me a chance. Or maybe they did not know better. They were probably ordered by the government to take me into care, or maybe it was all a conspiracy to fill the institutions. However, we stood tall. Even though I was just a child.

Now I look back at the movie *Gladiator*. It reminded me of Roman times. It seemed like I was in a dream. The long years in St. George's Approved School, St. Aidan's Approved, School, detention centres, Borstal scum, and all the prisons, marching every day, standing in corners for our punishments. The long walks home when they would let me out occasionally on weekends.

I remember the bus strike in 1969 in Liverpool when I had to walk home from the train station. It was quite a few miles, but I managed to do it. I would stand tall. In 1971, when I was the youngest prisoner in Risley Remand Centre, and then sent me off to detention in Derbyshire for military training, we had no choice. But I prevailed once again. Then I was recruited to St. Aidan's for more institutional abuse. We stood tall again when we ran away with my old friend, Franny Jones. We had stood against our abusers although we were recaptured and recommitted once again to St. Josephs.

After the countless beatings and sleepless nights from the Christian Brothers and priests, we never succumbed to weakness. What left us bruised only made us stronger and we stood tall once again. I was sent off to a Borstal scum system and an English reformatory system designed for youths between 16 and 21 years of age. Borstal's name came from the Anglo Saxon "burg-steal" fort a site or a place of refuge, likely referring to the hill there. The hill is now the home of Borstal scum. The Prevention of Crime Act rolls out Borstal Scum nationwide for males aged 16-20. Borstal was more about training, correction, and developing, and less about punishment. However, there was plenty of punishment, especially for me in solitary confinement over and over, but they never broke me. I had already served ten years, and

I was rebellious against the system. On some occasions, I would be put into solitary confinement for weeks, given only bread and water on the weekends. When I was released from solitary I was congratulated by members of the staff for my resilience.

I had demonstrated the importance of resilience in overcoming challenges and obstacles despite facing numerous setbacks and betrayals. I refused to give up and continued to fight for what I believed in. Once again, I stood tall. In 1982, the Criminal Justice Act abolished Borstal scum because of corporal punishments and children committing suicide.

However, their excuse was that it was an attempt to reduce the levels of youth crime, which only increased in the second half of the 20th century. Former Home Secretary, Willie Whitelaw and Margaret Thatcher, told leading criminologist Professor Dave Wilson that Margaret Thatcher had said the Borstal scum centres were run deliberately to put inmates under psychological and physical stress. That line alone between putting someone under stress and simply brutalizing them seemed to be inhuman. Once again, Margaret Thatcher had blood on her hands.

Treating other people as less than human, causing them to feel fear and suffering and humiliation, are violations of human dignity. Everyone has the right to be free from inhuman and degrading treatment.

After being treated inhumanely I found myself once again totally lost. I decided to go to Brighton to see my brother John. After a couple of drinks, I went to a local shop, Debenhams, and stole two shirts, which eventually led to my arrest under charges of theft for stealing two shirts. This, along with me getting beaten to a pulp by the Liverpool police and thrown through a plate glass window which severed my arm and cut an artery. After an emergency surgery to save my life, I just barely made it out of there with my limbs intact. I was paraded through the Magistrate's Court in Brighton and remanded into a local prison outside Brighton, Lewes Prison. Being banged up in Lewes was no joke. The cells were cramped. There was no heating, and the bitterly cold cells took the lives of some of the older prisoners.

The new prison took over from Gallows Bank where the last public hanging took place in 1831. Lewes had a long track record of being at the centre of famous criminal trials and this remains true up to the present day. A Lewes Coroner examined both visits of Jack the Ripper and unfortunately the crippled Elephant Man in 1799. A 17-year-old girl was sentenced to hang after being found Guilty of killing her newborn son. The hanging was in public and was apparently enjoyed by the locals in the same way as a country fair. The prison, as well as hosting its own ghost, has held at various times the revolutionaries of the Irish Rebellion, De Valera and Lawless, the Kray Twins, and Mick Jagger. George Wilton was charged with shooting Boer War prisoners and whom Winston Churchill helped set free, were held there. His story is told in the 1980s movie, *Breaker Morant.*

All of these foul deeds are well documented, and each has a twist in the tail. Unlocking the doors of the prison will reveal even more, but not until the murky case of the poisoned onion pie is told, and that leaves me standing in Lewes Crown Court in1973, facing the judge.

All I heard was, "you have done a bit of everything. You will be sentenced to two years in prison."

The judge said that he "had no mercy on me whatsoever."

I didn't feel anything. I was numb once again. I was placed back into Lewes prison, that dungeon, to serve my time. At least I was still standing.

Today, as I write this in 2024, Lewes prison is trapped in a cycle of rising violence, self-harm, and drug problems. After serving two months in Lewes prison, I was moved to a prison in London to serve my time. That prison was Wormwood Scrubs. The Scrubs has earned the opposite reputation over its 150 years of history. Its 1,000-man capacity had repeatedly been stretched to around 1,400. Over the years, it has grown infamous for poor hygiene, staff brutality, and riots. The Bible says it is a purely symbolic representation of Wormwood, and of bitterness that fills the earth during troubled times. It was also known for the Soviet spy, George Blake, who was housed in the Scrubs in 1966. Also, Keith Richards, from the Rolling Stones, was banged up for drug offenses.

I had spent three months in Wormwood Scrubs, mostly locked up 23 hours a day. One night I got involved in an argument over playing table tennis, which resulted in me hitting another prisoner. I would serve 21days in solitary confinement for that and placed on bread and water for the whole time. When I was released back into the main prison I was still standing.

I got notice one day that I would be transferred to my home-town, Liverpool, due to overcrowding in the Scrubs. The power I had used within me had beaten the dark underbelly of society.

The door opened early in the morning.

"Moogan!" a prison officer shouted, "get your kit packed, you're going to Walton Prison tomorrow."

I knew this was a good move for me. There would be local lads I knew. It was my hometown, after all.

Liverpool prison was constructed in 1848. It was called Walton Prison. It didn't escape the enemy bombing during World War II and was hit with high explosives hard in September, 1940. People were left trapped in the debris of the prison. The jail was hit again the following year in May, 1941, resulting in the loss of 15 lives.

The long drive to Walton was unbearable in a Black Maria police wagon, with handcuffs digging into my skin and bones. A slang term for it is 'paddy wagon.'

We stopped on the way at Winston Green for two hours for a sandwich and a cup of tea. Walton was another notorious prison, but it didn't mean anything to me. The poor prison guards had a miserable life. They would often shout through the cage to me. Some were decent and some were horrible men.

"You OK, Terry?"

We finally reached Walton Jail. The Black Maria pulled up alongside the metal doors.

"We have a prisoner from London. Moogan's his name."

The gates opened. I felt like this was home. This was my final destination. I was nearly 18 years of age and had spent ten years in Britain's institutions. As I arrived on the prison wing at least a dozen prisoners greeted me. They were all part of the institutions. Now, some I knew from the homes I was in and detention in Borstal scum many years ago.

After a month of settling down I had an altercation with a prison officer and told him to fuck off. I was taken yet again to solitary confinement and given 21 days in that block. It was summer, 1974. I was put on bread and water for three of those days. After twenty-one days, I was put back into the main wing in the prison. A few months after my 18th birthday, I would be released.

I had learned a valuable lesson throughout the institutions. Loyalty and betrayal. I was still standing. The hardest lesson I've had to learn as an adult is the relentless need to keep going, no matter how shattered I feel inside. This truth is both raw and universal. Life doesn't pause when our hearts are heavy, our minds are fractured, or our spirits feel like they are unravelling, it keeps moving, unrelenting, unapologetic, demanding that I move with it.

There's no time to stop, no pause for repair, no moment of stillness where we can gently piece ourselves back together. The world doesn't wait even when it needed to. We grow up on a steady diet of stories filled with unhappy endings, and happy endings, and most of all redemption and triumph, where it falls into place wearing my mask of strength when you're falling apart inside.

It's showing up when all you want is to retreat. It's choosing to move forward, step by painful step when your heart begs for rest. I stood tall and was brave through the heavy storms and believed that I was unbreakable to all the devils' forms.

I took the hits. I walked right back after all the crash landings. A man is not made for defeat; a man can be destroyed but not defeated. I feared nothing, for no one is taller than the last man standing. My struggle to survive and navigate a world where trust is a rare commodity highlights the importance of remaining true to oneself and others, even in the face of adversity. I am not what I have done. Fighting to be worthy is exhausting. I am what I have overcome. The world breaks everyone and afterward many are strong at the broken places. Courage is grace under pressure, the one thing that led me there. We didn't start the fights; we finished them with silence.

Fox News in America came calling one morning.

"Can we have your story?"

It was Stephanie Mohasco.

Elizabeth Taylor inspired bank robber to ditch life of crime and move to Hollywood, the headlines read, a working-class kid who beat the system.

I had gone through unusual challenges. I had knocked on God's door He let me in.

I am the last man standing. You will never walk alone. Amen.

THE STORY OF MY LIFE

I've had my share of life's ups and downs, but fate's been kind to me.

The downs have been many and quite a few. I guess you can say I've been lucky.

And I guess it's all because of you, God.

If anyone should write my life story, for whatever reason there might be, you'd be there between each line of fame and glory. Because you're the best thing that happened to me.

Lord, there had been times when life was hard. But always, somehow, I made it through. During every moment of hurting I've spent, there was a moment loving you, God.

Annette, Kelly, you're the best things that happened to me.

Amen.

ACKNOWLEDGEMENT

Much of my life story is not easy to read. It can bring tears, feelings of anxiety, outrage, and contempt for the many abusers who almost ruined me. My story is also one of triumph and standing tall.

One person who read, re-read, and read my manuscript again was author Jill Amadio who offered her opinion and worked on parts of the book with me. A fellow Brit, she perfectly understood my style of writing and kept it true to the way I needed to express myself.

Thank you, Jill.

If you have enjoyed this book, we appreciate your Amazon reviews and check out Terry Moogan's podcast interviews on Shaun Attwood's YouTube channel: From Liverpool Bank Robber to Hollywood Butler

OTHER BOOKS BY GADFLY PRESS

By Charlie Seiga:
Killer
The Hyenas
Liverpool's Notorious Jelly Gang

By John G Sutton:
HMP Manchester Prison Officer: I Survived Terrorists,
Murderers, Rapists and Freemason Officer Attacks in
Strangeways and Wormwood Scrubs

By Lee Marvin Hitchman:
How I Survived Shootings, Stabbings, Prison, Crack Addiction,
Manchester Gangs and Dog Attacks

By William Rodríguez Abadía:
Son of the Cali Cartel: The Narcos Who Wiped Out Pablo
Escobar and the Medellín Cartel

By Chet Sandhu:
Self-Made, Dues Paid: An Asian Kid Who Became an
International Drug-Smuggling Gangster

By Kaz B:
Confessions of a Dominatrix: My Secret BDSM Life

By Peter McAleese:
Killing Escobar and Soldier Stories

By Joe Egan:
Big Joe Egan: The Toughest White Man on the Planet

By Anthony Valentine:
Britain's No. 1 Art Forger Max Brandrett: The Life of a Cheeky Faker

By Johnnyboy Steele:
Scotland's Johnnyboy: The Bird That Never Flew

By Ian 'Blink' MacDonald:
Scotland's Wildest Bank Robber: Guns, Bombs and Mayhem in Glasgow's Gangland

By Michael Sheridan:
The Murder of Sophie: How I Hunted and Haunted the West Cork Killer

By Steve Wraith:
The Krays' Final Years: My Time with London's Most Iconic Gangsters

By Natalie Welsh:
Escape from Venezuela's Deadliest Prison

By Shaun Attwood:
English Shaun Trilogy
Party Time
Hard Time
Prison Time

War on Drugs Series
Pablo Escobar: Beyond Narcos
American Made: Who Killed Barry Seal? Pablo Escobar or George HW Bush
The Cali Cartel: Beyond Narcos
Clinton Bush and CIA Conspiracies: From the Boys on the Tracks to Jeffrey Epstein
Who Killed Epstein? Prince Andrew or Bill Clinton

Un-Making a Murderer: The Framing of Steven Avery and Brendan Dassey
The Mafia Philosopher: Two Tonys
Life Lessons

Pablo Escobar's Story (4-book series)

By Johnnyboy Steele:

Scotland's Johnnyboy: The Bird That Never Flew

"A cross between *Shawshank Redemption* and *Escape from Alcatraz*!" – Shaun Attwood, YouTuber and Author

All his life, 'Johnnyboy' Steele has been running. Firstly, from an abusive father, then from the rigours of an approved school and a young offenders jail, and, finally, from the harshness of adult prison. This book details how the Steele brothers staged the most daring breakout that Glasgow's Barlinnie prison had ever seen and recounts what happened when their younger brother, Joseph, was falsely accused of the greatest mass murder in Scottish legal history.

If Johnnyboy had wings, he would have flown to help his family, but he would have to wait for freedom to use his expertise to publicise young Joe's miscarriage of justice.

This is a compelling, often shocking and uncompromisingly honest account of how the human spirit can survive against almost crushing odds. It is a story of family love, friendship and, ultimately, a desire for justice.

By Ian 'Blink' MacDonald:

Scotland's Wildest Bank Robber: Guns, Bombs and Mayhem in Glasgow's Gangland

As a young man in Glasgow's underworld, Ian 'Blink' MacDonald earned a reputation for fighting and stabbing his enemies. After refusing to work for Arthur "The Godfather" Thompson, he attempted to steal £6 million in a high-risk armed bank robbery. While serving 16 years, Blink met the torture-gang boss Eddie Richardson, the serial killer Archie Hall, notorious lifer Charles Bronson and members of the Krays.

After his release, his drug-fuelled violent lifestyle created conflict with the police and rival gangsters. Rearrested several times, he was the target of a gruesome assassination attempt. During filming for Danny Dyer's Deadliest Men, a bomb was discovered under Blink's car and the terrified camera crew members fled from Scotland.

In *Scotland's Wildest Bank Robber*, Blink provides an eye-opening account of how he survived gangland warfare, prisons, stabbings and bombs.

By Michael Sheridan:

The Murder of Sophie: How I Hunted and Haunted the West Cork Killer

Just before Christmas, 1996, a beautiful French woman – the wife of a movie mogul – was brutally murdered outside of her holiday home in a remote region of West Cork, Ireland. The crime was reported by a local journalist, Ian Bailey, who was at the forefront of the case until he became the prime murder suspect. Arrested twice, he was released without charge.

This was the start of a saga lasting decades with twists and turns and a battle for justice in two countries, which culminated in the 2019 conviction of Bailey – in his absence – by the French Criminal court in Paris. But it was up to the Irish courts to decide whether he would be extradited to serve a 25-year prison sentence.

With the unrivalled co-operation of major investigation sources and the backing of the victim's family, the author unravels the shocking facts of a unique murder case.

By Steve Wraith:

The Krays' Final Years: My Time with London's Most Iconic Gangsters

Britain's most notorious twins – Ron and Reg Kray – ascended the underworld to become the most feared and legendary gangsters in London. Their escalating mayhem culminated in murder, for which they received life sentences in 1969.

While incarcerated, they received letters from a schoolboy from Tyneside, Steve Wraith, who was mesmerised by their story. Eventually, Steve visited them in prison and a friendship formed. The Twins hired Steve as an unofficial advisor, which brought him into contact with other members of their crime family. At Ron's funeral, Steve was Charlie Kray's right-hand man.

Steve documents Ron's time in Broadmoor – a high-security

psychiatric hospital – where he was battling insanity and heavily medicated. Steve details visiting Reg, who served almost 30 years in a variety of prisons, where the gangster was treated with the utmost respect by the staff and the inmates.

By Natalie Welsh:

Escape from Venezuela's Deadliest Prison

After getting arrested at a Venezuelan airport with a suitcase of cocaine, Natalie was clueless about the danger she was facing. Sentenced to 10 years, she arrived at a prison with armed men on the roof, whom she mistakenly believed were the guards, only to find out they were homicidal gang members. Immediately, she was plunged into a world of unimaginable horror and escalating violence, where murder, rape and all-out gang warfare were carried out with the complicity of corrupt guards. Male prisoners often entered the women's housing area, bringing gunfire with them and leaving corpses behind. After 4.5 years, Natalie risked everything to escape and flee through Colombia, with the help of a guard who had fallen deeply in love with her.

By Shaun Attwood:

Pablo Escobar: Beyond Narcos

War on Drugs Series Book 1

The mind-blowing true story of Pablo Escobar and the Medellín Cartel, beyond their portrayal on Netflix.

Colombian drug lord Pablo Escobar was a devoted family man and a psychopathic killer; a terrible enemy, yet a wonderful friend. While donating millions to the poor, he bombed and tortured his enemies – some had their eyeballs removed with hot spoons. Through ruthless cunning and America's insatiable appetite for cocaine, he became a multi-billionaire, who lived in a $100-million house with its own zoo.

Pablo Escobar: Beyond Narcos demolishes the standard good versus evil telling of his story. The authorities were not hunting Pablo down to stop his cocaine business. They were taking it over.

American Made: Who Killed Barry Seal? Pablo Escobar or George HW Bush

War on Drugs Series Book 2

Set in a world where crime and government coexist, *American Made* is the jaw-dropping true story of CIA pilot Barry Seal that the Hollywood movie starring Tom Cruise is afraid to tell.

Barry Seal flew cocaine and weapons worth billions of dollars into and out of America in the 1980s. After he became a government informant, Pablo Escobar's Medellin Cartel offered a million for him alive and half a million dead. But his real trouble began after he threatened to expose the dirty dealings of George HW Bush.

American Made rips the roof off Bush and Clinton's complicity in cocaine trafficking in Mena, Arkansas.

"A conspiracy of the grandest magnitude." Congressman Bill Alexander on the Mena affair.

The Cali Cartel: Beyond Narcos

War on Drugs Series Book 3

An electrifying account of the Cali Cartel, beyond its portrayal on Netflix.

From the ashes of Pablo Escobar's empire rose an even bigger and more malevolent cartel. A new breed of sophisticated mobsters became the kings of cocaine. Their leader was Gilberto Rodríguez Orejuela – known as the Chess Player, due to his foresight and calculated cunning.

Gilberto and his terrifying brother, Miguel, ran a multi-billion-dollar drug empire like a corporation. They employed a politically astute brand of thuggery and spent $10 million to put a president in power. Although the godfathers from Cali preferred bribery over violence, their many loyal torturers and hitmen were never idle.

Clinton, Bush and CIA Conspiracies: From the Boys on the Tracks to Jeffrey Epstein

War on Drugs Series Book 4

In the 1980s, George HW Bush imported cocaine to finance an illegal war in Nicaragua. Governor Bill Clinton's Arkansas state police provided security for the drug drops. For assisting the CIA, the Clinton Crime Family was awarded the White House. The #clintonbodycount continues to this day, with the deceased including Jeffrey Epstein.

This book features harrowing true stories that reveal the insanity of the drug war. A mother receives the worst news about her son. A journalist gets a tip that endangers his life. An unemployed man becomes California's biggest crack dealer. A DEA agent in Mexico is sacrificed for going after the big players.

The lives of Linda Ives, Gary Webb, Freeway Rick Ross and Kiki Camarena are shattered by brutal experiences. Not all of them will survive.

Pablo Escobar's Story (4-book series)

"Finally, the definitive book about Escobar, original and up-to-date." – UNILAD

"The most comprehensive account ever written." – True Geordie

Pablo Escobar was a mama's boy, who cherished his family and sang in the shower, yet he bombed a passenger plane and formed a death squad that used genital electrocution.

Most Escobar biographies only provide a few pieces of the puzzle, but this action-packed 1000-page book reveals everything about the king of cocaine.

Mostly translated from Spanish, Part 1 contains stories untold in the English-speaking world, including:

The tragic death of his youngest brother, Fernando.

The fate of his pregnant mistress.

The shocking details of his affair with a TV celebrity.

The presidential candidate who encouraged him to eliminate their rivals.

The Mafia Philosopher

"A fast-paced true-crime memoir with all of the action of Goodfellas." – UNILAD

"Sopranos v Sons of Anarchy with an Alaskan-snow backdrop." – True Geordie Podcast

Breaking bones, burying bodies and planting bombs became second nature to Two Tonys, while working for the Bonanno

Crime Family, whose exploits inspired The Godfather.

After a dispute with an outlaw motorcycle club, Two Tonys left a trail of corpses from Arizona to Alaska. On the run, he was pursued by bikers and a neo-Nazi gang, blood-thirsty for revenge, while a homicide detective launched a nationwide manhunt.

As the mist from his smoking gun fades, readers are left with an unexpected portrait of a stoic philosopher with a wealth of charm, a glorious turn of phrase and a fanatical devotion to his daughter.

Party Time

An action-packed roller-coaster account of a life spiralling out of control, featuring wild women, gangsters and a mountain of drugs.

Shaun Attwood arrived in Phoenix, Arizona, a penniless business graduate from a small industrial town in England. Within a decade, he became a stock-market millionaire. But he was leading a double life.

After taking his first ecstasy pill at a rave in Manchester as a shy student, Shaun became intoxicated by the party lifestyle that would change his fortune. Years later, in the Arizona desert, he became submerged in a criminal underworld, throwing parties for thousands of ravers and running an ecstasy ring in competition with the Mafia mass murderer, Sammy 'The Bull' Gravano.

As greed and excess tore through his life, Shaun had eye-watering encounters with Mafia hitmen and crystal-meth addicts, enjoyed extravagant debauchery with superstar DJs and glitter girls, and ingested enough drugs to kill a herd of elephants. This is his story.

Hard Time

"Makes the Shawshank Redemption look like a holiday camp."
– NOTW

After a SWAT team smashed down stock-market millionaire Shaun Attwood's door, he found himself inside Arizona's deadliest jail and locked into a brutal struggle for survival.

Shaun's hope of living the American Dream turned into a nightmare of violence and chaos, when he had a run-in with Sammy "the Bull" Gravano, an Italian Mafia mass murderer.

In jail, Shaun was forced to endure cockroaches crawling in his ears at night, dead rats in the food and the sound of skulls getting cracked against toilets. He meticulously documented the conditions and smuggled out his message.

Join Shaun on a harrowing voyage into the darkest recesses of human existence.

Hard Time provides a revealing glimpse into the tragedy, brutality, dark comedy and eccentricity of prison life.

Featured worldwide on Nat Geo Channel's Locked-Up/Banged-Up Abroad Raving Arizona.

Prison Time

Sentenced to 9½ years in Arizona's state prison for distributing ecstasy, Shaun finds himself living among gang members, sexual predators and drug-crazed psychopaths. After being attacked by a Californian biker, in for stabbing a girlfriend, Shaun writes about the prisoners who befriend, protect and inspire him. They include T-Bone, a massive African American ex-Marine, who risks his life saving vulnerable inmates from rape, and Two Tonys, an old-school Mafia murderer, who left the corpses of his rivals from Arizona to Alaska. They teach Shaun how to turn incarceration to his advantage, and to learn from his mistakes.

Shaun is no stranger to love and lust in the heterosexual world, but the tables are turned on him inside. Sexual advances come at him from all directions, some cleverly disguised, others more sinister – making Shaun question his sexual identity.

Resigned to living alongside violent, mentally ill and drug-addicted inmates, Shaun immerses himself in psychology and philosophy, to try to make sense of his past behaviour, and begins applying what he learns, as he adapts to prison life. Encouraged by Two Tonys to explore fiction as well, Shaun reads over 1000 books which, with support from a brilliant psychotherapist, Dr Owen, speed along his personal development. As his ability to deflect daily threats improves, Shaun begins to look forward to his release with optimism and a new love waiting for him. Yet the words of Aristotle from one of Shaun's books will prove prophetic: "We cannot learn without pain."

Un-Making a Murderer:
The Framing of Steven Avery and Brendan Dassey

Innocent people do go to jail. Sometimes mistakes are made. But even more terrifying is when the authorities conspire to frame them. That's what happened to Steven Avery and Brendan Dassey, who were convicted of murder and are serving life sentences.

Un-Making a Murderer is an explosive book, which uncovers the illegal, devious and covert tactics used by Wisconsin officials, including:

– Concealing Other Suspects

– Paying Expert Witnesses to Lie

– Planting Evidence

– Jury Tampering

The art of framing innocent people has been in practice for centuries and will continue until the perpetrators are held accountable.

Turning conventional assumptions and beliefs in the justice system upside down, *Un-Making a Murderer* takes you on that journey.

HARD TIME BY SHAUN ATTWOOD
CHAPTER 1

Sleep deprived and scanning for danger, I enter a dark cell on the second floor of the maximum-security Madison Street jail in Phoenix, Arizona, where guards and gang members are murdering prisoners. Behind me, the metal door slams heavily. Light slants into the cell through oblong gaps in the door, illuminating a prisoner cocooned in a white sheet, snoring lightly on the top bunk about two thirds of the way up the back wall. Relieved there is no immediate threat, I place my mattress on the grimy floor. Desperate to rest, I notice movement on the cement-block walls. *Am I hallucinating?* I blink several times. The walls appear to ripple. Stepping closer, I see the walls are alive with insects. I flinch. So many are swarming, I wonder if they're a colony of ants on the move. To get a better look, I put my eyes right up to them. They are mostly the size of almonds and have antennae. American cockroaches. I've seen them in the holding cells downstairs in smaller numbers, but nothing like this. A chill spread over my body. I back away.

Something alive falls from the ceiling and bounces off the base of my neck. I jump. With my night vision improving, I spot cockroaches weaving in and out of the base of the fluorescent strip light. Every so often one drops onto the concrete and resumes crawling. Examining the bottom bunk, I realise why my cellmate is sleeping at a higher elevation: cockroaches are pouring from gaps in the decrepit wall at the level of my bunk. The area is thick with them. Placing my mattress on the bottom bunk scatters them. I walk towards the toilet, crunching a few under my shower sandals. I urinate and grab the toilet roll. A cockroach darts from the centre of the roll onto my hand, tickling my fingers. My arm jerks as if it has a mind of its own, losing the cockroach and the toilet roll. Using a towel, I wipe the bulk of them off the bottom bunk, stopping only to shake the odd one off my hand. I unroll my mattress. They begin to regroup and inhabit my mattress. My adrenaline is pumping so much, I lose my fatigue.

Nauseated, I sit on a tiny metal stool bolted to the wall. *How will I sleep? How's my cellmate sleeping through the infestation and my arrival?* Copying his technique, I cocoon myself in a sheet and lie down, crushing more cockroaches. The only way they can access me now is through the breathing hole I've left in the sheet by the lower half of my face. Inhaling their strange musty odour, I close my eyes. I can't sleep. I feel them crawling on the sheet around my feet. *Am I imagining things?* Frightened of them infiltrating my breathing hole, I keep opening my eyes. Cramps cause me to rotate onto my other side. Facing the wall, I'm repulsed by so many of them just inches away. I return to my original side.

The sheet traps the heat of the Sonoran Desert to my body, soaking me in sweat. Sweat tickles my body, tricking my mind into thinking the cockroaches are infiltrating and crawling on me. The trapped heat aggravates my bleeding skin infections and bedsores. I want to scratch myself, but I know better. The outer layers of my skin have turned soggy from sweating constantly in this concrete oven. Squirming on the bunk fails to stop the relentless itchiness of my skin. Eventually, I scratch myself. Clumps of moist skin detach under my nails. Every now and then I become so uncomfortable, I must open my cocoon to waft the heat out, which allows the cockroaches in. It takes hours to drift to sleep. I only manage a few hours. I awake stuck to the soaked sheet, disgusted by the cockroach carcasses compressed against the mattress.

The cockroaches plague my new home until dawn appears at the dots in the metal grid over a begrimed strip of four-inch-thick bullet-proof glass at the top of the back wall – the cell's only source of outdoor light. They disappear into the cracks in the walls, like vampire mist retreating from sunlight. But not all of them. There were so many on the night shift that even their vastly reduced number is too many to dispose of. And they act like they know it. They roam around my feet with attitude, as if to make it clear that I'm trespassing on their turf.

My next set of challenges will arise not from the insect world, but from my neighbours. I'm the new arrival, subject to scrutiny about my charges just like when I'd run into the Aryan Brotherhood prison gang on my first day at the medium-security Towers jail a year ago. I wish my cellmate would wake up, brief me on the mood of the locals and introduce me to the head of the white gang. No such luck. Chow is announced over a speaker system in a crackly robotic voice, but he doesn't stir.

I emerge into the day room for breakfast. Prisoners in black-and-white bee-striped uniforms gather under the metal-grid stairs and tip dead cockroaches into a trash bin from plastic peanut-butter containers they'd set as traps during the night. All eyes are on me in the chow line. Watching who sits where, I hold my head up, put on a solid stare and pretend to be as at home in this environment as the cockroaches. It's all an act. I'm lonely and afraid. I loathe having to explain myself to the head of the white race, who I assume is the toughest murderer. I've been in jail long enough to know that taking my breakfast to my cell will imply that I have something to hide.

The gang punishes criminals with certain charges. The most serious are sex offenders, who are KOS: Kill On Sight. Other charges are punishable by SOS – Smash On Sight – such as drive-by shootings because women and kids sometimes get killed. It's called convict justice. Gang members are constantly looking for people to beat up because that's how they earn their reputations and tattoos. The most serious acts of violence earn the highest-ranking tattoos. To be a full gang member requires murder. I've observed the body language and techniques inmates trying to integrate employ. An inmate with a spring in his step and an air of confidence is likely to be accepted. A person who avoids eye contact and fails to introduce himself to the gang is likely to be preyed on. Some of the failed attempts I saw ended up with heads getting cracked against toilets, a sound I've grown familiar with. I've seen prisoners being extracted on stretchers who looked dead – one had yellow fluid leaking from his head. The constant violence gives me nightmares, but the reality is that I put myself in here, so I force myself to accept it as a part of my punishment.

It's time to apply my knowledge. With a self-assured stride, I take my breakfast bag to the table of white inmates covered in neo-Nazi tattoos, allowing them to question me.

"Mind if I sit with you guys?" I ask, glad exhaustion has deepened my voice.

"These seats are taken. But you can stand at the corner of the table."

The man who answered is probably the head of the gang. I size him up. Cropped brown hair. A dangerous glint in Nordic-blue eyes. Tiny pupils that suggest he's on heroin. Weightlifter-type veins bulging from a sturdy neck. Political ink on arms crisscrossed with scars. About the same age as me, thirty-three.

"Thanks. I'm Shaun from England." I volunteer my origin to show I'm different from them but not in a way that might get me smashed.

"I'm Bullet, the head of the whites." He offers me his fist to bump. "Where you roll in from, wood?"

Addressing me as wood is a good sign. It's what white gang members on a friendly basis call each other.

"Towers jail. They increased my bond and re-classified me to maximum security."

"What's your bond at?"

"I've got two $750,000 bonds," I say in a monotone. This is no place to brag about bonds.

"How many people you kill, brother?" His eyes drill into mine, checking whether my body language supports my story. My body language so far is spot on.

"None. I threw rave parties. They got us talking about drugs on wiretaps." Discussing drugs on the phone does not warrant a $1.5 million bond. I know and beat him to his next question. "Here's my charges." I show him my charge sheet, which includes conspiracy and leading a crime syndicate – both from running an Ecstasy ring.

Bullet snatches the paper and scrutinises it. Attempting to pre-empt his verdict, the other whites study his face. On edge, I wait for him to respond. Whatever he says next will determine whether I'll be accepted or victimised.

"Are you some kind of jailhouse attorney?" Bullet asks. "I want someone to read through my case paperwork." During our few minutes of conversation, Bullet has seen through my act and concluded that I'm educated – a possible resource to him.

I appreciate that he'll accept me if I take the time to read his case. "I'm no jailhouse attorney, but I'll look through it and help you however I can."

"Good. I'll stop by your cell later on, wood."

After breakfast, I seal as many of the cracks in the walls as I can with toothpaste. The cell smells minty, but the cockroaches still find their way in. Their day shift appears to be collecting information on the brown paper bags under my bunk, containing a few items of food that I purchased from the commissary; bags that I tied off with rubber bands in the hope of keeping the cockroaches out. Relentlessly, the cockroaches explore the bags for entry points, pausing over and probing the most worn and vulnerable regions. *Will the nightly swarm eat right through the paper?* I read all morning, wondering whether my cellmate has died in his cocoon, his occasional breathing sounds reassuring me.

Bullet stops by late afternoon and drops his case paperwork off. He's been charged with Class 3 felonies and less, not serious crimes, but is facing a double-digit sentence because of his prior convictions and Security Threat Group status in the prison system. The proposed sentencing range seems disproportionate. I'll advise him to reject the plea bargain – on the assumption he already knows to do so, but is just seeking the comfort of a second opinion, like many un-sentenced inmates. When he returns for his paperwork, our conversation disturbs my cellmate – the cocoon shuffles – so we go upstairs to his cell. I tell Bullet what I think. He is excitable, a different man from earlier, his pupils almost non-existent.

"This case ain't shit. But my prosecutor knows I done other shit, all kinds of heavy shit, but can't prove it. I'd do anything to get that sorry bitch off my fucking ass. She's asking for something bad to happen to her. Man, if I ever get bonded out, I'm gonna chop that bitch into pieces. Kill her slowly though. Like to work her over with a blowtorch."

Such talk can get us both charged with conspiring to murder a prosecutor, so I try to steer him elsewhere. "It's crazy how they can catch you doing one thing, yet try to sentence you for all of the things they think you've ever done."

"Done plenty. Shot some dude in the stomach once. Rolled him up in a blanket and threw him in a dumpster."

Discussing past murders is as unsettling as future ones. "So, what's all your tattoos mean, Bullet? Like that eagle on your chest?"

"Why you wanna know?" Bullet's eyes probe mine.

My eyes hold their ground. "Just curious."

"It's a war bird. The AB patch."

"AB patch?"

"What the Aryan Brotherhood gives you when you've put enough work in."

"How long does it take to earn a patch?"

"Depends how quickly you put your work in. You have to earn your lightning bolts first."

"Why you got red and black lightning bolts?"

"You get SS bolts for beating someone down or for being an enforcer for the family. Red lightning bolts for killing someone. I was sent down as a youngster. They gave me steel and told me who to handle and I handled it. You don't ask questions. You just get blood on your steel. Dudes who get these tats without putting work in are told to cover them up or leave the yard."

"What if they refuse?"

"They're held down and we carve the ink off them."

Imagining them carving a chunk of flesh to remove a tattoo, I cringe. He's really enjoying telling me this now. His volatile nature is clear and frightening. *He's accepted me too much. He's trying to impress me before making demands.*

At night, I'm unable to sleep. Cocooned in heat, surrounded by cockroaches, I hear the swamp-cooler vent – a metal grid at the top of a wall – hissing out tepid air. Giving up on sleep, I put my earphones on and tune into National Public Radio. Listening to a Vivaldi violin concerto, I close my eyes and press my tailbone down to straighten my back as if I'm doing a yogic relaxation. The playful allegro thrills me, lifting my spirits, but the wistful adagio provokes sad emotions and tears. I open my eyes and gaze into the gloom. Due to lack of sleep, I start hallucinating and hearing voices over the music whispering threats. I'm at breaking point. Although I have accepted that I committed crimes and deserve to be punished, no one should have to live like this. I'm furious at myself for making the series of reckless decisions that put me in here and for losing absolutely everything. As violins crescendo in my ears, I remember what my life used to be like.